T0367873

THEY CAN'T ALL BE TRUE

ANDY WRASMAN

WESTBOW°
PRESS
A DIVISION OF THOMAS NELSON
& ZONDERVAN

Scriptures taken from the Holy Bible, New International Version®, NIV®. Copyright © 1973, 1978, 1984, 2011 by Biblica, Inc.™ Used by permission of Zondervan. All rights reserved worldwide. www.zondervan.com The "NIV" and "New International Version" are trademarks registered in the United States Patent and Trademark Office by Biblica, Inc.™

WestBow Press books may be ordered through booksellers or by contacting:

WestBow Press
A Division of Thomas Nelson & Zondervan
1663 Liberty Drive
Bloomington, IN 47403
www.westbowpress.com
1 (866) 928-1240

Because of the dynamic nature of the Internet, any web addresses or links contained in this book may have changed since publication and may no longer be valid. The views expressed in this work are solely those of the author and do not necessarily reflect the views of the publisher, and the publisher hereby disclaims any responsibility for them.

ISBN: 978-1-4908-1929-7 (sc)
ISBN: 978-1-4908-1931-0 (hc)
ISBN: 978-1-4908-2981-4 (e)

Library of Congress Control Number: 2013922443

Printed in the United States of America.

WestBow Press rev. date: 03/04/2014

CONTENTS

THE STATE OF TOLERANCE

Having bought a supply of magazines, I was ready to board my flight to return for another year of teaching English in China. Flipping through the last American-published materials I would be able to purchase for many months, I landed on a picture of the good-luck charms a presidential candidate carried with him on the campaign trail. His hands cupped assorted charms, so many that I doubt they left much room in his pockets for keys or loose change, much less a smart-phone. I didn't recognize what all the charms were or what they each represented, but at least two of them were of religious origin: one derived from Christianity and another from Hinduism.

I smirked. This guy was good. Instead of polarizing himself, limiting his appeal to one ethnic group, religion, or cause by keeping just one good-luck charm in his pocket, he was able to nab members of multiple backgrounds with one photo of his eclectic collection. His choices were also obscure enough that many people wouldn't even recognize the affiliation of a particular charm unless they were adherents themselves, protecting some of the conflicting symbols from potential scrutiny.

I didn't follow much of the presidential campaign while living in China, but from my limited perspective overseas, the charm-toting candidate was running on a platform of diversity, peace, and tolerance, which appeared to be bolstered by iconic posters of himself with one-word slogans such as "Hope" or "Change." I found one of his campaign speeches online, and it was essentially a litany of divisions in social class, ethnicity, geographic location, political affiliation, and religious practice. The punch line was that, despite these differences, we were all Americans. In my mind, he was the coexist candidate, and it was refreshing to hear his words urging unity and peace within our American borders and abroad.

I didn't vote in that election, but all my Chinese students loved the outcome, as did all of my expatriate friends from Europe. The charm-carrying candidate won the election, and in 2008 President Barack Obama maintained the diversity platform on his way into the Oval Office, declaring in his inaugural speech:

> We are a nation of Christians and Muslims, Jews and Hindus, and non-believers. We are shaped by every language and culture, drawn from every end of this Earth; and because we have tasted the bitter swill of civil war and segregation, and emerged from that dark chapter stronger and more united, we cannot help but believe that the old hatreds shall someday pass; that the lines of tribe shall soon dissolve; that as the world grows smaller, our common humanity shall reveal itself; and that America must play its role in ushering in a new era of peace.[1]

These emotionally persuasive words were delivered with passion. Really, who wouldn't want all the differences in the world to dissolve away into peaceful harmony? What exactly would have to happen for "the lines of tribe to dissolve" among the religions named by President Obama?

Tolerance and Coexistence

Diversity. Respect. Tolerance. Coexistence. Before President Obama ran for office, these words began to make some noise as we entered into the twenty-first century. I remember the first time I saw a *Coexist* bumper sticker, around 2004 in Irvine, California. Coexist was spelled using symbols from various belief systems: a crescent moon for the *C*, a peace symbol for the *o*, male/female symbols were integrated into the *e*, the Star of David for the *x*, a Wiccan pentagram for the dot of the *i*, a yin-yang symbol for the *s*, and a cross for the *t*. I was mystified. I thought it was ingenious. I had never seen so many religions standing side by side to form a single word.

But what really floored me was the message itself. When these bumper stickers first hit the scene, America was at war in Iraq and Afghanistan. We had an openly Christian president who commonly used religious rhetoric when discussing the war on terrorism, and it couldn't be ignored that the men who hijacked the planes on September 11 were Muslim. Some saw the necessity to clarify that the hijackers were radical Muslims, but even the addition of that distinction didn't take away from the fact that America was attacked by Muslims on domestic soil; that American soldiers were fighting against Al-Qaida, a Muslim terrorist organization.

In such a context, *coexist*, spelled with religious symbols, had a significant implication. As humans, we ought to agree with its call for peace. After all, are we not better than the animals? As humans, we have the ability to strive to live together in peace without hating each other or killing each other over differences in race, culture, sexual orientation, politics, or even religion.

Trailing the coexist adhesive in popularity is the tolerance bumper sticker. Tolerance is at the heart of successful coexistence. By definition, the word implies that there are differences within the world's religions, and that the tensions caused by these differences must be resolved through practicing tolerance.

This should not be misconstrued as *agreement*, as some might interpret it. Tolerance is not agreement but a state of allowance. We must first recognize that individuals have the freedom of religious choice and expression. From there, the necessity to tolerate conflicting religious beliefs must exist if the preservation of human liberties is to continue. If we cannot muster the will to tolerate opposing beliefs, we resort to weeding out any belief other than our own. In the process, we kill all freedom of religious expression.

The coexistence and tolerance movements must be applauded for their calls for peace, but numerous people derive another message from these stickers. I have spent three years talking with students about their views on these two stickers at the University of California, Irvine (UCI) in the campus's freedom of speech zone. I have learned that many students think these stickers also imply that all religions are the same at their core, or that all religions lead to God. I have also learned that many students agree with this view and care enough to spend hours debating this position with me, even though I am a complete stranger to them. I have to admit to them that the idea that all religions are the same is a good sentiment. If it's true, there is no reason why we can't all get along.

If all religions led to the same positive outcome, we'd be able to move beyond simply tolerating religious differences to an arms-wide, open embrace of all faiths. Such an open acceptance can only be possible for someone who hasn't taken the time to study the world's religions. The shortest of studies of the sacred texts of just a few different religions would reveal contradictions in their fundamental teachings. If you want to see these fundamental teachings and the contradictions that arise from them, skip ahead to chapters two and three.

Social Pluralism vs. Literal Pluralism

Defining *pluralism* can be a challenge. It comes in all shapes and sizes, there are many different definitions available, and there are varying perspectives on what each definition actually means. Pluralism can refer to multiculturalism, the holding of numerous offices at once, dualism, and monism. Dualism is the idea that everything is either material or mental, physical or spiritual. One form of monism declares that everything consists of the same substance. Monism can also be a denial of dualism, the idea that there is no distinction between an object and the thoughts that perceive the object. As you can see, pluralism can't be easily pinned, but it can be broken into two camps. Pluralism can mean diversity, or it can mean that there are no differences at all; all is one, and one is all. I refer to these two camps as *social pluralism* and *literal pluralism*.

Social pluralism is the term I use to describe diversity in society. The diversity can be miniature or grand in size and in scope. Social pluralism can be observed at local, regional, national, continental, hemispherical, and global levels. Social pluralism can refer to the coexistence of multiple races, languages, political views, religious beliefs, or any number of categorical classifications. If two distinctions are made in any categorical classification, social pluralism is present. Therefore, social pluralism is alive and well, and it can't be avoided. Nowhere in America is without social pluralism, not red (Republican) states, blue (Democratic) states, not the wild of Alaska, or even the Southern Bible Belt. Despite the United States being called the melting pot of the world, differences still remain, and they always will. Even in communist countries like the People's Republic of China, or Islamic states like Iran, eradication of all differences cannot truly be achieved.

Metaphysical pluralism is the term I use to describe the view that everything is one, or true, despite apparent distinctions. I also like to call this view *literal pluralism* because in conversation I would ask a person, "When you say tolerance, are you advocating for *social* tolerance of the diverse races, languages, and cultures present in society, or do you *literally* believe that everything is one and the same?"

The interpretation of oneness isn't always the same, either. Literal pluralism can be divided into two camps: "all is one" or "all leads to one." In the discussion of religion, "all is one" means that all religions are the same; they all contain the same truth. "All leads to one" recognizes that each religion has different teachings and that they are not all the same, yet this camp of literal pluralism holds that all religions are spiritual paths leading to the same destination, so in the end everything eventually is one. For the remainder of the book, when I mention pluralism, I am referring to literal pluralism, and I will only make a distinction between the two camps of literal pluralism if it is necessary.

The Spread and Rise of Pluralism

Pluralism might be new in the West, but it is very old hat in the East. The oneness of reality is found in Hinduism, a religion whose origins date back as far as Judaism's beginning. The explanation for universal oneness is found in the Rig Veda, Hinduism's oldest collection of priestly chants. The Rig at one time claims that no one can know from where or how the universe began (Rig Veda 10.129),[2] yet it still offers an explanation for our origins. Everything results from the sacrifice of the cosmic man, Purusha (Rig Veda 10.90).[3] It is from Purusha's sacrificial body that everything that has been or whatever is to be is derived. Since everything consists of this one divine source, everything is at the core the same. In Hinduism, all are one, and one is all.

It is hard to pinpoint an exact moment that the monism (all is one) of Hinduism took root in the West. The sowing of the seeds began with the transcendentalism movement in the middle of the nineteenth century. Writers Ralph Waldo Emerson, David Henry Thoreau, and Walt Whitman were all prominent figures of this movement and today are required reading in many American schools. I read excerpts from all three of these writers in high school. Thoreau's *Walden* stood out to me the most because I was inspired by his experiment to live in the woods by Walden Pond for two years. I was enticed by the call to adventure; I'd rather be in the woods than in the classroom. *Walden* was also an invitation to be one with nature. This summons can be found in Hinduism through its teaching of seeking union with the divine at the heart of all things. All are one: nature, animals, and humans. Thoreau bares Hinduism's influence within the pages of *Walden*:

> In the morning I bathe my intellect in the stupendous and cosmogonal philosophy of the Bhagvat Geeta [Hindu text], since whose composition years of the gods have elapsed, and in comparison with which our modern world and its literature seem puny and trivial; and I doubt if that philosophy is not to be referred to a previous state of existence, so remote is its sublimity from our conceptions. I lay down the book and go to my well for water, and lo! there I meet the servant of the Brahmin, priest of Brahma, and Vishnu and Indra [Hindu gods], who still sits in his temple on the Ganges [the sacred river in India in which Hindus regularly bathe in ritual cleansing rites] reading the Vedas [four collections of Hindu priestly chants], or dwells at the root of a tree with his crust and water-jug. I meet his servant come to draw water for his master, and our buckets, as it were grate together in the same well. The pure Walden water is mingled with the sacred water of the Ganges.[4]

Ralph Waldo Emerson also scattered many seeds of pluralism. Some of the clearest can be seen in his essay "The Over-soul." In this essay, Emerson observes that we are many parts and particles and that we see the world in pieces. We make classifications and labels: that's the sun, that's the moon, that's an animal, that's a plant, and so on. But the whole of all of these is the soul. Emerson says that within us "is the soul of the whole; the wise silence; the universal beauty, to which every particle is equally related; the eternal ONE."[5] Emerson adds that this nature appearing in us all "is not social; it is impersonal; is God."[7] To receive a "revelation" from this soul, Emerson explains that one "must greatly listen to himself, withdrawing from all accents of other men's devotion" because "the Highest dwells with him; that the sources of nature are in his own mind."[7]

Though Emerson does not make any direct references to Hinduism in "The Over-soul," his teaching that the whole of all is the ONE, eternal soul synchs with Hinduism's teaching that there is one eternal essence to all things. Emerson and Hinduism both express this divine nature as being impersonal. Emerson insists that to hear divine revelation, one must only connect with the divine within oneself, which is also the striving goal of Hinduism – to become one with the divine, to no longer live in the illusion of the division.

Walt Whitman, who referred to Emerson with the title "Master," hints at similar pluralistic ideals in his poem, "Song to Myself," saying in the opening lines,

> I celebrate myself, and sing myself,
> And what I assume you shall assume,
> For every atom belonging to me as good belongs to you.[8]

As to the divine, in the same poem Whitman said, "I hear and behold God in every object."[9]

These three authors alone did not establish pluralism in the West— or more specifically America, since they were American writers—but they tilled the soil and planted the seeds, as did other members of the transcendental movement.

These quotations from over one hundred years ago show that pluralism hasn't appeared overnight. Through mandatory reading in educational systems, such works have been engrained across generations of Americans, even if the religious and philosophical implications of such works are not directly taught in the classrooms. At the very least, the words that come from such authors and their works have a stamp of authority due to their placement as required reading.

I want to close this discussion of the origin of Eastern philosophy's seed migration to the West with the words of John Muir, father of America's national parks system, that reflect almost identically the words shared by pluralists and New Agers today.

We all flow from one fountain Soul. All are expressions of one love. God does not appear, and flow out, only from narrow chinks and round bored wells here and there in favoured races and places, but He flows in grand undivided currents, shoreless and boundless over creeds and forms and all kinds of civilizations and peoples and beasts, saturating all and fountainizing all.[10]

The watering of the transcendental seeds came in 1893, in Chicago. It was the first meeting of the World's Parliament of Religions and is recognized as the first formal interfaith meeting of Eastern and Western religious leaders. It was here that Swami Vivekanada, a Hindu, delivered a series of addresses introducing America to Hinduism. His salutation, "Brothers and sisters of America," commenced his first address that proclaimed, "I am proud to belong to a religion which has taught the world both tolerance and universal acceptance. We believe not only in universal toleration, but we accept all religions as true."[11]

More decades of watering passed, and the seeds of the transcendental movement finally came to fruition in the 1960s. The countercultural movement sprang up in opposition to the Vietnam War and the draft that accompanied it. The movement included hundreds of thousands of youth questioning why they and their friends and families should risk, and possibly lose, their lives in a war that they couldn't justify. If drafted, their options were simple: go to jail, go to Canada, or "fight Charlie."

Beyond the antiwar sentiment within the "youth culture" of the 60s, the American government and the broader authorities of society came to be seen as oppressors of women and black Americans. Questions were raised, such as why were women kept from voting for so long? Why did so many have to struggle as part of the women's suffrage movement? Why are women still struggling to have workplace equality with men? With the civil rights movement still looming large, the youth of the nation had to ask, "Just how free are we as Americans? What should we be fighting for? Who should we be fighting against?"

The transcendentalists sought reprieve from authority and societal problems through alternative lifestyles, such as Thoreau's seclusion in the woods or Emerson's and Whitman's praise of individualistic and humanistic ideals. The countercultural movement took a similar approach.

They shared belongings and food, bypassing the system of capitalism that set America apart from communist Vietnam. Customary standards in dress and hairstyles were cast to the wind.

A bigger shift from traditional values came from the movement's rejection of the institution of marriage, opting instead for "free love." The use of marijuana and LSD also marked the movement. Sexual promiscuity and illegal drug use were great ways to undermine both governmental and religious institutions. Ethical values were now based upon one's subjectivity and not on time-honored authority and tradition.

The blossom of the counterculture movement came as the 60s drew to an end. The Woodstock Music Festival, three days of peace and music, attracted 300,000 to 500,000 youth, with estimates varying so widely because the fence around the festival grounds was torn down. Tickets could not be collected, and while many unticketed people were in attendance, many who did have tickets never made it to the festival because the New York State Thruway was shut down due to the unprecedented traffic.

What is usually forgotten about Woodstock is that it was originally billed as an "Aquarian Exposition." The Aquarius Age is linked with astrology, and for many members of the countercultural movement, its genesis was marked by their generation's arrival. This age was seen to be ushering in a new system: out with the old and in with the new.

And what exactly was new about the Aquarian Exposition seen by many as a defining moment, not only for rock music but a generation? Hinduism. Swami Satchadinanda opened the festival with an address. In it, he said,

> America is becoming a whole. America is helping everybody in the material field, but the time has come for America to help the whole world with spirituality also. And, that's why from the length and breadth, we see people—thousands of people, yoga-minded, spiritual-minded.[12]

In an exhortation to the festival-goers, Swami Satchadinanda delivered the following words: "So, let all our actions, and all our arts, express Yoga. Through that sacred art of music, let us find peace that will pervade all over the globe."[13] He also shared that "here the East has come into the West," and he closed his address by teaching and leading the festival attendees in a Hindu chant of "Hari Om" and "Ram."[14]

John Morris, the head of production for Woodstock, referred to Swami Satchadinanda's Woodstock address as "a blessing. It was like an invocation or whatever."[15] The embrace of Hinduism at Woodstock rolled on through the festival with yoga led from the stage as a time-filler while bands arrived and set up for their sets. Like most aspects of pluralism, words and practices were removed from their original context and application and cast into an eclectic conglomeration to meet the purpose and desires of any individual.

Calling Swami Satchadinanda's opening address "an invocation" doesn't mean the rest of what transpired at Woodstock was Hindu-related, as one would expect everything to be Christ-related after an invocation at a Roman Catholic mass. For example, the yoga at Woodstock was far removed from a spiritual path to oneness with Brahman. The practice was presented as just "another way to get high."[16]

As the counterculture movement faded and the hippies got their hair cut, found nine-to-five jobs, married, and had kids, the Age of Aquarius and its New Age musings weren't laid to rest as easily. The New Age movement has no single founder or central figure, authoritative text, official doctrine, or organizational structure; the same can be said for Hinduism. *New Age* is a term that is applied to an incredibly diverse group of people who, individually and in some cases collectively, practice and adhere to assorted spiritual disciplines such as connecting to past lives and lovers, communication with spirits or angels, astrology, tarot card reading, meditation, yoga, astral projection, interpreting dreams, using crystals for healing, mind-reading, palm-reading, magic, and witchcraft. Though a New Ager might not practice all of these, or even any of these, disciplines in their spirituality, New Agers commonly share beliefs in an impersonal, divine energy or force that is in all things. They believe that when we die, we will be reincarnated; that everything is united; and that all religions are one.

What's ironic about the New Age movement is that there isn't much new within it. Reincarnation is a central tenet of many of the longest-standing religions of the East. I've already mentioned that Hinduism teaches the unity of all, as does much of Eastern philosophy and mysticism. Astrology used to guide the fate of nations, empires, and people long before it was used in modern horoscopes to help a person know who to date and when to sell their stocks. The magic arts, divination, and various forms of communication via mediums have long been staples of occultism.

What's new about New Age beliefs is the popularity that these practices now have in the West. In most large bookstores, like Barnes and Noble, the New Age section and all that comes with it, including such popular topics as UFOs, the Mayan calendar (which isn't so popular now that 2013 has rolled around), and even vampirism, is as big or bigger than the Christian section. It definitely dwarfs other religions that have but one or two shelves each in most cases. With its pluralistic beliefs, the New Age movement has no boundaries.

It's now common for someone to say they are a blend of religions, claiming to be a Christian-Buddhist for example, or for a person to just claim to be spiritual while forming his or her own mixed bag of religious practices and beliefs. Another tendency is for a person to claim adherence to one specific religion, but actually hold New Age beliefs, or be simply syncretistic. A poll by the Pew Research Center's Forum on Religion and Public Life released in 2009 reveals that this is happening even within the incredibly exclusive religion, Christianity. According to the poll, large percentages of American Christians mix New Age practices with their Christianity. Twenty-nine percent say they have been in touch with the dead, 23 percent believe there are spiritual energies in trees, 23 percent believe in reincarnation, and 14 percent have consulted a psychic.[17]

Ask if Christians and Muslims pray to the same God, and a class in a Christian private high school will be torn over the answer. Neither will gain any ground in swaying the other position in the ensuing debate. I know because I have seen it happen firsthand on two different occasions. Of course, there is actually a third position present, one of ambivalence, which is another product of pluralism.

Even former president George W. Bush, who was always very vocal about his Christian faith, said that Christians and Muslims pray to the same God. Bush went an extra step into pluralism by moving outside of the Abrahamic religions, saying that those of *any* religion pray to the same God.[18]

The Heart of Pluralism

The 60s counterculture movement that questioned absolute truth and morality and the objectivity for measuring such standards did so because its members saw that people were being killed over differences that weren't directly affecting them in their personal freedoms. Different forms of government cause war, cultural clashes lead to hatred, racial differences bring oppression, the physically stronger sex suppresses the weaker sex, and religions ... well, I think we know the problems that arise from the interaction of diverse faiths vying for the ultimate authority on the most important questions of life, death, and the afterlife. The slogan that summed up the counterculture movement was "Make love not war," and this is the heart behind modern-day pluralism—love.

Those who imply pluralism when they use the words *tolerance* and *coexistence* are doing so from a correct heart position. From their standpoint, the often hateful reaction that intolerance offers in response to diversity is the root of humanity's self-inflicted pain and suffering. If we could only love one another, we could heal the world. If we could just get to that point where we recognize that we are all brothers and sisters, we could make the world a better place for ourselves and future generations.

Love covers a multitude of sins. Love trumps all ideologies, philosophies, and religions. If some refuse to hop aboard the love (pluralism) train because they are still elevating their beliefs above love, then all we have to do is convince them that the world's competing truth-claims are actually, at their core, the same. Differences are only apparent. All religions can be boiled down to one common denominator. That one common denominator is love. Love is all we need, and that is the heart behind pluralism.

Losing Truth and Love in Pluralism

Even if sincere love and conviction undergird the principles of pluralism, sincerity does not create truth. When I was young, I sincerely believed in the existence of a gift-giving Santa Claus who traveled the world with his flying reindeer on the eve of the celebration of Jesus' birth. It is quite possible to be sincere and still be wrong.

To the pluralist, discussions of what is true and what is false aren't necessary, because as Swami Vivekanada said, "all religions are true." In pluralism, absolute truth is beyond our capacity to discern. Truth becomes relative. This relativism has brought about a rejection of objective truth based on logic, reason, science, and the existence of a transcendent, personal God. The resulting vacuum has been filled with individual experience, feelings, and cultural background. These now serve as the guideposts for each person's unique, subjective conclusions on the nature of reality, which is ever in flux. Since I cannot have the same experiences as someone else, what's true for me may not be true for you. But neither of us is wrong.

Pluralism is the *zeitgeist*, the spirit of our age, that strives for unification, hope, peace, and change. The sacrifice for such progress is to jettison truth, a small price to pay for peace.

But is it? When truth becomes relative, the foundations of society are upended and humanity is placed on a slippery slope. If all truth is relative, words lose their meaning in a myriad of equally valid interpretations. Where can we draw the line on issues of morality, history, and interpreting literature?

A former student of mine wrote an opinion column in our school newspaper in which he shared what he had learned from watching annual marathons of the 1960s *Twilight Zone* television show. The Syfy Channel reruns them every New Year's Day. He wrote, "The moral ambiguity of the characters and the situations in the Twilight Zone led me to understand that there are two sides to every coin, and issues of ethics never exist in a black and white world."

I am pretty certain that this student doesn't truly believe that there are *never* any black and white issues in the realm of ethics, but for many born in the 1990s and 2000s, the gray areas of morality are rapidly expanding. This is largely because many of them have only been exposed to postmodern thinking, with its denial of an objective standard on which to base their moral judgments. If my black is your white, and we are both equally authoritative with no higher standard, we find ourselves in a very precarious moral dilemma.

When I meet individuals who truly profess that none of us can judge what is right and wrong for another person, I love to question them about the extremes of morality. If all truth is relative, can we say Hitler was wrong in the murder of six million Jews? If the person holds his ground and says no, I bring it closer to home, and speak of killing his family members, or his pets, since some people cherish their pets more than their next of kin.

Even this scenario isn't full-proof in bringing a person to acknowledge the need for an objective standard of morality. Once I spoke with a female student at the University of California, Irvine who was so adamant about not being able to judge others' actions that she wouldn't even say a person would be wrong if he raped her.

In most cases, relative moralists start to backpedal and form lines dividing black and white when the correct levers are pulled. When they make such judgments, I then press them on what grounds they can form their decisions. All they can usually offer is their personal feelings and experiences. But feelings and experiences can never serve as universal, objective standards. After such conversations, I am grateful that the law doesn't function on subjective terms. The words that make up the laws of the land have concrete meanings. At the end of the day, if there are contradictory interpretations of the meaning of a law or contractual agreement, both cannot be allowed to stand. Juries must give one verdict and one verdict only.

My faith even in the objectivity of the law is waning, since I recently read a news report that in the UK, a fourteen-year-old male raped a five-year-old he was babysitting. He was spared a custodial sentence because the judge ruled that it was the fault of society, due to the teen's exposure to pornography. Society received judgment, not the boy's actions. According to his cultural exposure, he couldn't receive blame. Judgment was still dealt by the law in this case, but it wasn't dealt in accordance with the letter of the law. Judgment was based upon the boy's life experiences and the judge's opinion. If the boy hadn't been exposed to pornography and had more parental supervision, then I assume the judge would have found him to be at fault, and the teenager would have received a custodial sentence.

As judges open the doors to question even the meaning of the words of the laws already on the books, the road ahead looks bleak. For the pluralists, however, it's sunny days ahead because, for them, their guiding compasses are their emotions. Happiness becomes the source and norm of life's conundrums. Unless, of course, the euphoria wears off and never returns, no matter how many times you remarry, change jobs, or incorporate new self-help fads or spiritual practices. It is possible to become so directionless, chasing the winds of an ever-changing reality, that you can get lost in your own subjectivity. What's true for you may not even be discernible anymore.

Finding Truth through Contradictions

Unification and truth cannot always coincide. When unification is forced, truth is lost; I believe that this chapter has shown that. Even love becomes subject to relativism. As long as the goal of literal pluralism is to bring about social pluralism, then the heart is in the right place, but the mind isn't. When people claim that all religions are the same or that all religions lead to God, they either haven't taken the time to study the world's religions, or they in fact are being intolerant by only embracing pluralistic religions. They reject all religions that assert exclusive truth-claims, such as Jesus' claim in John 14:6 to be "the way, the truth, and the life," the only way to God. Such a claim contradicts the claims of all other religions, to the point that if Christianity is true, then all other religions must be false.

The goal of this book is to evaluate the claims of religious pluralism in light of such apparent contradictions and to raise the level of true tolerance toward the world's religions by upholding and proclaiming what makes each religion unique and special to its adherents. If this can be accomplished, it swings wide the gates for interreligious dialogue among orthodox practitioners of contradicting worldviews. The end goal is to usher in the evaluation of religious truth-claims. Are any of them true? With what each religion claims about the purposes of life and the future of an individual after death, this is the most important question a person can ask for the here and now and for his or her eternal future.

THE MULTIPLE
RELIGIOUS PATHS

Religion has divided people. I don't think there's any
difference between the pope wearing a large hat and parading
around with a smoking purse and an African painting his
face white and praying to a rock.
—Howard Stern

Two roads diverged in a wood, and I—
I took the one less traveled by,
And that has made all the difference
—"The Road Not Taken" by Robert Frost

Is Howard Stern correct that, no matter what the facade of a religion appears to be, there's no difference between them? Or did Robert Frost nail it: are there diverging paths, and it makes all the difference which one you go by?

Religious pluralism would say it doesn't matter, because all paths are equally valid and true. *Tolerance* has lost its original meaning. It no longer stands for allowing people the freedom to believe whatever they want. Now it means people can't be judged for holding the beliefs that they profess and for living out such values. The new-order of tolerance necessitates an inclusive attitude and pluralistic worldview. The exclusive truth-claims of the old order of tolerance created true/false dichotomies that welcomed judgment and scrutiny, with the understanding that people who found differing conclusions would still have the right to believe what they chose to believe.

A modern example of blending multiple religious paths, and thus unifying them, can be found in the opening chapters of Elizabeth Gilbert's popular 2006 autobiographical book, *Eat, Pray, Love*, which was later adapted for the big screen with Julia Roberts playing Gilbert. Much of the book centers on experiencing God. Regarding the choice to use the word *God*, Gilbert explains that she "could just as easily use the words *Jehovah, Allah, Shiva, Brahma, Vishnu,* or *Zeus.* Alternatively, I could call God "That," which is how the ancient Sanskrit scriptures say it, and which I think comes close to the all-inclusive and unspeakable entity I have sometimes experienced."[1]

Taking Gilbert's words at face value, the divine figures she mentions from Judaism, Islam, Hinduism, and Greek mythology are interchangeable. Her reasoning is that this is possible because "He" or "She"—Gilbert also states that either pronoun is acceptable for God—can go by any name because God is so "all-inclusive" that human language is insufficient to properly name the being she chooses to call "God."

If you take note of Gilbert's explanations and those of other religious pluralists like her, their beliefs are based on their personal feelings, opinions, and experiences. To make the assertion that Jehovah, Allah, Shiva, Brahma, Vishnu, and Zeus are interchangeable names for God means that these names must be entirely divorced from the context from which they are derived. To believe religious pluralism is true apart from personal feelings, solely based on religious studies, a person must have less than a kindergarten knowledge of the world's religions. A brief reading of the religious texts of only a handful of religions reveals contradictions on fundamental levels.

As long as ignorance is bliss and subjectivity reigns, religious pluralism will continue to exist and even thrive. Studies indicate that such conditions exist in America, showing that most Americans are ignorant about the basic history, geography, and teachings of their own religious faiths and those of others.

The Pew Research Center's Forum on Religion and Public Life conducted a survey in 2010 to ascertain how much religious knowledge

Americans possess. A random sample of 3,412 adults were contacted via phone and asked thirty-two religious questions. The average score was 50 percent, or an F! The highest-scoring group was the atheists and agnostics; they got 65 percent, or a D. Mormons outscored Christians on questions about the Bible and Christianity.

Among all respondents, 54 percent knew that the Qur'an is the holy book of Islam. Fifty-one percent knew that Joseph Smith was Mormon. Forty-seven percent know that the Dalai Lama is Buddhist. Forty-six percent knew Martin Luther's role in Christian history. Only 38 percent knew that Vishnu and Shiva are connected with Hinduism. At least America passed with B-level scores on the questions regarding that Mother Teresa was Roman Catholic and that atheists don't believe there is a God.[2]

Such results explain why individuals can now call themselves Buddhist-Christians and why a devout Christian I know almost left the Christian faith after reading Gilbert's *Eat, Pray, Love*, having become convinced that Christianity's exclusive truth-claims must be false in light of Gilbert's open-mindedness and free-bird nature. These people lacked the necessary religious knowledge to be acquainted with the contradictory teachings of each religion.

Let me ask you some questions. Can you name the Ten Commandments? Do you know what the Passover is in Judaism and what it signifies? Which religion observes fasting during Ramadan and which celebrates Diwali? Which religion observes Hanukkah, and why? Do you know if Hindus and Buddhists should eat meat? Can observant Muslims drink alcohol? Do you know which religion practices yoga? Which religion seeks nirvana? Can you name the five pillars of Islam? How is the belief in one God different among Jews, Muslims, and Christians? Do you know the dates of the lives of the Buddha, Jesus Christ, and Muhammad, and where they lived and taught? Do all religions believe in a god? Do all religions pray? Do all religions believe in an eternal heaven or hell? Do any major religions believe in reincarnation? Do all religions have the same ethical laws of what is right and what is wrong, and if not, how are they different?

All of these questions are related to Hinduism, Buddhism, Judaism, Christianity, and Islam. These are considered by most scholars to be the world's major religions. Religions are usually classified as major or minor based upon the number of adherents. All of these religions, except Judaism, rank in the top five most followed religions. I keep Judaism in my list of major religions because it predates Christianity and Islam, and both of these religions trace their lineage and history to the founding patriarch of Judaism, Abraham, as well as to Adam and Eve, the first created humans. Most of the minor religions split from these five major religions or have similar patterns of beliefs and rituals found within these major five.

The goal of this chapter is to present the teachings of these five religions. I have chosen to present the key figures, places, events, historical dates, doctrines, and rituals for each of the following World Religions: Hinduism, Buddhism, Judaism, Christianity, and Islam. This glossary is not alphabetized. Instead it is sequenced for a coherent presentation of these religions' origins and basic beliefs and practices. If you know these hundred terms and their contexts within their given religions, you will have enough of a grasp of these major religions to answer the questions I posed two paragraphs before, as well as to score high on the religious survey given by the Pew Research Center.

The glossary will equip you with the knowledge needed to converse with adherents of these major religions, as well as followers of minor religions that are similar. Simply reading the glossary will expose apparent contradictions among these religions concerning what is considered divine, the ultimate problem of mankind, and how that problem can be overcome, as well as differences in the afterlife and the final destiny of mankind. Interested readers can learn more about these religions by consulting the following authorities: *The Oxford Dictionary of World Religions*, Michael Molloy's *Experiencing the World's Religions*, Stephen Prothero's *Religious Literacy*, and *ReligiousTolerance.org*.

Hinduism

Hinduism is one of the oldest religions still in practice and gets its name from the Indus River, the region Hinduism emerged from. It remains the dominant religion of India. It has no official creeds or organizational bodies for oversight. Hinduism is like a melting pot of thousands of gods and goddesses with various expressions of belief. It is a melting pot because it is not polytheistic; instead, these gods, goddesses, and practices come together in monism, or pantheism, meaning that all is one and all is God. Hindus believe in reincarnation, that the imperishable soul migrates from one body to another at death. The actions of a person or animal in this life direct the position of rebirth in the next life through karma. The ultimate goal is to achieve *moksha* and break free from this circle of life, escaping the yoke of karma.

1. Harappa Culture and Aryan Influence—The roots of Hinduism are traced back to the Harappa culture of the Indus Valley. It is one of the oldest known civilizations, and aspects of Hindu practices can be found in archeological digs there. Some scholars theorize there was a migration of Aryan tribes into India that mingled with the Harappa culture, whether forcefully or peacefully, and that the Aryan influence played a big role in forming the way Hinduism is today. The origin of the caste system can be attributed to this theory of outside influence, with the Aryan tribes rising to the top social class of the Indus Valley. Thus the caste system was used in a religious framework to ensure the Aryans would stay at the top. However, the Aryan influence theory is losing ground in contemporary thought, with preference now given to the theory of a single, continuous group in the Indus Valley giving rise to the conglomeration that is now Hinduism.

2. Vedas—The Vedas are the only divinely revealed sacred text of Hinduism. How they were received and who received them remains a mystery. They consist of four collections of priestly chants. The oldest and most popular Veda is the Rig Veda, which can be found in any large bookstore chain. The Rig Veda contains a creation story that explains Hindu beliefs regarding monism and pantheism. The Rig teaches that the god Purusha was sacrificed by other gods, and his body became the universe and everything within it. This narrative provides a good explanation for the caste system, the head of Purusha being the top caste and the other castes being formed from lower body parts.

3. The Upanishads—*Upanishad* means "sitting near." The image is that of a student sitting near a teacher. In the Upanishads, Brahmin priests wrote their reflections and meditations on the traditions of the Vedas. It is in the Upanishads that the theology of Hinduism becomes somewhat systematized, with explanations for practical applications of Vedic traditions to life. A parallel to the Upanishads would be the Talmud of Judaism, in which rabbis reflect on God's Word and then supply an application of the Scripture to God's people.

4. Brahman—Brahman is the divine reality at the heart of all things. Ultimately, this means that everything is God and everything is connected and one through Brahman.

5. Atman—Atman = Brahman. *Atman* is the term used to describe Brahman on an individual level. When speaking of the divine within a single person, the word *Atman* is used. When speaking on the universal level, *Brahman* is used. Also on the individual level, the word *shiva* refers to a person's soul.

6. Maya—The reason that we do not recognize the oneness and divinity of all things is because maya keeps this ultimate reality hidden from our senses. *Maya* means illusion. It is an illusion that we think we are separate and distinct individuals. In the movie *The Matrix*, the matrix was a construct created to pull the wool over our eyes to keep us from seeing what is real. The ancient Greek philosopher Plato, in his allegory of the cave, presented the idea that humanity is bound in a cave, staring at dancing shadows on a wall. The shadows were not what they perceived; there were real people behind them, dancing by a fire that no one could see. Both *The Matrix* and Plato's allegory of the cave present concepts similar to Hinduism's maya.

7. Samsara—Also known as "the circle of life" or reincarnation, samsara is the process whereby the divine soul of a person passes from one body into the next at death. This process is described in detail and explained in chapter two of the Bhagavad Gita.

8. Karma—This is likely the most-used Hindu word in Western culture. In the West, the word *karma* has taken on the meaning of "what goes around comes around" or "getting what is deserved." Good karma means someone will be financially or relationally blessed, while bad karma has been used to explain all sorts of misfortunes. Sharon Stone even blamed the devastating 2008 earthquake in Sichuan Province, China, as karma working against the Chinese government. Needless to say, she got blasted for such comments. Karma in Hinduism isn't the Western concept of "you reap what you sow." For Hindus, karma dictates the direction of one's next life. Good karma can send a person to a higher caste in the next life, and really bad karma can send a person back as an animal.

9. Caste System—Linked to the concepts of samsara and karma is the social caste system. There are four castes, and members of a caste should not socialize with members of other castes or marry someone from a different caste. Applying this caste system outside of India can be difficult, and in India's large cities, the castes are dissolving. In many rural areas of India, however, the caste system is very much alive and well.

The top caste is the Brahmin caste. Brahmins are Hindu priests. Priests often served as cooks, since as priests they could interact with those of lower castes. The caste below the Brahmins traditionally included warriors and rulers. The next caste belongs to those with a skilled trade. The bottom caste is comprised of unskilled workers.

Dalits are people who are not members of any caste. They are below the castes. Dalits are commonly referred to as "untouchables," because members of other castes never touch a Dalit.

9. Moksha—This is the highest goal of Hinduism. It is the breaking free from samsara, achieving union with Brahman. No longer will a person be under the yoke of karma and the illusion of maya. A person is unable to know if he or she has achieved moksha in this life; it isn't reached until death.

10. Yoga—*Yoga* means union. There are various forms of yoga in Hinduism, but they are all spiritual paths practiced to achieve a good reincarnation and union with Brahman. The yoga practiced in the West finds its origins in Hinduism and, for the most part, is stripped of its religious significance. The form of yoga that consists mainly of stretching, physical postures, movements, and breathing exercises is referred to as *hatha yoga* in Hinduism. *Bhakti yoga* is worship yoga in which practitioners devote themselves to worshiping a certain god or goddess, or multiple deities. Another form of yoga is *jnana yoga*, in which practitioners devote themselves to studying Hindu sacred texts, seeking union with Brahman through growth in knowledge. It is similar to the way that Christians study the Bible as a way of hearing God's voice and growing in their relationship with God.

11. Puja—A *puja* is a worship ritual in Hinduism. These rituals are numerous and diverse. Such rituals can be performed in devotion to a specific deity every day at a home altar, or in public at a temple. Special pujas are performed for festivals. The most important festival is Diwali, the festival of lights. A puja might involve numerous acts, including prayer, banging gongs, offerings of food, pouring of milk or water over a deity's idol.

12. Ganges River—The Ganges River is the most important geographic locale for Hindus. Its waters are regularly used for ritual purification, and it is a common practice to scatter the ashes of a deceased family member in the river in hopes of achieving moksha for the departed.

13. Guru—A spiritual teacher or guide is called a *guru*. A guru has come very near in experiencing oneness with Brahman and can serve as a guide to others in their pursuit of moksha.

14. Ashram—Religions are practiced in community, and Hinduism is no different. Although there are many ways for Hindus to be solo practitioners, communities of Hindus seeking union with Brahman have formed, and these are called *ashrams*. Ashrams are places for group practices of yoga and study of Hindu scriptures. The author Elizabeth Gilbert, in her book *Eat, Pray, Love,* shares her experiences of living in an ashram. Gilbert's experience of ashram life can be seen in the movie of the same name starring Julia Roberts.

15. Sacred Cow—Cows are sacred in Hindu belief. They are highly valued, right next to one's mother, and the connection to motherhood is in the provision of milk. Because of this, do not expect to have a hamburger in a McDonald's when visiting India. In fact, don't expect much meat at all in India. Hindus are vegetarians. This stems from the teaching of monism: even animals are divine and connected with humanity through Brahman. To kill an animal, even for food, is not good for karma.

16. Bhagavad Gita—This is an excerpt of the Hindu epic, the Mahabharata. It is the conversation between Arjuna and his charioteer, Krishna. The Bhagavad Gita finds Arjuna, a great warrior, on the brink of leading his army into battle against an army led by his cousins. Wars are never pretty, but civil wars are even worse, and Arjuna is conflicted about the situation. Isn't peace and losing ground better than shedding the blood of his relatives? Krishna gives advice concerning Arjuna's dilemma and convinces the warrior that sticking to his role in life, the duty he has been given, is a spiritual path to oneness with Brahman. This path is *karma yoga*, or action yoga. The Bhagavad Gita's teachings are very influential in encouraging Hindus to stay within their castes and the roles that come with those castes.

17. Avatar—An incarnation of a Hindu deity is called an *avatar*. Avatars are mostly associated with the god Vishnu.

18. Vishnu/Krishna/Rama—Vishnu is the most worshipped deity in Hinduism and is known largely through his avatars, of which there are ten. Not all of Vishnu's avatars are human in appearance; one was a fish and another a tortoise, for example. The two best-known avatars are Krishna and Rama. George Harrison of the Beatles sang a mantra to Vishnu, addressing both of these avatars by name in his solo song, "My Sweet Lord."

Krishna is the main figure of the Bhagavad Gita. Krishna and Rama both are depicted as having blue skin. James Cameron has openly said that these incarnations were the inspiration for the color of the Na'vi in his groundbreaking 3-D film, *Avatar*. The final avatar of Vishnu is said to come on a white horse, wielding a sword, to judge evil and end this cycle of the universe.

19. Trimurti—The Trimurti is commonly referred to as "the Trinity of Hinduism" among those most familiar with the Trinity of Christianity. The meaning of Trimurti is "three forms." It consists of the three deities Brahma, Vishnu, and Shiva. Each god plays a specific role. Brahma is the creator, Vishnu is the preserver, and Shiva is the destroyer. Destruction in Hinduism is not viewed in a negative light. Destruction is seen as similar to recycling; death gives birth to new life, the process of samsara.

20. Om—The symbol for om is commonly used to represent Hinduism. Om is thought to be the sound of Brahman, or even Brahman itself. In 1960s pop culture, om was discovered by the Moody Blues on their sophomore album, *In Search of the Lost Chord*.

Buddhism

Buddhism branched off from Hinduism in about the fifth century BC. It emerged from the teaching of Siddhartha Gautama, born a wealthy prince in or near what is present-day Nepal. He would become the Buddha, a title that means "Awakened One" or "Enlightened One."

In its conservative state, based on the teachings of the Buddha, Buddhism is an atheistic religion. The Buddha rejected the Hindu view that at the heart of all things there is one divine essence, Brahman. Because of its atheism, Buddhism in some circles is referred to as a philosophy rather than a religion.

The philosophy is essentially the Buddha's central teaching that life is suffering and that he had discovered the way to escape it. As Buddhism grew and spread throughout Asia, the teachings and practices of the Buddha blended with local religions and practices, gaining new precepts and even reincorporating aspects of Hinduism into Buddhist vocabulary and thought. Buddhism largely remains an Asian religion, but it is spreading to the West.

1. Siddhartha Gautama—There are varying versions of Siddhartha's life, none of which are authoritative, but they all follow the same basic outline. Siddhartha was miraculously conceived when a white elephant entered his mother's side, and he even had a miraculous birth, being born from her side as well. His mother died soon after his birth, and it was foretold by priests that he would either be a great king or a teacher. Siddhartha's father did not want the latter, striving to keep his son from exposure to pain or suffering of any kind. Siddhartha's father kept him within the palace grounds, providing him the best education and all the carnal pleasures of the world. However, Siddhartha disobeyed his father and left the palace. On this outing, he saw four sights of suffering that he had never imagined. These sights sparked his endeavor to learn why suffering exists and how it can be stopped. Once he reached enlightenment and suffering ceased for

Siddhartha, he spent the rest of his life teaching the middle path that is the end of suffering. A narrative of the Buddha's life is recorded in Hermann Hesse's novel *Siddhartha*.

2. The Great Going Forth—When Siddhartha left his father's palace, leaving behind his wife and son, to find answers to his questions, it is called the Great Going Forth. Living in a Hindu environment, Siddhartha followed numerous gurus and learned meditation. He lived the life of an ascetic, begging for his food and living outdoors. He went as far as starving himself, with the thought that he needed to separate himself from all physical desires and necessities to find the solution he sought. Nothing worked. But with the Great Going Forth, he swore not to return until he found the cure to suffering and, ultimately, death.

3. Bodhi Tree—Having lived life at both extremes, uberwealthy as a prince and starving as a wanderer, Siddhartha chose a middle path. In meditation under a tree one evening, he finally reached enlightenment. The tree under which he reached enlightenment is now called the bodhi tree. *Bodhi* means awakening or enlightenment.

4. Nirvana—When a person has reached enlightenment, he or she has achieved nirvana. Nirvana is the ultimate goal of Buddhism. Once it is reached, there is no more pain. It is also the end of karma and reincarnation. Unlike Hinduism's moksha, which is achieved after death, nirvana is experienced in this life, so an individual will know if he or she has found it while still living. Note: The Buddha retained the concepts of samsara and karma, with modification to fit his rejection of the Hindu teachings of Brahman, Atman, and the individual soul.

5. Three Jewels—Given the name *jewels*, three centerpieces are held in high esteem in the life of a Buddhist. They are the Buddha, the Dharma, and the Sangha.

6. Dharma—This word refers to the totality of the Buddha's teachings. This word entered American pop culture through the television show *Dharma and Greg*, which illustrated the clash between modernism and postmodernism and Western and Eastern philosophies through the marriage of Dharma, who was raised by hippie parents, and her lawyer husband, Greg, who was raised in a conservative, upper-class family.

7. Sangha—This term refers to a community of Buddhist monks and nuns who ideally live at a Buddhist temple.

8. The Three Marks of Reality—The Buddha recognized three universal experiences of reality. The first is suffering. Pain is a mark of reality. Note the use of the word *reality*; this is one of the divergences Buddhism took from Hinduism. Pain is illusory in Hinduism, a false perception brought about by maya; pain is reality in Buddhism.

The Buddha also observed that life is impermanent; everything is constantly changing. We don't always realize this because the change is gradual and we may not perceive it over time. Resistance to this change brings about suffering. Since our thoughts, personalities, and bodies are never the same from moment to moment, the Buddha discovered that we have no permanent identity. I may be called Andy for convenience, but what or who is Andy? I am many parts in motion; I am far different now after having lived in California, which is far different from my home state, Tennessee; and after having spent several years in China, I have a completely different view of America and my place in the world. People who knew me in high school, and even in college, will likely see many differences in my attitude, desires, goals, and mannerisms. With all these changes, am I still the same person that I used to be? And will I be the same at the end of my life?

The Buddha connected this teaching of no permanent identity to the concept of the soul, concluding that humans have no souls! In this the Buddha took another leave from Hinduism, denying Atman and Brahman, thus stripping away any sense of the divine that Hinduism holds central. The observations that we all suffer, that everything is constantly changing, and that we have no permanent self are called the Three Marks of Reality.

9. Anatman—This term means "no Atman." It denies the teaching that there is an eternal self, or soul, within individuals. It is linked with the mark of reality that there is no permanent self.

10. The Four Noble Truths—These four truths spring from the Three Marks of Reality. They summarize why there is suffering in life and how to end it. The First Noble Truth is "to live is to suffer." A very similar concept is found in the title of the Metallica song, "To Live is to Die." The Second Noble Truth is that desire causes suffering. Someone might crave designer fashion items, such as a Louis Vuitton purse, but not have the means to own them. Thus, that person suffers. A woman might desire to keep the beauty of her youth and suffer emotionally as she fights to retain it. A man might desire to lose weight, but then his host at a dinner party brings out dessert. The man suffers if he wants to eat it but doesn't, or he suffers from guilt if he gives in to the temptation. The same principle applies to anyone struggling with an addiction. The Third Noble Truth is a simple one: end desire, end suffering. The Fourth Noble Truth states that it is possible to end desire, and that is by following the eightfold path.

11. The Eightfold Path—The eightfold path isn't exactly a set of laws, although it might seem similar to some of the Ten Commandments from Judaism and Christianity. The eightfold path functions as a guide, a plan of action, that leads a person to Nirvana. The symbol for the eightfold path looks like a steering wheel for a boat; it has eight spokes, each representing one of the eight paths. The image of a circle is used because, although the eight paths are listed in a specific order, one is not more important than another; they are to be followed in unison. The paths are right view, right intent, right speech, right action, right occupation, right effort, right thought, and right concentration.

12. Ahimsa—This word means "no harm." A person should not cause or inadvertently bring harm of any kind to anything. This is the central aim of a Buddhist, and it springs from the eightfold path. The Buddhist temples I have visited in China contain turtle and fish habitats. Going beyond causing no harm, Buddhists will prevent harm. The turtles and fish at the temples have been rescued from food markets, purchased by Buddhists and then released at the temple to live out their lives in safety. Once I saw a comical sign at a temple that had provided the following English translation, "To release and protect, With one heart, Limited water resource, No release here please. – Full house to the coming tortoises and fishes." Apparently the practice can become too popular at the temples to accommodate the practice, so a Buddhist coworker explained to me that she releases fish at the famous West Lake, in Hangzhou, China, instead of at the nearest temple.

13. Theravada Buddhism—This is the conservative branch of Buddhism. Its name means "way of the elders." Theravada Buddhism strives to adhere to the original teachings of the Buddha, which means this branch of Buddhism focuses on life at Buddhist temples, where monks teach the Buddhist scriptures. Only monks can enter nirvana, and the way is found through detachment from desire achieved through meditation. Theravada monks typically wear orange robes.

14. Mahayana Buddhism—The name of this branch means "the big vehicle," depicting a giant wagon or boat that can fit many people. Thus for Mahayana Buddhism, nirvana is not limited to the monks. Instead of meditation as the way to attain enlightenment, one ought to pursue compassion. Mahayana Buddhism reincorporated the Hindu belief in Brahman, the divine nature within all things, and added to the Buddha's teachings the Buddha-nature, an eternal, ever-present, within all, cosmic Buddha energy. Siddhartha Gautama is seen as the incarnation of this Buddha-nature, and there have been multiple incarnations of Buddha, both before and after Siddhartha Gautama. The addition of bodhisattvas (see below) also distinguishes Mahayana Buddhism from Theravada Buddhism. The Mahayana branch of Buddhism has numerous schools, each with slightly different characteristics.

15. Bodhisattvas—Bodhisattvas are individuals who have reached enlightenment, but instead choose to reject nirvana and be reborn into the world to help others find the path they have realized. There are also heavenly bodhisattvas who now exist outside our world, but who still give aid and guidance from their heavenly residence. They have even from time to time broken into our physical plane to interact with us. They are a part of Mahayana Buddhism, but not Theravada Buddhism. Mahayana's view of the eternal Buddha-nature, coupled with the devotion and rituals directed toward the bodhisattvas and the Buddha, give this branch the typical appearance of a religion, with gods, offerings, and prayer.

16. Guanyin—In China, the most popular heavenly bodhisattva is Guanyin. She appears almost as often as, if not more often than the Buddha, and in some cases has her own temples. In most temples, the main room contains an image of the Buddha in meditation, sitting on a lotus flower. If a visitor walks behind the wall against which the Buddha sits, an image of Guanyin can often be found. She usually is depicted dressed in white in a standing position with a jar of water, or she is shown with a thousand arms, symbolizing her ability to reach out in compassion to everyone.

At the Hangzhou Orient Cultural Park in Xiaoshan, China, there is an eighteen-meter-high, man-made rock pillar that contains a Guanyin statue. The image emerges from the pillar to the sound of operatic music, smoke, and a water-fountain show. Water sprays from her jar onto the visitors below who have come to collect the water, catching it in bottles or umbrellas turned upside down. The water is said to have healing properties. The faithful take it home to ill family members or save it for when it's needed. The statue turns in a full circle as it sprays, and the crowd follows it around the rock pillar, catching as much of the water as possible. Others just kowtow to Guanyin as they are sprayed by her water. I have seen this firsthand, and I share it to illustrate the diversity of Buddhism. Conservatively, some argue Buddhism isn't a religion at all, because it has no God and no prayer. Liberally, Buddhism can have scenes like this with Guanyin, and other practices such as ancestor worship, prayers, and the worship of local deities that are far removed from anything taught by the Buddha himself.

17. Vajrayana/Tibetan Buddhism—This branch's name means "vehicle of the diamond" or "vehicle of the lightning bolt," indicating the speed at which this branch's followers are able to cut through to nirvana. Tibetan Buddhism, as it is commonly known in the West, is distinguished from other branches by the Dalai Lama, the spiritual leader and, for some, the political leader of Tibet. *Lamas* are monks or spiritual teachers, The Dalai Lama is considered to be a manifestation of Guanyin. It is believed that the Dalai Lama reincarnates after each life. A search is conducted to find who the new Dalai Lama is by seeing which baby recognizes personal items that belonged to the previous incarnation of the Dalai Lama.

Other traits that distinguish Tibetan Buddhism from other Buddhist branches are mandalas and prayer wheels. Mandalas are intricate designs consisting mostly of circles, squares, and arches. They are colorful and contain images related to Buddhism. Practitioners use mandalas for meditation. Tibetan prayer wheels come in various sizes and styles. Sometimes they are a rod with a cylinder top that can be spun by moving the rod in a circular motion. The top can be opened so a prayer written out on a piece of paper can be placed inside. There are also prayer pillars. Prayers are written on the sides of the pillars, and the petitioner need only spin the pillars as he or she walks by them. The concept is that the prayer emanates through the universe without the need for recitation. More prayers can be said through the spinning of multiple pillars than are possible for one person to recite.

18. Tripitaka—This is the name given to the Theravada scriptures. It means "three baskets." It is also sometimes called the Pali Canon. It comes in three parts: the first contains rules for monastic life, the second is a collection of the Buddha's discourses, and the third focuses on Buddhist doctrine formed from the Buddha's sermons. Mahayana Buddhism and Tibetan Buddhism do not share the same canon of scripture and have added many books not present in the Tripitaka.

19. Dhammapada—This is the most popular text from the Tripitaka, and English-language copies can easily be found at any major bookstore. It contains twenty-six chapters credited as the words of the Buddha.

20. Maitreya, Mi-lo-fo—An anticipated future Buddha who will usher in nirvana for everyone. The Sanskrit name for this Buddha is Maitreya. This future Buddha has numerous names and different images from culture to culture. I prefer to use the Chinese name, Mi-lo-fo. Mi-lo-fo is the image of the fat, laughing Buddha, which we Westerners commonly see at Asian restaurants. He is round and jovial, and is sometimes shown with a large bag of golden coins, because his arrival will be the end of all suffering. The image of the thin Buddha in meditation on the lotus flower is a stark contrast to the fat, laughing Mi-lo-fo. One focuses on the Buddha reaching enlightenment; the other focuses on the joy we will experience when nirvana comes to us all.

Judaism

Judaism is one of the oldest religions still in practice, and it is the first of the Abrahamic religions. Jews believe in one, eternal, transcendent God who is the creator of everything; before him there was nothing. He has many names and titles, but the key name he gave to Moses was "I AM." The Israelites then called him, Yahweh, "He is."

Yahweh has revealed himself to the world through the prophets he has sent to his chosen people, the Israelites. The history of the Hebrew Bible begins with the creation of the world and the first two humans, Adam and Eve. The origin of the Jewish nation, however, is in the covenant Yahweh made with Abraham: that Yahweh would bless Abraham, and Abraham's descendants would be a mighty nation whose numbers would be like that of the grains of sand on the shores. These descendants soon fell into slavery in Egypt, but Yahweh kept his promise. Through his chosen prophet, Moses, Yahweh led his people out of slavery with a series of miracles.

It was during this exodus from Egypt that the nation of Israel was established and another covenant was made with the Israelites. This covenant contained ordinances for festivals, sacrifices, and regulations to set the Lord's people apart from all other nations. The building of a temple was never a part of this covenant, but Yahweh allowed a temple to be built for him.

Throughout history, the Israelites have had two temples destroyed. They have been sent into exile and faced persecution again and again. The observance of their faith has adjusted to the loss of their temple and land, but they have always trusted in the promises of God to send them a savior whose kingdom will never end.

1. Tanakh/Hebrew Bible—The Hebrew Bible is formally called the Tanakh. It consists of three parts. The name of each part corresponds with the letters TNK, which is the abbreviated spelling of Tanakh in Hebrew.

T stands for *Torah*, the first five books of the Hebrew Bible, written by Moses. Torah, though commonly translated as "law," is more aptly translated as "teachings" or "instructions," since it contains more than just God's law. The Torah does contain the law, six hundred and thirteen commandments to be exact, but the Torah also contains the history of how Yahweh called the Jews, freeing them from Egyptian slavery and establishing them as his holy, chosen people.

N stands for *Nevi'im*, which means the prophets. The Nevi'im has eight books. The first books of the Nevi'im focus on the history of Israel, which are Joshua, Judges, Samuel, and Kings. The next books focus on the words Yahweh directly gave to the prophets Isaiah, Jeremiah, Ezekiel, and those found in the Book of the Twelve, to speak to the Israelites.

K stands for *Ketuvim*, which means the writings. The Ketuvim has eleven books. It contains narrative history, hymns, proverbs, and short stories.

In total, the Tanakh has twenty-four books. Although the Protestant Christian Old Testament is divided into thirty-nine books, it contains the same text as the Tanakh.

2. Covenant—*Covenants* are central to the Jewish faith. A modern-day word for covenant would be *treaty* or *contract*. There are numerous covenants recorded in the Tanakh, some of which were conditional and some that were not. Some of the key covenants were made with Noah, Abraham, Moses, and David. After a worldwide flood, the Lord promised

Noah that he would never destroy the world through water again. The Lord gave the rainbow as a seal of that promise. With Abraham, the Lord promised to make Abraham's descendants into a mighty nation. The covenant given to Moses on Mount Sinai after the exodus established the Israelites as the Lord's people. David was promised a descendant whose reign would never cease; that would be the reign of the expected Messiah.

3. Messiah—The word *messiah* means "anointed one." Anointing individuals with oil was a sign given by Yahweh to show that certain people were set aside for specific offices. Prophets, priests, and kings were anointed in ancient Israel. There are indications within the Tanakh that the expected "anointed one," will fulfill all three roles. "The Lion of the Tribe of Judah" in Genesis chapter 49 is an example of a title and a prophecy that is interpreted to foretell the coming of a warrior-king messiah. "Root of Jesse" and "Branch of David" are other messianic titles within the Tanakh.

4. Tabernacle, Temple—*Tabernacle* means "dwelling place." Part of the covenant given at Mount Sinai was that the Israelites would construct a tent where Yahweh would dwell among his people. Whenever the Israelites traveled, the priests moved the tabernacle with them, and thus Yahweh always accompanied his people. The tabernacle had a courtyard enclosed by a fence. The tabernacle was located in the western end of the courtyard, and it was divided into rooms by a thick curtain. The first room was called the Holy Place, and the innermost room was the Most Holy Place, sometimes called the Holy of Holies. The courtyard had an altar for burnt offerings. The Holy Place had a table for bread, an incense altar, and a lampstand. The Most Holy Place had the ark of the covenant, which served as the throne seat of the Lord. Yahweh's glory dwelled within the Most Holy Place. No one could enter into it without dying except for the high priest, and he only did this once a year on the Day of Atonement.

Once King David's enemies were defeated and he had settled in his palace, David did not think it fit for him to reside in a palace made of cedar while Yahweh was left to dwell in a tent. He desired to build a temple for God. Yahweh allowed the temple to be built by David's son, Solomon. This temple replaced the tabernacle and was built in 960 BC. The temple was destroyed by the Babylonians in 586 BC, when the Israelites were also sent into exile. The Book of Ezra records the rebuilding of the temple when the Israelites were called back from exile by Cyrus, king of Persia. This second temple was never destroyed, but it was renovated and expanded by Herod the Great, at which point it was called Herod's Temple. This temple was destroyed in AD 70, along with most of Jerusalem, by the Romans. Today the Muslim Dome of the Rock sits where the temple once stood.

5. Prophets, Priests, and Kings—All three of these were offices whose holders were appointed by Yahweh. The Tanakh records the anointing of some of Israel's prophets, priests, and kings as they were installed in their positions of service to God's people.

Prophets were representatives of Yahweh who spoke Yahweh's Word to his people and to other nations. The Jews consider Moses to be the greatest of the prophets. For a prophet to be a true prophet, all of his words that are declared to be from the Lord must come to pass.

Priests had to be from the tribe of Levi as instituted by God. They were men appointed to be intermediaries between Yahweh and his people. They were the ones who were allowed to conduct the rituals and sacrifices in the tabernacle, as spelled out in the Torah. The high priest was the only one who could enter the Holy of Holies to perform the required sacrifices on Yom Kippur, the Day of Atonement. Aaron was the first high priest.

God did not intend for the Israelites to have kings like other nations. He was to be their king. But the Israelites grumbled and wanted an earthly king. The Lord gave them the warning through his prophet Samuel that a king would abuse his position, misuse their sons in battle, and overtax them. The Israelites wanted to hear none of it; they wanted a king that they could see!

The first king was Saul, who disobeyed the Lord and lost favor with him. He was followed by David, who established Israel's borders and brought peace from their enemies. His son Solomon replaced the tabernacle with the first temple. The kings who succeeded Solomon either followed God or did not, and the Tanakh makes special note of which path a king chose to follow. There was usually much bloodshed and power struggle over the ascension of new kings, and eventually Israel was divided into two kingdoms. Both fell into the hands of the Babylonians, resulting in the destruction of the temple and the exile of God's people in 586 BC.

6. Holy—In Judaism, the Lord is holy. Israel is a holy people. The Hebrew language is even considered holy! *Holy* means "set apart." God is set apart from all things, for who is like him? The Jews are set apart from all other peoples. They are God's chosen ones, and their apartness is made visible through the external observances of the Law, such as male circumcision and following a kosher diet. The Israelites were told by God to be holy just as he is holy.

7. Sin—Breaking any of the laws given in the Torah is a sin. Man was not created sinful in the garden of Eden, but after the fall of Adam and Eve, the inclination of man's heart became evil from childhood. Since God is holy, sin causes separation between God and man. God must not allow the breaking of his laws to go without punishment. From the fall, it was revealed that death is a punishment for sin.

8. Sacrifices—To atone for their sins and be reconciled, God gave the Israelites various sacrifices they could offer. He also provided different offerings as voluntary acts of worship. The sacrifices, procedures, and purposes for them are laid out in detail in Leviticus. There were burnt offerings, grain offerings, fellowship offerings, sin offerings, and guilt offerings. The sacrificial victims included bulls, rams, birds, goats, lambs, bread, oil, flour, and grains. Since the destruction of the temple in AD 70, Jews have not offered sacrifices. Forgiveness of sins is still available to them because God desires mercy over sacrifice. A heart of repentance, brokenness, and contriteness over one's sins will bring forgiveness to those who trust in Yahweh's promises.

9. Decalogue—Another name for the Ten Commandments. In Exodus when these commandments were given, the Torah does not refer to them as commandments; instead, they are called "words." Hence, the Jews refer to them as the Decalogue, the Ten Words. These words were the start of the Sinai covenant. For the Jews and their numbering of the words, the first word isn't even a command. It is a proclamation from Yahweh. "I am the Lord your God, who brought you out of Egypt, out of the land of slavery." This opening proclamation defines the terms of the covenant: in essence, "I care for you and have set you free. I have your best interests at heart, so you can faithfully submit to me as I ask that you do x, y, and z." This is great news for the Jews. They weren't given a list of commands to follow to arouse Yahweh to rescue them, or to keep his favor. They were saved apart from the observance of the Law, before the Law was even given! This insight is generally lost in both Judaism and Christianity.

10. Sabbath—One of the commandments of the Decalogue is that the Jews would remember the Sabbath and keep it holy. The Sabbath is the seventh day of the week. Just as Yahweh created the world in six days and rested from creating on the seventh, so should man work for six days and rest from all of his labors on the seventh. The custom was to count days from sundown to sundown, so a day would begin at night. Because of this, Jews observe the Sabbath from Friday at sundown to Saturday at sundown. Thus, by current reckoning, Saturday is the Jewish Sabbath. The way the Sabbath is observed and what constitutes work varies among Jews today, but most observance-based sects attend worship gatherings at synagogues on these days, for prayer and readings from the Tanakh.

11. Yom Kippur—The first high holy day is Rosh Hashanah, which is the Jewish New Year's Day. It is commemorated by a day of rest and by the blowing of shofars, traditional Jewish trumpets, on the first day of the seventh month of the Jewish calendar. On the tenth day of the seventh month is the close of the high holy days with Yom Kippur. *Yom Kippur* means "Day of Atonement." This was the day the high priest was supposed to enter the Most Holy Place and make atonement for his sins with a bull, and for the sins of Israel with a goat. He took a live goat and confessed over it all the sins of Israel. A man appointed for the task then led the goat out into the wilderness, where it was left to die. This is where the term *scapegoat* comes from. This goat took the blame for the sins of Israel, and by being led into the wilderness, it symbolized that their sins had been removed. Leviticus chapter 16 lists the procedure for this day. However, none of those procedures can be followed today since the temple is destroyed. To observe Yom Kippur now, Jews fast all day and pray and repent for their sins at a synagogue.

12. Passover—The first observance of Passover was portrayed in the Charlton Heston movie, *The Ten Commandments*. After a series of plagues sent by Yahweh upon the Egyptians, the pharaoh still would not let Yahweh's people go. The final plague was the plague of the firstborn. The Lord sent an angel of death over Egypt that took the lives of the firstborn son of every household, unless the doorframe of the home was covered with the blood of a year-old, male lamb without defect. Every doorframe smeared with lamb's blood was passed over by the angel, and the firstborn son was spared. The families were ordered to stay indoors, eat the lamb in haste, and be prepared to flee Egypt. After the deaths of all the Egyptian firstborn sons, pharaoh commanded the Israelites to leave. The commemoration of the exodus is a lasting ordinance that is observed every year. For Passover today, Jews eat lamb with bitter herbs (to remember their suffering in Egypt). They remove all yeast from their houses and eat only unleavened bread (which symbolizes the haste in which they fled Egypt, having no time to wait for the bread to rise). The commemoration of Passover continues the next day with the Feast of Unleavened Bread, which is a seven-day feast.

13. Sukkot—This is a mandatory, seven-day festival. It is also referred to as "the Feast of Ingathering," because originally it was a harvest festival. The Jews lived in tents or booths for those seven days. This explains the other names Sukkot has, "the Feast of Tabernacles" or "the Feast of Booths." Living outdoors in tents commemorates the Israelites' wandering in the wilderness for forty years, from the time of the exodus to their entry into the Promised Land. It serves as a reminder of God's continual provision even now. Christians do not observe this festival, but if they did, it would remind them likewise that they are still sojourners in this land. Just as Yahweh provided for the Israelites in the wilderness and brought them safely home, so too shall he guide them through the wilderness of this life to their eternal home in heaven. Jews today live outdoors in *sukkahs*, covered booths. If they do not have a yard, they may set up a *sukkah* on a balcony, even if they live in a New York high-rise.

14. Hanukkah—Known by many as the "Jewish Christmas," Hanukkah is an eight-day festival. In the second century BC, Jerusalem was taken over by the Syrians. King Antiochus IV sacrificed a pig, an unclean animal to the Jews, to the Greek god Zeus within the Jewish temple. Needless to say, this upset the Jews mightily. Led by Judas Maccabeus, the Jews took back the temple by force. They needed to cleanse and rededicate the temple. One aspect of the temple regulations was that the lampstand in the Holy Place had to remain lit at all times. They only had enough oil to keep it burning for a day, but they began the rededication anyway. Miraculously, the oil lasted for eight days until they could get more. This is why Hanukkah lasts for eight days. Each night of the festival, Jews light one branch of a nine-armed menorah, give gifts, and play games in celebration. At the end of the festival, all nine branches of the menorah are lit at once. The ninth (extra) candle is the one that is used to light the others.

15. Kosher – The word *kosher* means "proper" or "clean." It refers to ritually correct food and beverage consumption and preparation. The rules are extensive, but here are a few of the key regulations: do not eat an animal with a cloven hoof, do not mix dairy and meat products, do not eat any meat with blood still in it, and do not eat shellfish. This means that Jews should not eat pork or shrimp. They should not eat their meat medium rare. The regulation about mixing dairy and meat products stems from the law that an animal should not be cooked in its mother's milk. We cannot be certain if this is happening or not since we rarely track our dairy and meat products from the farm to our house, so the rule is simply don't mix dairy and meat. This means that Jews should only eat vegetarian pizzas. Some Jews even have separate pots and dishes for preparing and serving dairy and meat products, and a few go so far as to have separate kitchens to preserve a kosher diet. Apartments with two kitchens are more common in New York because of this. I learned about this custom firsthand when I was an electrician's apprentice. We were working at a private Jewish elementary school in Tennessee that had two completely separate rooms for cooking.

16. Shema—This is the most important prayer for Jews and is recited daily, often before meals and before going to sleep. It doesn't by nature appear to be a prayer; it is more like a doctrinal statement about the monotheistic nature of Yahweh and how the Jews should keep all of the Lord's words close to their hearts. The Shema gets its name from the first word of the prayer, *hear*, which in Hebrew is *shema*. The beginning of the prayer draws from Deuteronomy 6:4–9, which reads, "Hear, O, Israel: The Lord our God, the Lord is one. Love the Lord your God with all your heart and with all your soul and with all your strength. These commandments that I give you today are to be upon your hearts. Impress them on your children. Talk about them when you sit at home and when you walk along the road, when you lie down and when you get up. Tie them as symbols on your hands and bind them on your foreheads. Write them on the doorframes of your houses and on your gates."

17. Observance-Based Divisions—Jews are divided based upon how they observe the Law. Many questions arise as to how to follow laws that were given over three thousand years ago in today's society without a temple. Orthodox Jews are the most conservative branch. They follow the letter of the Law to the best of their abilities in the twenty-first century. This means that the men do not cut their beards or the hair on the sides of their heads, and they wear *kippahs*, or skullcaps. Orthodox synagogue services are conducted entirely in Hebrew, and on the Sabbath they don't drive cars, cook, or flip a light switch. These prohibitions come from a law that on the Sabbath, a person shouldn't start a fire: starting the car involves ignition, and flipping a light switch involves sparks of electricity. Orthodox Jews sometimes turn on the lights they need the day before the Sabbath and then leave them on, so they don't "start a fire" on the Sabbath. If they anticipate needing to go into their refrigerators, they will unscrew the light bulbs the day before. I know someone whose Christian church shares a lot with an orthodox synagogue. When the Jews needed to turn on a light on the Sabbath, they came over and asked for assistance from the Christians. Orthodox Jews bind *talits*, boxes that contain verses from the Tanakh, to their arms to ensure that they are following the Shema, and they have mezuzahs on their doorframes that contain words from the Torah.

Conservative Jews adhere to the Law, but not as strictly as Orthodox Jews. For instance, they will likely drive to the synagogue. Reform Jews, on the other hand, are much more liberal. They actively seek to bring Judaism into the modern age. The men cut their hair. Families may skip synagogue gatherings, or not fast on Yom Kippur, or only observe select festivals. Services aren't restricted to the Hebrew language, and women can be rabbis.

Reconstructionists are the most liberal observance-based division of Judaism – they are sort of like the relativists discussed in the first chapter. Judaism is seen as constantly changing and can be different from one person to the next. The Tanakh may be literal or may be metaphorical; you can make of the Hebrew Bible whatever you wish.

18. Resurrection—There is not much written in the Tanakh concerning the afterlife. There is a clear teaching of an end-time resurrection in Daniel, which reads, "Multitudes who sleep in the dust of the earth will awake: some to everlasting life, others to shame and everlasting contempt" (Daniel 12:2).

19. Pharisees, Sadducees, Zealots, and Essenes—It is commonly recognized among the Jews that prophecy has ceased; there were no more prophets of Yahweh after Malachi. The Jews came under Roman rule and in some cases were forced to worship other gods or pay tribute to emperors who claimed to be gods. To fill the void left by the prophets and to counteract Roman influence, various groups emerged in the second century BC.

The Pharisees focused on the observance of the Law. They cast a wide safety net around the Law, adding to the Law in order to prevent the Jews from breaking the Law. If someone broke one of the laws the Pharisees had established, that person might not have broken God's Law. The Pharisees came to believe that if all of Israel could observe the Law in its totality for one day, the Messiah would come and establish his everlasting kingdom, free from Roman tyranny.

The Sadducees were from the tribe of Levi, the priests. They only accepted the Torah as canonical and rejected the rest of the Scripture. They also did not believe in the resurrection of the dead.

The Zealots were a revolutionary group that sought freedom from Rome through military force. The Essenes responded to Roman influence in a completely different manner. They left the city and lived a monastic lifestyle in the wilderness outside Jerusalem. They were scribes, and it is from them that we received the Dead Sea Scrolls.

20. Talmud—The Talmud is like a giant, interpretative footnote to the Tanakh. It contains additional details about the history of events recorded in the Tanakh, and it provides traditions, legends, cultural practices, and events not even mentioned in the Hebrew Bible. Rabbis through the ages have recorded their interpretations and applications of Mosaic Law in the annals of the Talmud. It is the size of an encyclopedia and is second to the Tanakh as an authoritative text.

Christianity

Christianity grew out of Judaism, emerging in the first century AD based on the teachings of Jesus of Nazareth. He and his earliest followers taught in the areas surrounding Jerusalem. By the beginning of the fourth century, Christianity had become the dominant religion of the Roman Empire.

Christians believe that Jesus is the incarnate Son of God, that he is fully human and fully divine, and that he came to save mankind from its sinfulness. They believe that Jesus is the Christ, the promised Messiah from the Hebrew Bible. Unlike the first century Jewish expectation of a Messiah who would overthrow the Romans and establish a kingdom that would last forever, Jesus came to lay down his life as an atoning sacrifice, worthy of the forgiveness of all of humanity's sins, past, present, and future.

He died by Roman crucifixion. On the Sunday after Jesus' death, his tomb was found empty. Later Jesus was seen raised from the dead by many of his followers, as many as five hundred at one time.

In Christianity, salvation, the forgiveness of one's sins, comes from having faith in the message of Jesus Christ's death as a substitute for the penalty that each of us deserves. Christians believe he conquered the grave and has the power to raise us from the dead upon his return to judge the world.

Christians recognize the ceremonial laws and the history of the Jews found in the Hebrew Bible as pointing to Jesus and being fulfilled by him. For instance, on the day Jesus rode into Jerusalem before his crucifixion, the Israelites hailed him as king, expecting him to at that time lead them in revolution. On this same day, the Jews were to select their Passover lambs; unknowingly, they selected Jesus to be their Passover lamb.

The lamb for Passover was supposed to be without defect and, when it was slaughtered, was not supposed to have any bones broken. Christians believe Jesus was sinless. Pontius Pilate, who sentenced him to crucifixion on the demand of the Jews, did so while finding no fault in him. To hasten death, the Romans would sometimes break the legs of those being crucified. Jesus had already died by the time they went around breaking the legs of those being crucified that day.

For Passover, Jews were to put the lamb's blood on the door frames of their homes; Jesus' blood on the cross is the doorway into the household of God.

The first exodus was an escape from slavery under the Egyptians; the second exodus with Christ was freedom from slavery to sin and the penalty that it brings. Instead of passing through the parted waters of the Red Sea as the Jews fled their old life in Egypt, Christians pass through the waters of baptism as their old, sinful nature is put to death and they are made alive in Christ.

As the Jews wandered the desert for forty years, following God to the Promised Land, so too Christians follow God in the wilderness of this life, waiting to cross over Jordan into their heavenly home.

1. Trinity—The doctrine of the Holy (which means "set apart") Trinity truly does set Christianity apart from Judaism and Islam, the other Abrahamic religions that claim there is only one God. Jews and Muslims sometimes claim that Christians do not worship one God but three gods. Christian doctrine, however, maintains that there is only one God. Historically, Christian teaching has been that there is only one God who exists in three persons, all of whom share in the same divine essence. These three persons are the Father, the Son, and the Holy Spirit. All three are self-conscious and can think, act, and feel on their own accord. They are distinct and recognizable from one another, yet they are all one in deity. All three are eternal, not created nor made. All three are omnipotent (all-powerful), omnipresent (everywhere), and omniscient (all-knowing).

The necessity of this teaching is seen in the role that all three persons play in salvation. The Father sent his eternally begotten Son, Jesus, to die as an atoning sacrifice for the sins of mankind. Jesus fulfilled all righteousness, never stumbling in any area of the Law, and died as a worthy substitute for the sins of mankind. The Father received and accepted that sacrifice. The Holy Spirit raised Christ to life and is the giver and sustainer of faith in the lives of believers. Such an exchange allows for God to be just, punishing wickedness, and still merciful and loving.

2. Incarnation—*Incarnation* refers to God assuming a human nature in the person of Jesus Christ. The incarnation began at the conception of the Virgin Mary. At that moment, Jesus assumed a human nature. He was now fully human and fully God. This seems like a contradiction, but it is not. His divinity was not restrained or restricted in any way within a human body, because God, to be God, must retain his nature and always be omnipotent. In his incarnation, for a time, Jesus chose not to make use of his divine powers. Out of his will, he chose to make himself nothing, taking on a human nature. God can do anything, including adding a human nature to himself, without losing any of his divine prerogatives.

The incarnation is absolutely essential to salvation. If Jesus were not fully God, he would not be able to fulfill all righteousness. If he were not fully human, he would not be able to be tempted or die. If he were not God, he would not be able to serve as a worthy substitute for the sins of all of mankind.

3. Christ—*Christ* is the Greek equivalent of the word *messiah* in Hebrew. It means "anointed one." In ancient Israel, three offices were distinguished by anointing with oil: prophets, priests, and kings. Jesus, as the Christ, was anointed by the Holy Spirit at his baptism and served in all three offices. As a prophet, he spoke the Word of God, and this office continues today as Christians proclaim his Word. As a priest, he served not in the Levitical priesthood, because he was born of the royal line of David in the tribe of Judah. Instead he served as high priest in the priestly order of Melchizedek, the first priest in the Hebrew Bible, who was a priest before the Law was given to the Israelites at Mount Sinai and before the Levitical priesthood was established. As high priest, he was able to offer an atoning sacrifice for the sins of all of Israel. Unlike the other high priests, who had to offer a sacrifice to cover their own sins before entering into the Most Holy Place, Jesus had no sins of his own that needed to be covered. Instead of offering the blood of bulls, goats, and lambs, in his holiness Jesus was able to offer himself. As king, Jesus' kingdom is not of this world. He sits on a heavenly throne and his reign will never end.

4. Revelation—*Revelation* with a capital *R* is a book written by the apostle John that closes the New Testament. Revelation can also be written with a lowercase "r," meaning God's revelation of himself to mankind, or how he has made himself known to humanity. He has revealed himself to mankind in two ways: through what he has made and through direct interaction with us in history. General revelation is God's revelation of himself through his creation. From what has been made, all can see that there is a God and know his divine attributes. This knowledge, however, is not enough to bring any of us into a relationship with God. It does not reveal who God is, what he thinks of us, or what he demands of us. This knowledge only brings us into condemnation. God has also directly shown himself to humanity through special revelation, which comes specifically through his Word as recorded in the Bible and through the historical revelation of himself in the person of Jesus Christ. This knowledge is necessary to come into a right relationship with God.

5. The Bible (Old Testament/New Testament)—God has directly revealed himself to humanity through the Bible. Christians maintain that the Tanakh, or the Hebrew Bible, is the Word of God. The name given to the Tanakh in Christianity is the Old Testament (OT). The OT text is the same as the Tanakh, but the ordering and division of it is different. Instead of twenty-four books, there are thirty-nine books. Some Christian denominations, such as the Roman Catholic Church, have more books they include in the OT. The Christian Bible also contains the New Testament, twenty-seven books that include four biographies of Jesus (Matthew, Mark, Luke, and John), a historical account of the early church, focusing on Peter and Paul's ministries (Acts), letters from Paul and other apostles and first generation disciples, and an apocalyptic writing from the apostle John (Revelation).

6. Inspiration—The text of the Bible came through the inspiration of the Holy Spirit. The writers of the Old and New Testaments wrote as they were led by the Spirit to write. Unless they were directly quoting the Lord, they were not taking down dictation word for word from God. The Holy Spirit retained and worked through the personalities and characteristics of the individual writers. Even though the words are God's, Matthew still comes through as the author of the gospel of Matthew.

7. Church—This word has many meanings within Christendom. The word can be used to refer to a building where Christians regularly gather for prayer, listening to instruction from God's Word and the study of it, singing praises to God, conducting special services, sharing communion, and celebrating baptisms. *Church* can also refer to a local group of Christians who band together for such acts of worship. Usually they hold to a common set of beliefs in the interpretation of the Bible. This use of the word *church* can also be expressed using the word *congregation*. *Church* can also refer to many congregations that are united by a common confession of belief. Such a church usually has a governmental organization that oversees the preservation of doctrinal unity, church discipline, and practice among the congregations that form such a union. This use of the word *church* can also be expressed with the word *denomination*.

There are many denominations within Christianity: Roman Catholic, Episcopalian, Eastern Orthodox, Greek Orthodox, Lutheran, Presbyterian, Methodist, Baptist, Church of Christ, Assembly of God, and many others. Denominations have divisions within themselves. There are even congregations that call themselves nondenominational. Sometimes these congregations form denominations as they plant new congregations, as Calvary and the Vineyard have done, both having started in Southern California.

Despite such divisions, and despite so many different uses of the word *church* within Christendom, a precise doctrinal use of the word refers to all true Christian believers from all times. The myriad of subtle differences in teachings and emphases amongst the Christian denominations leads to much dispute over what exactly must be believed for one to be a "true" believer, but among the denominations, they all hold to the same understanding of the doctrine of the Trinity. They also confess Jesus to be the Savior of the world and that forgiveness of sins comes through him though there are differences on how that forgiveness is received. Some denominations credit some degree of work to the individual, while others attribute all work in salvation to God alone.

8. The Reformation—The first big split within the church, called the Great Schism or the East-West Schism, came about in 1054, and it broke the church into the Roman Catholic Church in the West and the Eastern Orthodox Church in, as the name indicates, the East. The split was more political and cultural than theological. The Roman Catholic Church struggled with another split about three hundred and fifty years later over who the pope was, again not a theological split. The first huge theological split came in the sixteenth century and is known as the Protestant Reformation or simply the Reformation.

Martin Luther is credited with starting the Reformation when he nailed the Ninety-five Theses to the church door in Wittenberg (which, by the way, wasn't an offensive act, as some might think, because the church door served as a bulletin board for such debate in Luther's day). Central to Luther's Ninety-five Theses and the Reformation as a whole was a call to reform the extrabiblical works required of believers by the Roman Catholic Church, such as the buying of indulgences and making religious pilgrimages to pay to see sacred artifacts. Such acts were ways of ensuring a person would not have to go to purgatory, a hell-like place where unpardoned sins were cleansed before a soul was admitted to heaven. These works could even be performed on behalf of the soul of a departed loved one to lessen their time in purgatory.

Luther saw that these practices and teachings, along with many others, as undermining the saving work of Jesus Christ. Though Luther did not seek to split the church, a split inevitably occurred when Luther's calls for reform were not met. Central to the disagreements were different sources for Christian doctrines. The Reformers claimed *sola scriptura*, by Scripture alone, as the only guide for Christian theology. The Roman Catholic Church claimed Scripture and sacred tradition, as interpreted by the pope and his magistrates.

9. Justification/Sanctification—*Justification* and *salvation* are essentially synonymous. If a person is justified, or righteous in God's sight, that person is saved. If a person has justification from God, that person has salvation from God. The Reformers stressed that justification (salvation) came by grace, through faith in Christ. The moment a person has faith, or believes, in Jesus Christ and his atoning work on the cross, that person is justified. With this view, justification is *instantaneous*. The moment I have faith, it is "just as if I'd never sinned."

Linked with justification is the term *sanctification*. In justification, a person is *declared* righteous, or holy. That does not mean the person literally *is* righteous. A person who is justified before God is simultaneously a sinner and a saint. That person still sins. Sanctification is not a declaration of holiness; it is being *made* holy. The moment a person has faith in Christ and is justified, the *process* of sanctification begins. It is a life-long process that will never be complete this side of heaven. However, in this life, the Christian should expect to grow in holiness, to bear more and more righteous fruit, and to sin less and less.

Certain Christian denominations do not keep this Reformation view of justification and sanctification, but instead mingle justification and sanctification by making a person's justification contingent upon his or her progress in the realm of sanctification, instead of the saving work of Jesus Christ received through faith.

10. Total Depravity—There is much debate and division within Christianity over how individuals are justified and what people must do to be saved. The Reformers saw that all of mankind suffers from total depravity as the result of inherited sin, the sinful nature we all are born with. Being totally depraved means that we are dead in our sins and trespasses, born deaf, dumb, and blind enemies of God, unable to approach him or please him in any way. Such a view means we do not even have the ability to accept or choose to have faith in him before we are made alive in Christ. Christian denominations that hold to the doctrine of total depravity believe that we have absolutely no role to play in our salvation; we are saved solely by the grace of God. Christian denominations that deny total depravity focus on the individual's ability to accept Jesus in justification. A human work is inserted, and in some cases justification and sanctification are mingled. Justification becomes a process based upon how well we are following Christ.

11. Law/Gospel—*Law* is what God demands of us. All have fallen short of God's standard (or have sinned, which in Greek is an archery term that literally means "missed the mark") and deserve eternal punishment. Christians look at God's Law and see that it is divided into several types: ceremonial, civil-political, and moral.[3] There are ceremonial laws that pertain to sacrifices and the observance of festivals, such as Passover and Sukkoth. Others pertain to observances such as circumcision and a kosher diet. These laws pointed to Christ, have been fulfilled by him, and no longer are required to be followed under the New Testament. Some of these laws can be followed if desired, such as a kosher diet, but others, such as sacrificing animals, would now be sinful, since Christ's death is seen by Christians as the once-for-all atoning sacrifice.

Within Scripture there are also civil-political laws, which were laws given specifically to the nation of ancient Israel. Since that nation established by God no longer exists, people no longer have to observe those laws. If those laws are contrary to the laws of the nation in which a person currently resides, it would be sinful to follow them now, unless of course the civil-political law overlaps with God's moral law. Moral laws are timeless, unchanging laws that apply to all people in all places, such as the Ten Commandments.

Gospel means "good news." The good news is that Jesus Christ has paid the full penalty for the sins of the world. He has risen from the grave, conquering sin, death, and the Devil. The gospel does not place any demands (laws) upon us. The gospel is free for us, but not free for Jesus, who had to pay dearly for us to receive God's grace.

12. Conversion—This word describes the moment a person becomes a Christian. Like justification, conversion is instantaneous. A person either is a Christian or is not a Christian. There is not a middle ground where a person could say, "I am half Christian, on my way to becoming fully Christian." There might, however, be a lengthy process leading up to conversion. The apostle Paul describes the process as gardening; one person might till the soil (prepare a person to receive the gospel message), another might plant the seed (the gospel message), another might water the seed. God is the one who makes it grow, meaning God is the one who finally converts a person.

13. The Great Commission—Jesus' last words to his disciples in the gospel of Matthew are called the Great Commission. These words are, "All authority in heaven and on earth has been given to me. Therefore go and make disciples of all nations, baptizing them in the name of the Father, and of the Son, and of the Holy Spirit, and teaching them to obey everything I have commanded you. And surely I am with you always, to the very end of the age" (Matthew 28:18-20). With these words, Christians today have been given the imperative to share the gospel message with others. It is through hearing this message that people may come to have faith in Jesus Christ and be saved.

14. Baptism—Commanded by Jesus Christ, Christians make disciples through baptizing in the name of the Triune God and teaching everything Jesus commanded. *Baptize* means "to wash." When water is applied to a person in the name of the Father, and of the Son, and of the Holy Spirit, it is baptism. (Some Christians claim the application of the water must be through full body immersion.)

Denominations have differing interpretations on the meaning and significance of baptism. Some denominations believe that baptism is a means of grace, meaning that baptism delivers grace to an individual. Several Bible verses indicate that in baptism a person is connected to Jesus' death and resurrection, that they are buried and raised with him through the waters of baptism, and that their sins are washed away. Others interpret such verses as being purely symbolic. Those who take a symbolic view of baptism usually view baptism as a person's public proclamation of the decision to follow Christ and generally don't baptize infants, since they believe a confession of faith is a necessary prerequisite to baptism.

15. Communion—"The Lord Jesus on the night when he was betrayed took bread, and when he had given thanks, he broke it, and said, 'This is my body which is for you. Do this in remembrance of me.' In the same way also he took the cup, after supper, saying, 'This cup is the new covenant in my blood. Do this, as often as you drink it, in remembrance of me'" (1 Corinthians 11:23–25). These words are known as the words of institution spoken at the Last Supper, the last meal Jesus shared with his disciples. He told them to remember him in this meal and to take it together often.

Following his command, Christians observe this meal with bread and wine (or grape juice). As with baptism, there are differences in interpretation among Christians about what exactly this meal is and what it means. Some view communion as a means of grace, that there is forgiveness of sins received through its taking. Those with this view believe that Jesus' body and blood are present in the meal, either physically or spiritually. Other Christian denominations see communion simply as a commanded act of symbolic remembrance. This meal has many names in different Christian circles: the Eucharist, the Lord's Supper, the Lord's Table, Communion, the Breaking of Bread, and the Sacrament of the Altar. Early Christians even called it a Love Feast.

16. Sacrament—This is an extrabiblical word, like the words *Trinity* and *Bible*. Therefore it is not used by every denomination. *Sacrament* is used to describe baptism and communion, but some extend the term to other Christian rituals or practices. Those who call baptism and communion sacraments believe the promise of forgiveness of sins is attached to those who receive them. Grace would still be delivered to an individual who receives them apart from faith, but only in faith can a person receive the benefits of that grace.

17. Pastors/Priests—*Pastor* or *priest* is the title used to describe the leader of a local church congregation. Priests were the only ones who could offer sacrifices in the temple to God in the Old Testament. This title carries over into the New Testament era for the Roman Catholic Church and the Eastern Orthodox Church, which is fitting since both consider Communion, also called the Eucharist, as a bloodless sacrifice that is offered to God by their priests. Most other denominations use the term *pastor* to describe the leaders of their congregations. *Pastor* means "shepherd," and the title indicates that the person who holds this office guides and protects God's people who are under his care.

18. Apostles—Jesus had twelve selected disciples who lived with him and received private instruction from him during his earthly ministry. One of them, Judas, betrayed him and committed suicide before Christ's resurrection. Jesus after his resurrection commissioned the eleven and sent them out to the ends of the world to make disciples, to be his church-planters. The word *apostle* means "sent one." These eleven were personally sent by Jesus. The eleven saw it foretold in the psalms that Judas should be replaced, so they chose one of those who had been with them from the beginning of Jesus' ministry. The lot fell to Matthias, so there were twelve apostles again. Paul, formerly named Saul, became a thirteenth apostle through his personal encounter with the risen Christ and from the instruction Paul received from him. Because of their intimate instruction and time with Jesus, the apostles had authority on doctrinal matters in the first generation of the Church. Only books that came out of the apostolic circle are included in the New Testament canon of Scripture.

19. Disciples—Jesus was a rabbi, a teacher. *Disciple* means "student." Those who followed and learned from Jesus were called disciples. Any follower of Jesus today can also be called a disciple.

20. Heaven/Hell—The New Testament greatly expands upon the Old Testament revelation of the afterlife. Direct explanation about the resurrection of all the dead on the last day is provided on numerous occasions. This resurrection of the dead will coincide with the return of Christ. He will come to judge the living and the dead. He will separate all people. Those who are righteous will go to heaven. Those who are wicked will go to hell. Both heaven and hell are eternal, and those who go to each will go with their newly resurrected bodies intact. In heaven all things will be made new, and God will be with his people. There will be no more pain or suffering. In hell, there will be darkness, pain, suffering, and the absence of God. All people deserve hell, but for Christ's sake, for his innocent, bitter sufferings on the cross, those who have faith in Jesus shall not be put to shame, but have eternal life.

Islam

Islam means "submission." *Muslim* means "one who submits." Muslims submit to Allah. The central belief of Islam is that there is only one God, and he is Allah! Muhammad was Allah's messenger. He was the last of the prophets. Muslims believe that many of the prophets of Judaism and Christianity were also prophets of Allah, such as Moses and Jesus, and that there were messengers who received Allah's word before Muhammad.

Muslims believe that the Tawrat (Book of Moses), the Zabur (Book of David), and the Injeel (Book of Jesus) all came from Allah, but that these books were corrupted, lost, or changed over time.[4] Allah's word as revealed to Muhammad was sent to rectify the corruptions of these previous works. This word is revealed in the Qur'an, Islam's holy book, and was received by Muhammad over a period of time ranging from AD 610 until his death in AD 632.

Muslims follow what are called the five pillars of Islam and do so in hopes that when they face Allah's judgment at the end of their lives, they will receive his mercy and enter into paradise.

1. Muhammad—He was born in Mecca, located in modern-day Saudi Arabia, in AD 570. He was a traveling caravan driver. This occupation brought him into contact with Judaism, Christianity, and the pagan religions of Arabian society. In AD 610, he received his first revelation from the angel Gabriel. The angel delivered a series of messages from Allah to Muhammad for the remainder of Muhammad's life. The messages were delivered word for word as Allah sent them. Muhammad only had to recite the messages he received, and recite them he must, because Muhammad was illiterate.

Muhammad did not receive a warm welcome as a prophet in Mecca, which was already a site for religious pilgrimage. Many idols of local tribes stood in the city and were worshipped. The polytheistic audience didn't take well to Muhammad's central message that "Allah is the only true God!" It's never a welcome message to say someone else's religion is wrong (which I guess is the motivation for this book), but the claim that Allah was the only true God was also bad for business. It cut out the idol carvers and religious tourism.

Under persecution, Muhammad and his followers fled to a nearby city, Medina. It was in Medina that Muhammad's following grew and was able to establish the forces necessary to re-enter Mecca and cleanse it of idolatry. Muhammad died in AD 632, and the messages he received from Allah are recorded in the Qur'an.

2. Night Ascent—this is also known as the night journey. As Muhammad faced persecution for the proclamation of the messages he received from Allah, he began to doubt his calling as a prophet. Ten years after his first revelation from the angel Gabriel, Muhammad was taken to Jerusalem and up into paradise. He saw and even spoke with all the prophets of Allah that had come before him, including Moses, David, and Jesus, before seeing Allah himself. This experience comforted Muhammad and reassured him that he was a true prophet of Allah, despite the struggles he was encountering in Mecca as he proclaimed the message of Allah.

3. Qur'an—Also commonly spelled *Koran*. Muhammad is called "the seal of the prophets." He is the last of the prophets. The messages he received from Allah through the angel Gabriel are unchanged and stand as the very words of Allah. Previous messages from Allah given to earlier prophets have been corrupted over the course of time, and the Qur'an has restored those messages to his people. The word *Qur'an* means "recitation." It indicates that Muhammad received Allah's messages and recited them exactly as they were given to him. The Qur'an was not intentionally recorded in a written form until after the death of Muhammad. When it was written down, it was recorded by his nearest followers. Differing texts quickly arose, and the caliph Uthman, the third leader of Islam after Muhammad, ordered that one definitive text be established and that all variant texts be destroyed.

Muslims only consider the Qur'an to be authoritative in its Arabic form. Any translations are not considered to be the Qur'an. The Qur'an consists of 114 chapters, called *suras*. The chapters are arranged from longest to shortest, not in the order in which Muhammad received them.

4. Allah—Muslims believe there is only one God, *Allah*, which means "the God" in Arabic. Although Muslims call Allah simply "the God," Allah has ninety-nine names, or titles, within the Qur'an. Some examples of his names are "the Provider," "the Subduer," "the Loving," "the Bringer of Judgment," and "the Kind." In connection with the name "the Bringer of Judgment," Muslims believe that there will be a final judgment in which a person's life and works shall be judged by Allah. Based on this judgment, the individual will spend eternity in either hell or paradise. No Muslim is certain if his or her good works have been enough to merit a place in paradise, but if one submits to Allah and follows the five pillars of Islam, one can be more hopeful of receiving Allah's mercy.

5. The Five Pillars—Similar to the Ten Commandments, the five pillars of Islam serve as the central tenets to be followed by Muslims. There are, of course, more rules and expectations set by Allah, but these are the most important ones. Whereas the Christian faith speaks of the teachings of the prophets and the apostles as being the foundation upon which the Christian faith is built, Islam speaks of pillars that uphold the ceiling, or roof of a building. The five pillars support and uphold the Islamic faith. Therefore, orthodox Muslims stringently adhere to the five pillars. It is through strict observance of these pillars that anyone may have hope of escaping the wrath of Allah's final judgment, although such adherence does not provide certainty of receiving paradise. The five pillars are the *shahadah* (creedal confession and faith), *salat* (prayer), *zakat* (charity), *sawm* (fasting during Ramadan), and *hajj* (pilgrimage to Mecca).

6. Shahadah—This is the first of the five pillars. The shahadah is a one-sentence creedal statement of belief: "There is no God but Allah, and Muhammad is his messenger." If a person recites this creed in faith, he or she has converted to Islam and has become a Muslim. The first words whispered into the ears of infants who are born into Islamic families are the words of the shahadah.

7. Salat—*Salat* means "prayer." Salat is the second of the five pillars, and it can also be spelled *salah*. Muslims are to pray five times a day, at set times, facing toward Mecca when they do. The prayers are recited while the petitioner alternates forward and backward through three different positions: standing, kneeling, then prostrate. The prostrate position involves pressing the forehead to the ground and stretching the arms in front of the head, palms on the ground. In Islamic nations, there are calls for prayer throughout the land at the set times, and everyone stops and prays together. The times follow the position of the sun in the sky: approximately at sunup, noon, afternoon, sunset, and late at night. Muslims must wash themselves before the prayers.

8. Zakat—This is the third of the five pillars. *Zakat* means "alms-giving" or "charity." Muslims give 2.5 percent of their wealth to charity: to the poor, to the sick, and to those in need. Muslims may always give more if they choose, and many do.

9. Sawm—*Sawm* refers to fasting during the month of Ramadan. Ramadan is the ninth month of the Islamic calendar. During this month, Muslims are required to abstain from food, drink, and sex during daylight hours. At nightfall, it's game on. There is much feasting at night in Islamic communities during Ramadan. The fast during the day is to encourage self-control and restraint in the individual. As Muslims fast, the time that would be spent on eating and drinking is turned to Allah through additional prayers and more readings from the Qur'an.

10. Hajj—The fifth of the five pillars is the *hajj*, a pilgrimage to Mecca. A *hajji* is one who has taken the pilgrimage to Mecca. All Muslims are required to make this pilgrimage once in their lifetimes, as long as they are physically and financially able. Today, with the ease of air travel, Muslims have no trouble arriving at Mecca during the special month of pilgrimage, the twelfth month of the Islamic calendar. At that time, they can partake in a special series of events with all the pilgrims from the seventh day of the month to the tenth day of the month.

On the seventh day and throughout the rest of the hajj, the men dress in an *ihram*, two white sheets of cloth. Women may dress as they desire, so long as they dress in accordance with Islamic rules for being in public. Women usually wear white too. A preparation, or purification, on this day includes entering the Great Mosque and walking around the Kaaba seven times. Days eight through ten include several hikes outside of Mecca to Mina and the Plain of Arafat. Pilgrims camp outdoors and perform specific rituals each day, such as praying all night, sacrificing an animal, throwing stones at pillars, and cutting one's hair. The hajj concludes on the tenth day with a final visit to the Kaaba.

About two million Muslims travel to Mecca each year for the hajj. The Muslims I have talked with who have made the pilgrimage speak of experiencing the sheer number of Muslims from all over the world, sharing in unison the rituals of the hajj, as being the highlight of their pilgrimage.

11. Kaaba/Black Stone—The Great Mosque of Islam is located in Mecca. Its significance is similar to Judaism's former temple, which was destroyed by the Romans in AD 70. The Great Mosque might also be referred to as the Sacred Mosque or the Grand Mosque, or by its Arabic name, Masjid al-Haram. At the center of the Great Mosque is the Kaaba, a cubical, black shrine. When Muslims face toward Mecca for prayer, the Kaaba is what they are actually facing. It is significant because the Kaaba contains the Black Stone, which is affixed to one of the walls of the Kaaba. The Black Stone is a meteorite that was a gift from Allah and was venerated by both Adam and Abraham. Abraham constructed the Kaaba, but at some point the Black Stone lost its connection to Allah and became venerated in connection with pagan religions. Once Muhammad received his revelations from Allah and cleansed Mecca of all its idols, the Kaaba returned as a shrine dedicated to Allah.

12. Halal—Similar to the Jewish practice of maintaining a "proper" or "clean" diet, *halal* refers to the foods that are permissible for Muslims. A halal diet forbids the eating of pork and any blood. It also provides criteria for how animals should be cared for and how they should be slaughtered. Muslims are restricted from drinking any wine by the Qur'an, which is why Shiraz wine, which originated in Iran, is no longer produced in that Islamic nation. The word *wine* has been broadened in contemporary practice to include any alcoholic beverages.

13. Sharia—There are plenty of dos and don'ts of Islam that extend beyond the five pillars and maintaining a halal diet. The totality of all these laws for society, families, and individuals is called *sharia* law. It varies slightly among Muslim groups and from Muslim nation to Muslim nation. A well-known example is the expectations for modest dress by women in public. Some Islamic cultures require women to be completely covered except for their eyes, others say the face may be uncovered, and still others allow for the hair to be uncovered also. Sharia law provides guidance for business, marriage, divorce, judicial systems and penalties, hygiene, rituals for the five pillars, and rules for social order. Sharia law is derived from the Qur'an and the Sunnah, found in the Hadiths.

14. Hadiths—Second to the Qur'an in importance for Muslims are the Hadiths, recollections of the sayings of Muhammad. The Hadiths are necessary for interpreting the Qur'an, since the Qur'an is not written in chronological order or with much narrative. Sometimes as the revelations were received by Muhammad, questions were asked by Muhammad and others who witnessed Muhammad receiving the messages. Answers were given, but since the Qur'an only contains the words of Allah, the questions were omitted from the Qur'an. The Hadiths serve to fill in the gaps and give a backdrop for understanding the Qur'an. The Qur'an also contains very little about the life of Muhammad, so the example of living in submission to Allah that Muhammad demonstrated is contained in the Hadiths. The history of the Hadiths, however, is questionable, particularly with regard to which sayings of the prophet are authoritative and which are not. The two main branches of Islam, the Sunnis and Shiites, have different collections of Hadiths.

15. Sunni—The Sunni branch of Islam is the largest branch, with as many as 90 percent of Muslims belonging to this group. *Sunni* essentially means "traditional," and Sunnis try to emulate precisely what they consider to be the example demonstrated by Muhammad through his sayings and actions. Since Muhammad's death, Sunni Muslims believe that guidance should come from the words of Allah found in the Qur'an and that leadership should belong to elected leaders and teachers.

16. Shiite—The Shiite branch of Islam is mostly found in Iran and Iraq. This branch believes that the succession of leadership after Muhammad should have been hereditary. Since Muhammad had no surviving sons, leadership should have gone to his cousin and adopted son, Ali bin Abu Talib. For the Shiite, Ali was and is the true successor of Muhammad, despite the election of Abu Bakr, Muhammad's close and trusted friend, who is held to be the rightful successor by the Sunni.

The successors to Muhammad are called *imams*. There are differences among the Shiite with regard to how many imams followed Muhammad. Many believe that there were twelve imams and that the twelfth imam, Muhammad al-Mahdi, did not die and that he will return. This belief is similar to the way that Muslims believe that Jesus did not die, and will return to bring justice to the land and convert the whole world to Islam. Such beliefs were publicly proclaimed by the former Iranian president Mahmoud Ahmadinejad. He expressed the desire to take over Israel and incite enough chaos to usher in the return of the twelfth imam, Muhammad al-Mahdi.

17. Sufi—Sunni and Shiite Muslims focus on adherence to the external observance of rules in the Qur'an and the Hadiths as the path to pleasing Allah. Sufis focus on the internal heart position one has toward Allah and the personal experience of a relationship with him. Sufis wear white robes and tall, brown, cylinder-shaped hats, sometimes called dervish hats. They are most known for their swirling dances in which the bottom of their robes furl out to make the dancers look like upside-down spinning tops. Essentially, Sufi Muslims practice a form of mysticism similar to Christian mysticism and Hindu disciplines, in which practitioners attempt to draw nearer to God by losing themselves in various meditative practices. Sufi Muslims are far from orthodox, and their practices cannot be clearly derived from the Qur'an or the Hadiths. Many Sunni and Shiite Muslims do not view Sufis as actual Muslims.

18. Mosque—A place of worship for Muslims is called a *mosque*. Mosques often have domed ceilings. The majority of the space in a mosque is devoted to the prayer hall. Men and women may pray together in the prayer hall, but it is customary for women to pray behind the men or in a separate area. The mosque I visited in southern California had a second-floor loft overlooking the prayer hall, designated for women. Prayer halls are generally wide open, without any furniture for seating, so Muslims may prostrate themselves on the floor. No images may be made of Muhammad, special scenes, events, or places of Islam, since to do so is construed as making idols. If there are decorations, they will be decorative text from the Qur'an or from Islamic prayers. Muslims and visitors take off their shoes when entering a mosque. There are washing areas for purification, either in the restrooms or in designated courtyards that contain special bath sinks for fully washing the body. The five daily prayers are held at mosques, but Muslims may pray them anywhere they are at the proper time. Friday at noon, however, attendance at a mosque is obligatory. The Friday noon service is unique because it includes a sermon.

19. Imam—Shiite Muslims call the initial successors after Muhammad imams, but this title is also used for all Muslim religious leaders. The chief prayer leader of a mosque, who also gives the Friday sermon, usually carries the title imam.

20. Jinn—Along with good and evil angels, entities that Judaism and Christianity also believe in, Islam teaches the existence of *jinn*, or genies (think Aladdin and his wonderful lamp). The teachings about jinn are not very detailed in the Qur'an, and most of the beliefs and practices concerning them are derived from Arabian culture before Islam. The Qur'an, however, shows that jinn can become Muslims, submitting to Allah's will. At the final judgment, jinn who do wrong in the sight of Allah will stoke the flames of hell, while jinn who do good will be in paradise.

ENACTING THE LAW OF NONCONTRADICTION

He hoped and prayed that there wasn't an afterlife. Then he realized there was a contradiction involved here and merely hoped that there wasn't an afterlife.
—Douglas Adams

The equation A ≠ Non-A represents the law of noncontradiction. The law doesn't mean there are no contradictions. It simply means that if a statement is true in one context, the exact opposite of that statement cannot also be true in the same context. When this law of logic is applied to religious truth-claims, it's as if the Death Star of *Star Wars* is fully operational and has been aimed at religious pluralism. In *Star Wars*, the rebel forces launched a counterstrike upon the Death Star and successfully stopped its future use. In the case of the pluralists' defense against the law of noncontradiction, the tactic is a full-frontal assault of an ad hominem nature. Instead of addressing the contradictions that arise when applying the law of noncontradiction to religious truth-claims and the arguments for the exclusive nature of those claims, pluralists opt to attack the character of the nonpluralists. The nonpluralist faces such accusatory questions as, "How can you be so arrogant as to think you are right and everyone else is wrong?" or derogatory statements like, "Only a bigot would think his religion is the only right religion!"

Being painted as a villain ought to be expected if one is taking an affirmative stance against a pluralist, but in all reality, out of love, truth must be proclaimed despite any unpleasantness that might arise. It might be seen as intolerant to make the claim that all religions can't be true. But in light of reason and logic, making that claim is in the best interest of the pluralists if one of those religions is exclusively true.

For example, Christianity's truth-claim that Jesus is God contradicts Islam's claim that Jesus is just a human prophet, which in turn contradicts Judaism's claim that he is a false prophet. Plugging these statements into the equation of the law of noncontradiction, we see that "Jesus is the incarnate Son of God" (A) ≠ "Jesus is not the incarnate Son of God" (Non-A).

With this one simple example, it becomes apparent that, based on the laws of logic and reason, all religions cannot be true. This, however, does not mean that one religion is true—all religions could be false! If Jesus is not the incarnate Son of God, the only way to the Father (John 14:6), then Christianity must be false. The reverse must then be true; if Jesus is the incarnate Son of God, the only Savior of the world, then all other religions must be false. This comes solely from the law of noncontradiction.

The Contradictions Abound

The contradictions among the world's religions go beyond teachings related to Jesus. Ethics and morality are often pointed to as being the unifying factors, but religions contradict each other even in their moral codes. They contradict in regard to specific laws as well as in the objective of the given set of laws (some religions might even reject the use of the term *laws*).

Dogmatic studies of religions commonly use categorical topics to guide comparative investigation and to serve as tools for organizing the resulting information about each religion. The categories I have chosen for comparing the teachings of the world's religions are:

Views of the Divine
Nature of the Universe
Nature of Man
Humanity's Ultimate Problem
Solution to Mankind's Problem

Views of the Afterlife
Sacred and Authoritative Literature
Code of Ethics

Since the previous chapter presented the teachings of five major religions in detail, I will bullet-point the information from that chapter under the headings for each of the categories. I will also provide the beliefs of a few minor religions within each category and strive to present the teachings using direct quotations from each religion. This approach should make the contradictions apparent.

Views of the Divine

- **Judaism**—Monotheistic. Unitarian. God is transcendent and he is called Yahweh. Deuteronomy 6:4 states, "Hear, O Israel: The LORD our God, the LORD is one."
- **Islam**—Monotheistic. Unitarian. God is transcendent and he is called Allah. The shahadah, the Islamic creed of faith, states, "There is no God but Allah."
- **Christianity**—Monotheistic. Trinitarian. God is transcendent and exists in three persons: the Father, the Son, and the Holy Spirit. Matthew 28:19 lists the three persons as just one name that disciples are to be baptized in, and the three are listed together throughout the New Testament.
- **Hinduism**—Polytheistic/pantheistic. There are many gods and goddesses who can be worshipped. Yet everything, including the many gods, is at the core the same divine essence, called Brahman. Taittiriya Upanishad 2.6 says, "Who denies God, denies himself. Who affirms God, affirms himself," and Chandogya Upanishad 6.12–14 says, "An invisible and subtle essence is the Spirit of the whole universe. That is Reality. That is Truth. THOU ART THAT."[1]
- **Buddhism**—No god. The Buddha denied Brahman and the individual soul when he split from the teachings of Hinduism. Belief and worship in a god can actually be a hindrance in reaching nirvana because following a supreme power produces fear, as explained by the Buddha in the Dhammapada: "Men in their fear fly for refuge to mountains or forests, groves, sacred trees

or shrines."[2] Refuge does not come from a god but from the Four Noble Truths.

- **Wicca**—Pantheistic and other views. Everything is a manifestation of the divine, which is identified as a female being called the Goddess.   Some descriptions of the Goddess give the impression of energy, like the Force in *Star Wars* that connects all things. Some Wiccans are monotheistic, and others say there are a transcendent God and Goddess. Some say that both the God and the Goddess are one, being of the same divine essence.

- **Scientology**—There is a Supreme Being, but the Church of Scientology has no set doctrine concerning God to which its members must subscribe. One's view of God is contingent upon each individual's level of spiritual awareness.

- **LaVeyan Satanism**—Each man is his own God.

- **Atheism**—There is no God.

Nature of the Universe

- **Judaism**—Genesis 1:1, the first verse of the Tanakh, clearly states, "In the beginning God created the heavens and the earth." The universe and everything in it was created by God. Except for humanity, which was uniquely created, the first man from the dust of the ground and the first woman from the side of man, and except for God, who is eternal, everything has come into existence out of nothing from the spoken word of God. It is taught in the Genesis account that the Lord created all in six days and rested on the seventh. It is from this structure that the command for humanity to work six days and rest on the seventh is derived (Exodus 20:8–11). Nature is objective and distinct and separate from a personal, transcendent God.

- **Christianity**—The Christian Bible incorporates the teachings of the Tanakh concerning creation and adds more details to them. The first verses for the gospel of John state, "In the beginning was the Word, and the Word was with God, and the Word was God. He was with God in the beginning. Through him all things were made; without him nothing was made that has been made" (John 1:1-3). Christianity also shows that God is the sustainer of the universe, as Colossians 1:17 states: "In him [Jesus] all things hold together." Nature is objective, distinct, and separate from a personal, transcendent God.

- **Islam**—The Qur'an does not have the detailed narrative of creation found in Judaism and Christianity. Namely, it lacks the order of creation that the Genesis account gives. But it is not mute on the subject, and retains the idea that Allah created the heavens and the earth in six days (Surah 7:54). Nature is objective, distinct, and separate from a personal, transcendent God.
- **Hinduism**—The Rig Veda states that no one knows the origin of the universe, because no one observed it. It also gives an explanation that the universe came into existence through the cosmic sacrifice of the god Purusha, with everything being made from his body parts. The Purusha explanation is the basis of Hinduism's teaching that all of creation is one, and that all is eternally divine. However, this monistic reality is masked by an illusion. As souls are subject to reincarnation, the universe is subject to cycles of death and regeneration.
- **Buddhism**—Buddhism doesn't have a specific teaching about the origin of the universe. A Buddhist's belief concerning the universe is that all things are constantly changing, in the sense that there is a different universe every moment. Linked to this permanent shifting is a complete lack of personal identity. If you are never you, and I am never me, and everything is only classified for convenience's sake, then what is the universe but nothing?
- **Jainism**—"Some foolish men declare that a Creator made the world. The doctrine that the world was created is ill-advised, and should be rejected. If God created the world, where was He before creation? . . . How could God have made the world without any raw material? If you say He made this first, and then the world, you are faced with an endless regression . . . Know that the world is uncreated, as time itself is, without beginning and end. And it is based on principles . . ." (Ācārya Jinasena in Mahāpurāna).[3]
- **Sikhism**—The universe is created by the one and only true God. According to Guru Granth Sahib, "He established the earth, the

air and the sky, the water and the oceans, fire and food. He created the moon, the stars and the sun, night and day and mountain; he blessed the trees with flowers and fruits."[4]

Nature of Man

- **Judaism**—Man was created in the image of God, which indicates that man was created holy, immortal, and with the ability to reason. The first two humans were Adam and Eve. God formed Adam from the dust of the ground and breathed life into him. Eve was made from the side of Adam. Due to their disobedience to God's law, they became subject to death. Now, man is no longer perfect, but there isn't a formalized doctrine of mankind's total depravity. All have propensity to do good and evil, with the ability to choose one over the other.[5] Humans have both bodies and souls.

- **Christianity**—Christianity has the same view of mankind as Judaism, except Christians have the doctrine of Original Sin, the teaching that all of humanity is born with sin passed on from Adam. Romans 5:12–14 states, "Just as sin entered the world through one man, and death through sin, and in this way death came to all men, because all sinned—for before the law was given, sin was in the world. But sin is not taken into account when there is no law. Nevertheless, death reigned from the time of Adam to the time of Moses, even over those who did not sin by breaking a command, as did Adam."

- **Islam**—Instead of teaching that Adam was made from the dust of the ground and Eve from Adam's side, the Qur'an teaches that Allah made humanity from clots of blood (Surah 96:2). This is not a contradiction, since neither the Genesis creation account nor Surah 96 says that God "only" made Adam from dust or from clots of blood, but this is a noteworthy discrepancy between the creation details. Islam does not have a doctrine of Original Sin as Christianity has, so individuals are considered good at birth with potential to do good and evil.

- **Hinduism**—Each person is divine, as all things are one in Brahman. The Svetavatara Upanishad teaches, "May God who is hidden in nature, even as the silkworm is hidden in the web of silk he made, lead us to union with his own Spirit, with Brahman. He is God, hidden in all beings, their inmost soul who is in all."[6]

- **Buddhism**—There is no eternal nature. There is no individual soul, just constant change, so "you" are never truly "you." There is no personal identity, no personal self.

- **Zoroastrianism**—Yasna 37:1 states that Ahura Mazda has created "all existing things that are good."[7] Humanity has the free will to choose to do good or evil.

- **LaVeyan Satanism**—The seventh of the nine satanic statements that open the Satanic Bible reads, "Satan represents man as just another animal, sometimes better, more often worse than those that walk on all-fours, who, because of his 'divine spiritual and intellectual development,' has become the most vicious animal of all!"[8]

- **Scientology**—Humans are spiritual beings. A spiritual being is a *thetan*, and according to the Church of Scientology, "The thetan is immortal and has lived—and will continue to live—through countless lifetimes. One *is* a thetan who *has* a mind and who *occupies* a body. The thetan animates the body and uses the mind."[9]

Humanity's Ultimate Problem

- **Judaism**—Adam and Eve disobeyed God. Their rebellion brought mankind under a curse that involves struggle between the sexes, painful labor (both in childbearing and work), and ultimately death. The prophet Isaiah recognizes that such lawlessness has cut mankind off from God as he warns Israel, "Your iniquities have separated you from your God; your sins have hidden his face from you, so that he will not hear" (Isaiah 59:2).
- **Christianity**—Romans 3:23 states that "all have sinned and fallen short of the glory of God." Romans 6:23 teaches that the penalty of that shortcoming by stating, "The wages of sin is death."
- **Islam**—Allah knows all and sees all. Nothing is hidden from him. A day is coming when Allah shall bring judgment to everyone (Surah 69:18). Each individual will be held responsible with no second chances. The Qur'an warns, "Guard yourselves against a day on which no soul shall stand for another: when no ransom shall be accepted from it, no intercession avail it, no help be given it" (Surah 2:123).[10] Humanity's problem is facing Allah's judgment on human actions in life and ensuring that the good of an individual's life outweighs the evil. Only Allah can be the judge.
- **Hinduism**—"Who sees the many and not the ONE, wanders on from death to death. Even by the mind this truth is to be learned: there are not many but only ONE. Who sees variety and not the unity wanders on from death to death."[11] Our minds are deceived by the illusion called maya that keeps us from seeing the oneness of things. This deception causes us to live within a cycle of death and rebirth. We must find the path that leads to immortality and

escape samsara, the cycle of reincarnation. There are many paths available, and we must find the one that works best for each of us.

- **Buddhism**—The reality of this life is found in the mind's perception of what is real and what is lasting. The world is always changing, always in flux, and our minds and bodies, with their desires and cravings, resist change. If our minds can't acknowledge and accept this constant impermanence, pain and suffering are the natural byproduct. The origin, or cause, of this suffering is our desires for gratification and success. The Buddha taught, "The mind is fickle and flighty, it flies after fancies wherever it likes: it is difficult indeed to restrain."[12]

- **Christian Science**—Mankind's ultimate problem is being deceived by the illusion of sin, suffering, and death. To the question, "Is there sin?" the answer provided in Mary Baker Eddy's *Health and Science* is, "All reality is in God and His creation, harmonious and eternal. That which He creates is good, and He makes all that is made. Therefore the only reality of sin, sickness, or death is the awful fact that unrealities seem real to human, erring belief, until God strips off their disguise. They are not true, because they are not of God. We learn in Christian Science that all inharmony of mortal mind or body is illusion, possessing neither reality nor identity though seeming to be real and identical."[13]

- **Atheism**—If you are reading this text, you are alive, but the greatest problem you and everyone else who is alive has is death. At death, you no longer exist, and that is mankind's ultimate problem: our mortality. Rocker, writer, and speaker Henry Rollins expresses the atheistic view as, "I don't believe in an afterlife; you step on a bug, it dies; I shoot you in the face, you die, and you don't come back. That's my belief. OK? There are no ghosts; there's no afterlife; I'm not a spiritual person; I'm kind of a cash and carry type of guy, wash and wear."[14] Based on Rollins' words, it can even be said that there isn't an ultimate problem for mankind. We just are, and then we are not.

Solution to Mankind's Problem

- **Judaism**—Jews believe in a resurrection of the dead in the world to come upon the arrival of the messiah. At this resurrection, each man will be rewarded or punished on account of his deeds in this life. An individual has free will to choose to do good and reap a better life in the messianic age. Salvation is determined by the actions of each individual. The Web site *Being Jewish* explains, "In Judaism, it is entirely up to you. If you do good, you will get good."[15] For Jews, this is ensured through the observance of the covenant given to Moses on Mount Sinai, of which many of the laws are no longer applicable without the temple. Non-Jews are bound to the seven Noahide laws, laws that God gave to Noah after the flood. If a non-Jew adheres to these, he or she will partake in the life to come.[16]

- **Christianity** – Salvation and forgiveness of sins can only be found through faith in Christ, who died as an atoning sacrifice for the sins of the world. Romans 4:4–5 explains the role of human effort in salvation: "Now when a man works, his wages are not credited to him as a gift, but as an obligation. However, to the man who does not work but trusts God who justifies the wicked, his faith is credited as righteousness." In Christianity, the merit of our deeds brings only eternal condemnation and wrath, but "the gift of God is eternal life in Christ Jesus our Lord" (Romans 6:23). One receives this gift through coming into contact with the gospel of Jesus Christ and having faith in that message. In Ephesians 2:8–9, Paul reminded the church in Ephesus, "For it is by grace you have been saved, through faith—and this not from yourselves, it is the gift of God—not by works, so that no one can boast."

- **Mormonism**—2 Nephi 25:23 says, "For we labor diligently to write to persuade our children, and also our brethren, to believe in Christ, and to be reconciled to God; for we know that it is by grace that we are saved, after all we can do."[17] This sounds remarkably similar to Christianity, but Mormonism involves our works. After we have done "all we can do," then grace covers the rest. Our works are involved in salvation.

- **Islam**—Surah 95:8 proposes the question, "Is God not the best of all judges?"[18] While no Muslim is certain how he or she will fare on the day of Allah's judgment, obeying his commands found in the Qur'an will help one find favor in Allah's sight. Hope must lie in the fact that Allah is merciful and the best of judges; better to be judged by Allah than a man. Surah 20:112 reads, "Those who are burdened with sin shall come to grief: but those who have believed and done good works shall fear no tyranny or injustice."[19]

- **Hinduism**—Liberation from samsara and karma lie ultimately in the mind. The Maitri Upanishad says, "A quietness of mind overcomes good and evil works, and in quietness the soul is ONE: then one feels the joy of Eternity. If men thought of God as much as they think of the world, who would not attain liberation?"[20] The paths to liberation are numerous, and the paths are called *yogas*. These spiritual paths are taught most clearly in the Bhagavad Gita and involve studying Hindu scriptures, devoting one's self to the work assigned in life, and meditation. The path most often followed by Hindus is devotion to a specific deity, as described in the words of Krishna: "Though engaged in all kinds of activities, My pure devotee, under My protection, reaches the eternal and imperishable abode by My grace."[21]

- **Buddhism**—Detachment from worldly desires and cravings of the flesh is how one can escape suffering. Entering into this state of existence is to have attained nirvana. Nirvana is achievable in this life before death. To achieve nirvana, to end suffering through ending all desire, a person must adhere to the noble eightfold path. This teaching is directly stated in the Buddha's "Sermon at Benares" through the following brief excerpt, "Now, this, O bhikkhus [monks], is the noble truth concerning the way which leads to the destruction of sorrow. Verily, it is this noble eightfold path; that is to say: Right views; right aspirations; right speech; right behavior; right livelihood; right effort; right thoughts; and right contemplation. This, then, O bhikkhus, is the noble truth concerning the destruction of sorrow. By the practice of loving-kindness I have attained liberation of heart, and thus I am assured that I shall never return in renewed births. I have even now attained Nirvana."[22]

- **Scientology**—Higher states of spiritual awareness can be achieved through *auditing*. Auditing is performed by ministers of the Church of Scientology. During auditing, a minister will ask a *preclear*, a person who is receiving the audit, a series of questions with the assistance of an e-meter to pinpoint areas of spiritual distress within the preclear's life. The auditing process should help an individual obtain his or her "full spiritual potential."[23]

- **Jainism**—To reach perfection is to destroy karma, which rids one of all misery. Perfection comes through right knowledge, faith, conduct, and austerities. Each of these have certain requirements for obtaining deliverance, but the one that is most commonly associated with Jainism is conduct. Its nature is seen through the extreme practice of *ahimsa*, harming no living being, which for Jainism extends even to plants.

Views of the Afterlife

- **Judaism**—At the end there will be a resurrection of the dead, some to everlasting life and others to everlasting contempt. Daniel 12:2–3 speaks this belief directly, saying, "Multitudes who sleep in the dust of the earth will awake: some to everlasting life, others to shame and everlasting contempt. Those who are wise will shine like the brightness of the heavens, and those who lead many to righteousness, like the stars forever and ever."

- **Christianity**—Each person has one life that will determine his or her eternal fate. At the end of this age, all the dead will be raised back to life and judged by Christ. Christ's followers will enter heaven to live with God forever, while all others will be sentenced to eternal damnation in hell. Hebrews 9:27–28 explains this life and the one to come: "Just as man is destined to die once, and after that to face judgment, so Christ was sacrificed once to take away the sins of many people; and he will appear a second time, not to bear sin, but to bring salvation to those who are waiting for him."

- **Islam**—There will be a final judgment from Allah that all people will have to face. Both the beliefs and deeds of individuals will be weighed by Allah to determine the rewards or punishments deserved by every person. Submission to Allah in accordance to the revelation he has given in the Qur'an is the surest way to receive Allah's approval at the final judgment. The Web site, *The Religion of Islam,* explains the Islamic view of the final judgment with respect to Jews and Christians, who also received prophets of Allah: "Jews declare paradise to be a birthright of the 'chosen people,' Christians claim 'not to be perfect, just forgiven,' and Muslims believe that all who die in submission to the Creator are eligible for redemption. Those who followed the revelation and prophet of their time will be successful, whereas those who forsook the revelation and prophet of their day did so to the compromise of their souls."[24]

- **Hinduism**—"As the embodied soul continuously passes, in this body, from boyhood to youth to old age, the soul similarly passes into another body at death" (Bhagavad Gita 2:13).[25] After death there is a transmigration of the soul from one body to a different body. The new body could be that of a human or animal. The goal is to attain moksha, liberation from this cycle of reincarnation and union with Brahman.

- **Buddhism**—The Buddha denied an individual soul and the existence of a permanent identity. Despite denying the individual, the Buddha taught that there is continuation from one life to the next through reincarnation. When a person finally reaches enlightenment, nirvana is achieved. *Nirvana* means "blown out," indicating that a person is no longer reborn, that all desires have been extinguished, and that sorrow is no more. The Buddha explains this achievement and his endeavors to obtain release from suffering in this way: "I have gone round in vain the cycles of many lives ever striving to find the builder of the house of life and death. How great is the sorrow of life that must die! But now I have seen thee, housebuilder: never more shalt thou build this house. The rafters of sins are broken, the ridge-pole of ignorance is destroyed. The fever of craving is past: for my mortal mind is gone to the joy of the immortal NIRVANA."[26]

Sacred and Authoritative Literature[27]

- **Christianity**—The Holy Bible.
- **Jehovah's Witnesses**—All current Watchtower publications, including the *New World Translation of the Holy Scriptures* (a version of the Bible), *Reasoning from the Scriptures, You Can Live Forever in Paradise on Earth, Watchtower* magazine, and *Awake!* magazine.
- **Mormonism**—*The Book of Mormon, Doctrine and Covenants, Pearl of Great Price*, plus the Bible (King James Version or Joseph Smith's Inspired Version) which is seen as less reliable than *The Book of Mormon*. Authoritative teachings of Mormon prophets and other general authorities. *Ensign* and *Liahona* magazines.
- **Unification Church**—*Divine Principles* by Sun Myung Moon, considered the "Completed Testament," *Outline of the Principle, Level 4*, and the Bible.
- **Christian Science**—*Science and Health with Key to the Scriptures, Miscellaneous Writings, Manual of the Mother Church*, and other books by Mary Baker Eddy; the Bible; *Christian Science Journal; Christian Science Sentinel*; and other official periodicals.
- **Unity School of Christianity**—*Unity* magazine, *Lessons in Truth, Metaphysical Bible Dictionary*, and the Bible.
- **Scientology**—*Dianetics: The Modern Science of Mental Health* and other writings by L. Ron Hubbard, and *The Way to Happiness*.
- **Wicca**—No official sacred text; however, *The Book of Shadows*, first compiled by Gerald Gardner, is widely used by Wiccans.
- **New Age** – No official sacred text; however, almost any religious text can be used, as well as texts on astrology, mysticism, and magic.
- **Islam**—The Holy Qur'an and the Haddiths.
- **Nation of Islam**—The Qur'an. In addition, *Message to the Blackman in America, Our Savior Has Arrived*, and other books guide the views of the Nation of Islam.
- **Judaism**—The Tanakh and the Talmud.
- **Hinduism**—The Vedas, the Upanishads, and the Bhagavad Gita.

- **Hare Krishna**—Swami Prahbuhpada's translations and commentaries on Hindu scriptures, especially the Bhagavad Gita.
- **Buddhism**—The Mahavastu, the Jataka Tales, and the Tripitaka.
- **The Church of Satan**—*The Satanic Bible* by Anton LaVey.
- **Daoism**—Tao Te Ching, Zhuangzi, and Daozang.
- **Confucianism**—The Analects of Confucius.
- **Shinto** – The Kojiki, Nihon Shoki, and Rikkokushi.
- **Sikhism**—The Sri Guru Granth Sahib (or Adi Granth).

Code of Ethics

On this topic, I will diverge from the bullet-point style because it is in this category that I have heard the largest number of arguments that all religions are the same. The stance is taken that all religions call for us to love one another as we love ourselves; all religions are about love. Another position broadens the spectrum of moral exhortation, likely recognizing that there must be differences among religious laws. This broader position claims that all religions have the same basic code of moral conduct without defining what that code actually is.

I met a Hare Krishna lady outside a Walmart, proselytizing and handing out literature tracts and pamphlets. I struck up a conversation with her to see what exactly she believed. From my questions, she must have assumed I was a Christian. She assured me that it didn't matter if I believed in Jesus or not because Jesus and Krishna are the same.

Not rolling over too easily, I asked, "How are they the same?"

She told me, "They are the same person; they have the same teachings. They taught don't kill. Don't eat meat."

I ignored the first part of her answer about the two being the same person and went to her next claim that neither of them ate meat, informing her, "Oh, you are mistaken. I know that Jesus ate meat. He was a Jewish rabbi and observed Passover, which involved slaughtering a lamb and eating its meat, as commanded by God. Jesus also had disciples who were fishermen. He never forbade their work. In fact, he aided them in catching fish, and he fed his disciples fish on occasion. No. I'm sorry. You are mistaken on that point. Jesus definitely ate meat and never told people not to do so."

She quickly dismissed me by saying, "I don't know about that."

From this one example alone, it's obvious that all religions don't have the same code of ethics. Jainism goes so far as to avoid killing anything across all classifications of life. Jains who hope to reach perfection walk with a broom, carefully sweeping the path in front of their feet to ensure any bugs are gently removed from the danger of being crushed. They drink filtered water to keep from killing microscopic bacteria or organisms. Face masks are worn to ensure no life form is accidentally inhaled. They starve themselves, eating the fewest possible vegetables to sustain life.

A most interesting interpretation of the famous Ten Commandments of Judaism and Christianity comes from Martin Luther, the sixteenth-century monk turned church reformer. Luther boils all of the commandments down to one command, the first one: "You shall have no other gods." If all religious laws are the breaking of this one law in Luther's interpretation of the Ten Commandments, then how could one harmonize the moral codes of all religions?

Does the Law of Noncontradiction Fully Invalidate Pluralism?

Side-by-side comparisons of doctrinal teachings from the world's religions, as has just been demonstrated, reveal direct contradictions. It soon emerges that some religions teach that the divine is not personal. Rather, the divine is an impersonal essence or force that permeates all things, constructing a divine and eternal universe. These religions contradict the religions that espouse the existence of a personal Creator God who is distinct and separate from the universe he has created; this God alone is divine.

Usually religions that have a pantheistic view of the divine lean toward reincarnation and karmic laws of cause and effect, whereas religions with a monotheistic, transcendent view of God believe that each of us has only one life before facing a judgment day that decides one's eternal fate.

It becomes obvious that all religions can't be true when the logical equation of $A \neq Non\text{-}A$ is applied. The mutually contradictory teachings among the world's religions necessitate such a conclusion. However this doesn't immediately put the nails in the coffin of religious pluralism.

In the first chapter, "The State of Pluralism," I said that there are different types of pluralism. *Social pluralism* and *literal pluralism* were the two views I presented. I used these terms because in conversation I would ask a person, "When you advocate for tolerance, are you asking for *social* tolerance among the diversity of religious options, or are you *literally* suggesting that everything is one and the same?"

Literal pluralism presents itself in two ways: "all is one" and "all leads to one." In the discussion of religion, "all is one" means that all religions are true, and it is this view that the law of noncontradiction squelches. Pluralism that maintains that "all leads to one" cannot be so swiftly dismissed for containing a logical fallacy because, at its root, it acknowledges the contradictions.

Climbing the Holy Mountain

The "all leads to one" breed of pluralism depicts religions as different spiritual paths that eventually converge at a single destination. It is commonly expressed as "All religions lead to God."

As I demonstrated earlier, pluralism arises from Hindu theology. Huston Smith confirms Hinduism's inclusivism in his immensely popular book, *The World's Religions*. He concludes his section on Hinduism by sharing an image of many religious paths winding their way to the top of a holy mountain:

> It is possible to climb life's mountain from any side, but when the top is reached the trails converge. At base, in the foothills of theology, ritual, and organizational structure, the religions are distinct. Differences in culture, history, geography, and collective temperament all make for diverse starting points. Far from being deplorable, this is good; it adds richness to the totality of the human venture. Is life not more interesting for the varied contributions of Confucianists, Taoists, Buddhists, Muslims, Jews, and Christians?[28]

The heart behind this form of pluralism cherishes and seeks the good in differences. It maintains the differences, and even acknowledges that they are often contradictory, but confesses that the contradictions are merely apparent, not real.

As long as the holy mountain analogy is coming from a Hindu framework, as Huston presents it, then God must be expressed through Brahman alone. Hindus have no qualms about saying that the gods of other religions are just different faces with different names that are all manifestations of Brahman, the divine essence in all things. In Hinduism's pantheistic cycle of death and rebirth, all does finally lead to God, since all is one and all is God.

The catch is that this context of pluralism is not saying that all religions are true, although some might claim that it does. In fact, it only has room for Hinduism to be true. All other religious claims, especially those of exclusive Christianity and Islam, are false. In this sense, it is not violating the law of noncontradiction.

It's still possible for this analogy to be employed outside of Hinduism or other pluralistic religions without violating the law of noncontradiction. The law of noncontradiction holds that all religions could be false; they just can't all be true due to their contradictory teachings. This means it is entirely possible for the holy mountain analogy to be true, but most, if not all, of the religions represented in the analogy would have to be false.

For example, if Christianity says God is V, Judaism says God is W, Islam says God is X, Buddhism says God is Y, and Hinduism says God is Z, it's possible for all of these religions to lead to the same God and their adherents all share in the same eternal fate, but only if God isn't V, W, X, Y, or Z. God would have to be represented by a different letter not already claimed by the world's religions; let's say G. In this scenario, all religions could lead to G, but in the end, V, W, X, Y, and Z must be put aside due the fact that they contradict each other and are not G. In such a scenario, no violation of the law of noncontradiction has been committed. God, as represented by G, is either unknown or only partially known through the religions current in this state and at this time.

Touching the Sacred Elephant

Another popular analogy that depicts an "all religions lead to God" form of pluralism is the story of several blind men touching various parts of an elephant and being unable to agree on a single description of the creature they're touching. This story has connections to Jainism, Buddhism, Hinduism, and even Sufi Islam, a mystical branch of Islam. The story is found in the teachings of the Buddha within the Pali canon of Theravada Buddhism. One of the most popular versions comes from a nineteenth-century poet, John Godfrey Saxe, who rewrote the story in rhyme.

Though there are minor discrepancies among the versions, they all present the same basic scenario: since each blind man is touching a different part of the elephant, they disagree on what the elephant actually is. The one touching the tail might think the elephant is a broom; the one touching the side of the elephant might think the elephant is a wall; the one touching the elephant's trunk might think the elephant is a snake. Individually, they each know a part of the elephant accurately, but not the sum total of the animal. They fail to grasp what the elephant actually is because of their blindness. Their dispute is futile since they are all mistaken.

It is pretty clear how this story can be used within the framework of pluralistic relativism. Christians, Jews, Muslims, Hindus, Buddhists, and the like are all touching the same sacred elephant, God. But because all of humanity is spiritually blind, we are incapable of knowing God as he actually is. Any fighting among religious faiths is thus futile.

On the flip side, the good news within pluralism is that every religion is true based on what its adherents have experienced of the sacred reality. Since all religions have touched the sacred elephant, all religions lead to the same divine truth. Religious pluralists argue that if humanity could only come to "see" this predicament, all religious fighting could stop. We could recognize what each religion has learned about God and, by compiling the parts of the whole, come to a better understanding of who or what the nature and personhood of the sacred reality is.

The view of the divine expressed by the sacred elephant analogy is plausible and worth considering. Before considering the accuracy of its assertions, I want to stress the pluralistic uses of the story. Far from saying all religions are true, the story of the blind men and the elephant takes all religions and throws them under the bus, where they are left broken in their false perceptions of ultimate truth. As hopeful as this story can appear, in reality it just drops the bomb on absolute truth, at least absolute truth concerning God. The blind men show us that truth concerning God is unobtainable due to our limited faculties.

Skepticism toward God doesn't invalidate this brand of pluralism. The problem lies within itself. Nestled within the story of the blind men and the elephant is a self-contradiction that makes the entire claim crumble in on itself. The pluralists claim that God is unknowable; every religion is wrong about its perceived understanding of the divine. However, in making this claim, the pluralists also implicitly declare they have an inside track on who God is. If no one is capable of knowing God due to our lack of sight in the realm of the divine, then what prescription glasses have enabled the pluralists to know the nature of God with such certainty? Pluralists are rejecting all exclusive truths concerning God, but making one themselves.

The Law of Noncontradiction Cannot Reveal Which Religion Is True

Sifting the world's religions for the ultimate answers in life can be a daunting task. The pages of the sacred texts of just the major religions number into the thousands, and studying them can require such detail that doctorate degrees are obtainable. Agreement among the religions can be found on superficial levels, but they contradict each other on fundamental doctrines. Recognition of these contradictions brings us no closer to knowing the truth, nor does pluralism's eradication of all their points of conflict.

The law of noncontradiction serves to illustrate what cannot be true— namely, two contradictory statements. This law of logic leaves us to admit that all religions cannot be equally true and valid. The law doesn't dictate that any of them must be true; however, the door is left open for at least one to be true. The law of noncontradiction doesn't deny the existence of truth.

This book could close now, and its title, *Contradict - They Can't All Be True*, would be defended. But the goal of this book isn't to reject the possibility of knowing the truth, so more must be written. My aim is to launch religious contradictions deep into the heart of pluralism so that they must be acknowledged and tested, in the hope of finding the truth!

There must be absolute truth, because the laws of nature and logic are true and enduring. Such laws allow for and in fact give birth to inquisitive investigation. To this end, the law of noncontradiction is the catalyst that sets the gears in motion, but if the law of noncontradiction alone is used, we fail to find which claim is true, if any. The time has come to launch from the apparent contradictions into the realm of testing religious truth-claims.

FINDING A RELIGIOUS
LITMUS TEST

The American Heritage Dictionary defines the word *test* as "a procedure for critical evaluation of the presence, quality, or truth of something." Another definition given is "a basis for evaluation or judgment."

The tests that most of us are familiar with are academic tests, which certainly fit the definition. But instead of discovering the truthfulness of something, academic tests discover a student's retention of what has been taught. When it comes to determining which religion is true, if any, a religious litmus test is required. A litmus test uses a single indicator to yield a verdict.

A pregnancy test tests for only one thing—pregnancy. The test result indicates "pregnant" or "not pregnant." A coroner's test for life tests for only one thing—the presence of life.

The first litmus test I learned was the one I used in the backyard growing up, the one we used to test the water in our pool. I forget the specifics, but the test provided a simple answer based on a strip of paper that changed color. Instead of an answer framed as yes or no, it yielded "too much" answers concerning acidity and basicity.

I saw Henry Rollins perform at the Orange County Fair in 2005. To introduce a song, he said something to effect of, "In this life there is a line that divides. It divides what's right and what's wrong, what's black and what's white. You can't straddle the line. You can either be in the black or in the white. There is no gray. You must pick a side. This song is called 'Black and White.'"

That same approach needs to be directed toward religions. Pluralism attempts to straddle the lines of contradiction. We can't stake our beliefs in both the black and white at the same time by creating a "gray" ground on which to stand. We need a test to prove which beliefs are false and which are true if we want to have any certainty in religious matters.

Religions Aren't Falsifiable—or Are They?

Agnostics declare that there is no test for evaluating religious truth-claims. Concerning the "God Question," an agnostic pleads that the existence of God is neither provable nor improvable; such information cannot be acquired. The word *agnostic* comes from the Greek root words *a* and *gnosis*. *A* means "without" and *gnosis* means "knowledge." In religious matters, agnostics claim that we do not know what is true and that we cannot *ever* know because the claims of religions cannot be tested through the scientific method. This position is grounded in the philosophy of the eighteenth-century atheist David Hume, who emphasized *empiricism*, the theory that all knowledge is derived from our sensory perception. Since God cannot be directly experienced by our senses, we are incapable of knowing anything about God.

Karl Popper, considered by many to be the greatest philosopher of science in the twentieth century, proposed that for a hypothesis to be falsifiable, it "must be capable of conflicting with possible, or conceivable, observations."[1] Popper also viewed *falsifiability* and *testability* as interchangeable terms. For Popper, something was testable if it could be subjected to investigation through the scientific method, which requires all tests to be not only observable, but also repeatable.

Since there is not a possible or conceivable, much less observable or repeatable experiment that can be conducted to test the existence of God, then claims concerning the existence of God are not falsifiable claims, according to Popper.

Karl Garret Vanderkooi, PhD in biochemistry from the University of Rochester, explains how logical-positivism, a position similar to Hume's empiricism, plays a role in guiding the process of working scientists.

> Logical-positivism defines two main categories of statements: meaningful and meaningless statements. Meaningful statements have been variously defined as those which are verifiable, falsifiable, or confirmable by empirical observation. All other statements are labeled as meaningless (except, of course, analytic statements which are true by definition). Hence any ideas or concepts which do not have what would loosely be called a scientific (i.e. verifiable) basis are considered meaningless. The logical positivist abhors unprovable, metaphysical assumptions, just as the empiricist did.[2]

Empiricism, logical-positivism, and strict guidelines that say only statements that can be tested via the scientific method are falsifiable have led many to believe there is no possible way of proving or disproving the existence of God. The result is that religion has been excommunicated from the field of science. Jeffrey Burton Russell, professor emeritus of history at the University of California, Santa Barbara, provides the following critique of "bracketing out" religion and any nonempirical realities from science:

> This bracketing out—the refusal to consider realities beyond the physical—is not inherent in knowledge; the Latin *scientia* refers to all knowledge. The word "scientist" is first attested in 1834. Scientists define their fields as limited to the physical. This definition is reasonable and probably necessary. But it does not mean that entities outside their fields can't exist. Science is supposed to be based on evidence, and there is no evidence that every phenomenon is physical.[3]

Granted, agnostics don't say that God doesn't exist; that is what atheists do. Agnostics just say that the existence of God is unknowable, untestable, nonfalsifiable, and nonverifiable. Ultimately they are standing with empiricism and the scientific method.

The error is that most of life's most important realities can't be classified as falsifiable through the scientific method, such as love and moral ethics, nor observed, such as the gravitational pull that keeps us safely planted on this earth's surface. Agnostics fail to realize that there are tests that can be applied to the God Question, and it's a form of testing that is widely accepted and practiced in day-to-day life. It's the historical forensic test.

Can the Past Be Known Since It Can't Be Seen? And What Does That Have to Do with God?

At University California, Irvine, I had a discussion with an undergrad student who argued that religious truth-claims could not be tested. His objection was that there is no possible test that we can readily produce that could verify God's existence with the "five senses," so there is no possible way of proving or disproving the existence of God.

I asked him, "If you were arrested and charged with murder, is there a way that you could prove your innocence?" He paused and laughed because he knew that there was no way a murder trial could be evaluated by a scientific method that relies on observation; the murder can't be repeated at will.

I followed up that question by asking, "Is there any way to know what happened in the past to verify the claims of history? How can we prove that yesterday happened? Or how could you prove tomorrow that we had this conversation over cups of coffee?"

He said, "It's easy to know the truth about current events, because there are still many eyewitnesses alive who *do* have empirical experience with the event."

I agreed with him and admitted that we can possess knowledge apart from what we have personally experienced with our senses or from what can be repeatedly observed.

Springing off his statement that recent events are easier to verify, I said, "Shows like *CSI* demonstrate the process behind investigating events of the past. We evaluate the evidence that remains after an event. We interrogate witnesses and look for corroboration. Still, cases run cold and are eventually closed. As time continues to pass by, it becomes increasingly difficult to determine the truth of what occurred.

"But we want to know the past! It's vital for the present," I exclaimed. He pondered and nodded while sipping his coffee, probably wondering where I was going. I had a captive audience, so I continued to keep him engaged with another question. "So how can we know the truth concerning the past? Is there a way to test it?"

"I'm not sure." He shrugged. "But there must be a way to know with relative certainty, or all the history classes I've taken over the years are meaningless."

"Let's pick an example from history, then. George Washington," I proposed. "How can we know that he existed, that he was a general, that he was the first president of the United States of America?"

He didn't want to share his answer, likely because he knew it would show a blind trust he had demonstrated most his life. He answered really slowly, "I … know … what I … know … about … George Washington … from history books."

"And from the one-dollar bill," I added.

"Yeah, sure," he conceded.

"But what makes those history books trustworthy?" I asked.

Having never considered it before, he shot from the hip. "I'm sure we have correspondence to and from George Washington, official documents from his time in the military and the presidency, and other historical documentation concerning the events of his life. Since he was the first president of the United States of America, we probably have a lot of documents about him and even images of him from his lifetime that were *intentionally* recorded and preserved for future generations."

"I bet you are right. But how can we trust everything written about him? Is it all true? Is there a way to separate the fact from the fiction, objectively?"

"I'm sure there is, and historians must have a way to do so."

"And if we're able to do so with George Washington, wouldn't the same criteria be applicable to other historical persons and events, such as determining if Julius Caesar was killed by Roman senators on the ides of March?"

"Sure. But I imagine it's harder to do so, since Julius Caesar is further removed than George Washington and lived in a time before the printing press," he answered.

"Good. So we're on the same page that there must be some sort of objective test applied to determine the truthfulness of historical claims. Otherwise all history books are a waste of trees. I'd even go a step farther and say that the recorded results of scientific tests would be useless too, since they also occurred in the unobservable past."

"Of course; we're on the same page."

"But we weren't initially," I reminded him. "At first you said that we couldn't know anything apart from what we can observe with our five senses."

"That's true, but we were talking about religion. I really meant in regard to God. There is no way of knowing he exists without empirical experience, of which there is none."

"So you conclude that God is a personal being, if he exists?" I asked.

"Where do you get that?"

"Well, you used 'he' to describe 'him.' So if there is a God, do you conclude that God is a personal being who can think and act?"

"I think that's right. *If* there is a God, I think he'd *have* to exist in some fashion as to be able to think, act, and feel. Otherwise, how is he God? How would he exist if he wasn't?"

"Does that mean God would have senses, just as we have senses?" I asked.

"Maybe not as we do, but certainly he has some nature that provides him the ability to experience the cosmos."

"That's cool. I agree with you on this point. But it's all based on assumptions, which I *assume* you realize, which is also why you haven't taken an affirmative stance on the existence of God."

"Otherwise it would be blind faith."

"I trust things blindly all the time," I told him. "I believe Africa exists, although I have never been there. I trust recipes will work without having seen them cooked by someone else first and without seeing someone else taste them first. I trust that elevators work safely and properly without checking to see if the certification is current or expired; I just get in it and hit the floor I want. What about you? Have you seen your professors' PhD diplomas?"

"Okay, you make good points. I, as we all do, believe things blindly, but not irrationally! I trust the authorities or organizations that provide the type of qualifications that you mention."

"I think it's wise to do so, but it's still blind trust if we just take it all in as true without checking their sources or comparing one author's report with another's. No one has time to do that with every issue in life. We have to sometimes trust authority on certain subjects. But when it comes to God, I think it's smart to question the subject deeply and not just blindly accept the answers of any one source of authority on the subject."

"I hear you. So what's the test for God that you keep alluding to?"

"It's what's called the historical test or the historiographical method, which is why I wanted to know where you stood on our ability to discern the past. It's also why I was curious if you thought God, if he exists, could interact with the world. What I suggest doing, if you want to test religious truth-claims, is to sift through the religions and find a historical event within their teachings that can be evaluated according to the standard principles of evaluation that would be applied to any other historical event. The event needs to prove or disprove the existence of God. In particular, you'd want to find an event in which God is claimed to have directly interacted with humanity within history."

Historiography—a Threefold Test of Evidence

There must be a set method of testing the trustworthiness of any document of antiquity for its historical reliability. This method must be of a nature that it can be applied to all texts—official government records, mythical epics, poems, plays, historical reports, and biographies, even biographies found in religious texts such as the Bible. Military history professor Chauncey Sanders, in his book *An Introduction to Research in English Literary History*, provides a threefold test for historiography. Sanders writes, "The evidence upon which we must rely in attempting to solve problems of authenticity and attribution may be classified as external, internal, and bibliographical."[4] Standard methods of collecting and testing these three categories evidence can be applied to any document of antiquity to gauge its trustworthiness as a credible historical witness.

For the bibliographic test, Sanders focused on the ability to discern if a document is what it is claimed to be; that is, whether a document is genuine or a forgery.

If someone came forward with a document that he claimed was a newly discovered Shakespeare play written in Will's own hand, how would you know if it was or if it wasn't? This is a predicament that most of us don't consider because we don't deal in resolving such matters, but there are numerous tests that can be applied bibliographically to determine if William Shakespeare actually wrote the play. These include the material used for writing, the material it was written on, and the method by which it was written. Sanders explains, "Ordinary ink turns brown with age; hence one cannot very well execute an allegedly old inscription with modern ink."[5] Paper and binding methods have changed over time, and if a method that didn't arise until the eighteenth century is attributed to the sixteenth century, we have unveiled a forgery. The font of type or style of handwriting can also be a giveaway for age, as both of these things have changed throughout history.

Once the bibliographic test is complete and the document is determined to be authentic in its dating, the internal evidence is addressed. What is in the text itself and how does that contribute to its authenticity or authorship? Examining the literary style, word choices, spelling, vocabulary, and dating within the questioned text are all aspects of the internal test. If we know an author is prone to misspell a certain word or to use a certain literary technique or word choice regularly, but in a document attributed to the same author we find none of these occurrences, we can assume the document was written by a different author. If the references within the document date it to 1452, but the author to whom it's attributed died in 1438, we know someone else had to have written it. Such is the internal evidence test as expressed by Sanders.[6]

The external test looks to evidence outside of the document in question that can verify the text. Sanders gives an extreme example of the external test at work: "If we know that a Latin work was written in a certain village at a certain time, the fact that only one person living in the village at that time knew Latin would be prima facie evidence of his authorship of the work."[7] Other external evidence can be the words of the author found in a different text and referring to the text in question. If the attributed author says someone else wrote the text, we can trust that the attributed author didn't write it, especially if we have other external evidence from contemporaries who attribute the work to someone else.

These three tests laid out by Sanders give an excellent method for determining a document's authenticity and attribution to a specific author. For our investigation into the reliability of a text's accounting of a specific historical person or event, the scope of these three tests will need to be broadened, but nonetheless retain the same elements.

For the bibliographic test, all the aspects mentioned by Sanders for determining the date of a document will be employed. Additional work will be textual criticism. This will verify if the copies of a specific work accurately portray the original autograph. Since we don't have the original manuscripts of the scriptures of any major religion, this is an important aspect of the bibliographic test. Accuracy in transmission over time is determined by comparing all the copies of a work to see if they relay the same text. If all the copies we have of a text, early and late, are closely related, or if missing portions are filled in by other copies in the same way, we can trust that the original autograph manuscript, though no longer in our possession, has been accurately preserved through the copies.

For the internal evidence test, we'll still inspect the document for attribution as Sanders did, but we'll also investigate what the author says about his or her relation to the historical events under examination. Is the author an eyewitness, or reporting hearsay, or writing from generations removed? Is the author writing fiction or nonfiction? Does the text have internal contradictions to make it unreliable? These are questions we will ask during the internal test.

For the external evidence test, we'll ask the same questions as Sanders, but we'll also turn those questions towards the specific historical event that is under our investigation. What did others say about the event, and do their reports corroborate or contradict the religious text's claims?

These tests result in conclusions that are not absolutely certain. Historians must work in the realm of probability because new information could always arise, or possible explanations currently unimaginable might one day be discovered. With the evidence at hand, and the data acquired through historiographical research, judgment calls must be made. When there is a preponderance of evidence, however, a person can weigh that evidence and say that beyond a reasonable doubt, or with reasonable certainty, that X occurred in the past.

A.J.M. Wedderburn explains the scenario this way: when historians "assert that something is certainly true, what they mean in practice is that something has been established 'beyond a reasonable doubt', that is, the level of probability has become so high that the falsehood of the assertion is highly improbable."[8]

Searching Religions for a Testable/ Falsifiable Religious Event

Now that a method for testing historical claims has been established, religions must be combed for a falsifiable event. The event should be one that, if proven to be false, discredits the entire religion. Such an event needs to be objective, which means it needs to have been an external event that can be evaluated by factual evidence. If it is discernible only by personal feelings and subjective reasoning, that event is not falsifiable and won't prove helpful for discerning religious truth.

Most of the events central to religious narratives do not fit the needed criteria for objective, historical evaluation. Maybe the agnostics are correct; the truth concerning God is unknowable, even through historiography.

Hinduism—The Vedas are considered to be the only divinely revealed texts of Hinduism. It is from these texts that the teachings of the Upanishads and other Hindu texts derive. The problem is that the Vedas don't bode well for the historical testing. We don't know who first received them, how they were received, when they were received, where they were received, or who finally wrote them down. The main claim in Hinduism is that everything is divine because everything came into existence through the separation of divine substance, but the Vedas themselves deny the certainty of this claim because no one witnessed it.

Buddhism—Buddhism centers on the historical event of Siddhartha Gautama attaining enlightenment sitting underneath the bodhi tree. He spent the rest of his life teaching others how they too could reach enlightenment.

Did the Buddha really attain enlightenment? Attaining enlightenment means reaching nirvana, which means there is no more suffering. It begins in this life, not after death. There is no way to objectively say that the Buddha reached nirvana; he was alone when it happened, so no one witnessed the actual moment. Even if there were witnesses, enlightenment and the escape from suffering are strictly subjective, not susceptible to being factually verified.

Judaism—There are key events within Judaism that are certainly objective and can fit the criteria, such as the lineage of the patriarchs. Did Abraham, Isaac, Jacob, and Joseph exist? Did all of mankind share one common language at the time of the Tower of Babel? Were the Jews enslaved in Egypt? Did they have a ten-plague, miraculous exodus and wander in the wilderness for forty years before entering into the land promised to their forefather, Abraham? For certain, if the Exodus occurred as the Tanakh claims, then one would expect there to be evidence of such an event in the annals of history apart from the Tanakh. Thus, the external test can also be applied.

Judaism's religious claims fare much better for historical evaluation than most religions, but the key parts that directly concern God interacting with his people are largely subjective. How could one prove that Noah and Abraham spoke with God? Did Moses actually receive the covenant from God directly? There weren't witnesses. How could one prove that Jacob and Joseph actually had dreams from the Lord? Did Ezekiel and Isaiah really see visions? Such events were not externally experienced and can only be evaluated by the person who subjectively experienced them.

Christianity—Like Judaism, Christianity records a lot of events in the New Testament that can be objectively evaluated. Was Jesus a historical person? If so, is there a specific event in his life or works that would prove or disprove the Christian faith? If so, is there a way to objectively verify that event?

The claim of Christ's divinity began with his virgin conception. If he was not born of a virgin, then Jesus would just be a mortal man who died on a cross. But how could we know if Mary was actually a virgin when she gave birth?

Islam—The word of Allah is the Qur'an. It was delivered to the prophet Muhammad by the angel Gabriel. Muhammad recited what he received from the angel, and the words he recited were written down and canonized after his death. This revelation that Muhammad received over a period of twenty-three years is certainly a historical claim that, if falsified, would falsify all of Islam, since Islam stands squarely on the belief that the Qur'an is the word of Allah and Muhammad is his messenger. The problem is that such a delivery of God's word isn't objective; only Muhammad heard and saw the angel.

Can any religion provide a historical event that qualifies as falsifiable—that is, testable through accepted means of evaluating history? Would any religion in its sacred text provide an objective event upon which the religion literally stands or falls? Or are all religions built upon subjective experiences?

There is one religion that has at its core a falsifiable event that, if proven false, would falsify the entire religion. That event was laid bare by its greatest missionary, the apostle Paul.

> For what I received I passed on to you as of first importance: that Christ died for our sins according to the Scriptures, that he was buried, that he was raised on the third day according to the Scriptures, and that he appeared to Peter, and then to the Twelve. After that, he appeared to more than five hundred of the brothers at the same time, most of whom are still living, though some have fallen asleep. Then he appeared to James, then to all the apostles, and last of all he appeared to me also, as to one abnormally born.
>
> For I am the least of the apostles and do not even deserve to be called an apostle, because I persecuted the church of God. But by the grace of God I am what I am, and his grace to me was not without effect. No, I worked harder than all of them—yet not I, but the grace of God that was with me. Whether, then, it was I or they, this is what we preach, and this is what you believed.
>
> But if it is preached that Christ has been raised from the dead, how can some of you say that there is no resurrection of the dead? If there is no resurrection of the dead, then not even Christ has been raised. And if Christ has not been raised, our preaching is useless and so is your faith. More than that, we are then found to be false witnesses about God, for we have testified about God that he raised Christ from the dead. But he did not raise him if in fact the dead are not raised. For if the dead are not raised, then Christ has not been raised either. And if Christ has not been raised, your faith is futile; you are still in your sins. Then those also who have fallen asleep in Christ

are lost. If only for this life we have hope in Christ, we are to be pitied more than all men.

But Christ has indeed been raised from the dead, the firstfruits of those who have fallen asleep. For since death came through a man, the resurrection of the dead comes also through a man. For as in Adam all die, so in Christ all will be made alive. But each in his own turn: Christ, the firstfruits; then, when he comes, those who belong to him. Then the end will come, when he hands over the kingdom to God the Father after he has destroyed all dominion, authority and power. (1 Corinthians 15:3–24)

Paul makes it very clear. If a person can produce evidence that Jesus did not rise from the grave, he or she can disprove Christianity. Paul is pulling down the collar of his shirt and saying, "Here's my jugular."

Let's put Paul's invitation to the test. We'll submit the resurrection accounts to Chauncey Sanders' threefold test: bibliographic test, internal evidence test, and external evidence test. Let's see where the chips lie, at least for one religion.

5

TESTING THE TESTABLE

I was raised in a Christian household in Tennessee. I was taught that Jesus is God, that he died for my sins and he rose from the grave, that the Bible is the Word of God, and that the Bible is true. I believed this along with other stories I was taught about Santa Claus and the Easter Bunny.

Like most children, I shook my beliefs in the fantasies of the Christian holidays, but I clung on to the stories about Jesus' birth, life, death, and resurrection. Also like many people who grew up being taught the Christian narrative and believing it, I began to have healthy questions about the validation for those beliefs. I asked, "Why can we be certain that the Bible is the Word of God?" The answers I received all through high school were simply Bible verses that proclaimed the nature and trustworthiness of the Bible. Essentially, I only received, "The Bible is the Word of God because the Bible says it is the Word of God," or "Just pray and ask God to reveal himself to you. If you do so sincerely, he will show himself to you and answer your questions in your heart. Then you'll know the Bible is true."

Fortunately or unfortunately, living in the Bible Belt of America, I rarely met anyone who openly claimed to not be Christian. There were of course a few exceptions, but the culture was largely Christian. My public high school football team said the Lord's Prayer together before games, I had science teachers who openly spoke about their Christian faith, and I had coaches who stressed, "God first, family second, school third, and football fourth."

It wasn't until I left Tennessee for California in my early twenties that I began to interact with people who were hostile to Christianity. In some cases I met people from other countries who had never even heard the gospel message of Jesus. This was shortly after the turn of the century. Now I imagine the religious climate in Tennessee has shifted closer to that of California than the traditional Bible Belt stereotypes.

In August 2004, I took a class at Concordia University–Irvine called Christian Apologetics. The professor was Rod Rosenbladt, and the subject was entirely foreign to me. Our main text was *History, Law, and Christianity*, by John Warwick Montgomery. It was this course and this text that first introduced me to the bibliographic, internal, and external tests of historiography that I shared from Chauncy Sanders' work in the previous chapter. Montgomery's book showed how the gospel of Jesus Christ fares when confronted with the rigors of these investigations.

I firmly believe that knowing the results that such historiographic tests yield when applied to the resurrection of Jesus Christ are the most valuable information a person may receive, because the conclusion one comes to in the realm of theology is the most important decision a person can make. That decision has bearing on eternity. To know for certain if Jesus rose from the grave is the best place to begin to make that decision. The resurrection of Jesus is the only religious claim (to the best of my knowledge) that can be historically evaluated to prove or disprove a religion.

The Bibliographical Test Applied to the New Testament

Since many people do not read Greek or Hebrew and do not have access to the Old and New Testament manuscripts from which our English translations of the Bible are derived, it is usually taken for granted that we know exactly what the original biblical texts contained. We do not. We no longer possess any of the original texts of the Bible, or any original copies of other ancient manuscripts for that matter. We don't even have any original copies of Shakespeare's plays written in the sixteenth and seventeenth centuries, so not having original copies of biblical texts shouldn't come as shocking news.

What we have for the books of the Bible are copies of copies of the originals. In many circumstances, we are likely looking at copies far removed from the original manuscripts. Moreover, all the copies we have do not relay the exact same message. Some of the copies are missing sections or are merely fragments—just a few verses in some cases!

The art of textual criticism takes these copies and meticulously compares them. If they all relay roughly the same text, then likely we have an accurate transmission of the original work. Christians who know this process of compilation teach that, properly speaking, only the original biblical documents were inspired by God and inerrant. As the copies stand now, they are in error, as they are not identical, and there is no way of knowing which, if any, serve as an exact match of the original text.

This does not mean that the biblical texts or any other ancient documents are unreliable. The three historiographical tests introduced in the last chapter need to be employed before any verdicts on reliability are levied.

To discern if Jesus rose from the grave, we need to start with the bibliographical test for the New Testament books. We start here because these books contain four biographies of Jesus Christ written in the first century, within about forty years of Jesus' death, give or take a decade or two depending on the biography. These four sources are where we obtain the majority of our knowledge of Jesus' short life and ministry. The other New Testament books provide additional insight into Jesus' words and deeds and contain numerous direct references to Jesus' resurrection and the significance of that event for all of humanity.

The goal of the bibliographic test in our inquiry is to determine if the New Testament texts we possess accurately represent the original manuscripts. In our technologically advanced era of electronically stored, written communication that can be quickly retrieved and mass-produced at will, we have lost sight of the challenges to written transmission from previous centuries. Copying manuscripts by hand is time consuming and open to errors. For ancient works, the more copies of a manuscript we hold for comparison, the more certain we can become that the copies are faithful to the original if, after comparison, we conclude that all the copies are analogous. If we only have ten copies of a specific work and every copy is drastically different in word choice, we know that the transmission of the original hasn't been very accurate. However, the text might still be reliable if the missing portions or scribal errors do not change the overall message or theme.

For the Bible, we have a great wealth of copies for comparison—well over five thousand copies in the original Greek language. That may not sound like much when we think of a *New York Times* bestseller that tops a million copies, but for an ancient document this is a staggering number of copies. Having twenty copies of an ancient document is considered exceptional, and many documents from antiquity exist today through ten copies or fewer.

The total count of New Testament manuscripts is constantly growing too, as more copies are discovered. In 1925, A. T. Robertson numbered the Greek manuscripts at over four thousand,[1] and in 2001, Norman Geisler and Peter Bocchino placed them at 5,686 copies.[2] How many more copies might we discover over the next century?

This total count can be deceiving. It does not mean that we actually have 5,686 Greek copies of the entire New Testament. Some of these manuscripts are just fragments, a few verses at times, as in the case of the the Rylands Library Papyrus P52, which only contains John 18:31–33 and 37–38. However, we do have entire copies of the New Testament, and I'll mention the most important of these copies in a moment.

To further support the Greek manuscripts, we have copies of New Testament translations in Latin, Ethiopic, Slavic, and Armenian, pushing the total number of manuscripts to over 24,000.[3] Even if we did not have any of these copies, we could still piece together the New Testament text from the many direct quotations and citations made by early Christian writers in their commentaries, letters, and sermons.[4] Again, such numbers are mountainous in comparison to other works. For instance, a contemporary of the gospel writers, the Jewish historian Josephus, wrote *The Jewish War*, and it has come to us through nine surviving manuscripts.[5] Caesar's *The Gallic Wars* remains through ten extant copies, and Aristotle's *Poetics* through just five copies.[6] The work that has the greatest number of extant manuscripts next to the Bible is Homer's *The Iliad*, raking in fewer than 650 copies.[7]

The numbers game doesn't necessarily prove the Bible was transmitted accurately. All of the texts could contain a different message. The insertion or deletion of a single word, such as *not*, could make a huge difference. If half the copies say, "Jesus is the Son of God," and the other half say, "Jesus is not the Son of God," then we can't be certain what the original text actually contained.

If the differences were this huge in the biblical texts, then the Christian faith would be standing on shaky ground. Don Stewart, graduate of Talbot Theological Seminary, explains the nature of most of the discrepancies that arise within the texts we have, so we know that the differences are not as damning as the example I just supplied.

> A variant reading can be defined as any place in the text where two given manuscripts disagree with each other. For example, in John 1:18 there is a variant with regard to a description of Christ. Some manuscripts read the "only begotten Son" while other manuscripts read the "only begotten God." Therefore, we have a variant in the manuscripts. Whenever two manuscripts disagree with regard to word order, spelling, grammar, etc. it constitutes a variant. Few variations in the text actually exist. There is complete agreement among the manuscripts in about 95 percent of the text. The 5 percent where there is any question consists of trivialities such as word order and spelling.[8]

The superior preservation of the New Testament doesn't end here. Most ancient manuscripts have huge time spans between the date of the original manuscript and the date of their surviving copies. Not so with the New Testament documents. Sir Frederic G. Kenyon, the former director and principal librarian of the British Museum, explains the time interval comparison between the New Testament documents and other ancient works in this way:

> In no other case is the interval of time between the composition of the book and the date of the earliest extant manuscripts so short as in that of the New Testament. The books of the New Testament were written in the latter part of the first century; the earliest extant manuscripts (trifling scraps excepted) are of the fourth century—say, from 250 to 300 years later. This may sound a considerable interval, but it is nothing to that which parts most of the great classical authors from their earliest manuscripts. We believe that we have in all essentials an accurate text of the seven extant plays of Sophocles; yet the earliest substantial manuscript upon which it is based was written more than 1400 years after the poet's death. Aeschylus, Aristophanes, and Thucydides are in the same state; while with Euripides the interval is increased to 1600 years. For Plato it may be put at 1300 years, for Demosthenes as low as 1200.[9]

Imagine that we lived in the year 4013 and the first mention we had of the theory that the Mayan calendar predicted the end of the world was from handwritten copies dated 3150 of New Age books first written in 2009. If all we had were these copies, over a thousand years removed from the first manuscript, how could we be certain the text wasn't changed in 2300 or 2500? That's the sort of time span we're working with concerning events of ancient history and the documents that record them.

Now imagine that the first handwritten copies we had were dated 2350 and not 3150. If I told you that most historians in the year 4013 trusted the accuracy of the document transmission that recorded history in the early to mid–2000s, even though the oldest available copies of these manuscripts were from the 3000s, wouldn't you then expect a copy dated 2350 to be considered very trustworthy in its transmission of the original document, since there was less time for scribal errors or intentional alterations to have taken place?

That's exactly the dating scenario we have for New Testament documents in comparison with all other ancient documents. Plus, remember, the number of copies is far greater too.

The oldest fragment of the New Testament we have is from the collection of papyri in the John Rylands Library. It's labeled p52 (papyrus 52). On one side it contains John 18:31–33 and on the other 18:37–38. It can be viewed online at the University of Manchester Library's Web site.[10] The document is generally dated from AD 110 to AD 140. Considering that the gospel of John is dated from AD 60 to AD 90, we have a range of twenty to eighty years from when the gospel of John was first written to the earliest surviving copy. It's just a fragment of one chapter of John's gospel, but it's nonetheless amazing in comparison with the thousand year gap most ancient documents suffer.

The Bodmer Papyri are manuscripts kept in the Bodmer Library in Geneva, Switzerland. They contain p66, 72, and 75. The Foundation Martin Bodmer says, "The Papyrus Bodmer II (P66) is a remarkable document. It is a transcription of the oldest known example of the complete Gospel According to Saint John. The manuscript, which dates back to the end of the 2nd century, gives an insight into how Christian texts were written less than 100 years after the Gospel was drafted."[11]

It is already great news that there are fragments and a complete book from the New Testament dated so close to the time of the original writings. As I quoted from Kenyon earlier, we also have complete copies of all the New Testament books that date to the fourth century. This first complete copy of the New Testament is called Codex Sinaiticus, which dates to the middle of the fourth century, and it also happens to contain the complete Old Testament. An earlier work, Codex Vaticanus, contains most of the Bible, but is lacking a few of the New Testament books. Codex Sinaiticus is scanned and viewable online at www.codexsinaiticus.org.

Having fragments less than one hundred years removed from the original text and complete books beginning at about one hundred years greatly helps with distinguishing which of the variant readings is mostly likely what the original text contained. If 70 percent of the texts say "Cephas" and 30 percent say "Peter," then it's likely the original said "Cephas"—unless, of course, the 30 percent were all dated earlier than the 70 percent. Even then, the discrepancy wouldn't matter unless it touched upon a substantive issue. In this case, we know that Cephas was another name for Peter, so there is no substantive issue.

Two great examples that illustrate how the dating of manuscripts helps us determine what the original text was are Mark 16:9–20 and John 5:4. Open up a copy of the Bible to the last chapter of Mark. Most English translations will have a special note in the middle of the chapter. The New International Version has a black line across the middle of the chapter with a bracketed comment underneath it. I think most readers just skip past that bracketed comment and pick up reading at verse 9, but that bracketed material reads, "The earliest manuscripts and some other ancient witnesses do not have Mark 16:9–20." This means there is a strong likelihood that Mark 16:9–20 wasn't in the original text; therefore, it's not actually a part of the Bible.

Now turn to John 5:4. Can you find the verse? I bet you can't. Most English translations don't have it. You'll see verse 3, and then verse 5. It's not that verse 4 is missing; it's just that the earliest manuscripts don't contain it. The footnote in the New International Version lists the additional verse that "less important manuscripts" contain.

What's great for textual criticism and the reliability of the New Testament documents is that scholars actually can draw lines in the middle of chapters and add footnotes to point out textual uncertainties. We can only do this because we have so many copies of the New Testament from such a wide range of dates that we can recognize portions that were likely inserted later. We do not have to worry about the missing sections of Scripture. We just have to decipher the questionable additions; of course, we have.

Again, most of the discrepancies are irrelevant, on the level of did the original text say, "Jesus Christ," "Christ Jesus," or just "Christ"? Does it matter? When the variants are more drastic, we can recognize that the text is in doubt, yet also claim with certainty that no Christian doctrines are affected by the discrepancy.

At the conclusion of this bibliographic test, one must face the reality that the New Testament books pass with flying colors. The results of this test led Dr. John Warwick Montgomery to the following conclusion, which is often quoted from his book, *History, Law, and Christianity*: "To express skepticism concerning the resultant text of the New Testament books is to allow all of classical antiquity to slip into obscurity, for no documents of the ancient period are as well attested bibliographically as the New Testament."[12]

This of course does not automatically mean the text of the New Testament is true. This test is for the textual authenticity of the New Testament books, not the historiography. We can trust that the New Testament documents have been successfully transmitted to us from their original state, but this doesn't mean that their words are pure fact without a trace of legend. For instance, I can trust that the copies we possess of the first edition of *Action Comics*, the first recorded appearance of Superman, accurately represent the original author's message. That doesn't automatically mean it's true that there is a man from another planet, now living on Earth, who possesses superpowers and wears red, white, and blue underwear with a cape. To ascertain if the New Testament documents contain fact, legend, or fiction, two more historical tests remain to be applied: the internal and external tests.

Internal and External Tests

The internal evidence test turns to the document in question and sees what it has to say about itself. Does the document indicate whether it is to be interpreted as fact or fiction? Does the author claim to be an eyewitness, or reporting hearsay, or writing generations removed from the event? Does the text have internal contradictions that make it unreliable? Does the author make statements that go against known facts?

Note that a document's credibility should be questioned if it goes against *known* facts, not the unknown. On numerous occasions, the validity of the Bible has been doubted on the basis of our lack of knowledge of the existence of a specific place, person, or event mentioned in the Scripture. However, as time passes and archeology advances, new discoveries have corroborated biblical testimony.

As you can see, the external test has already been utilized in affirming the internal evidence of the documents. These two tests are often interrelated. The same questions asked in the internal test are asked of other documents in the external test to determine what others have reported about the events in question. Do their reports corroborate or contradict the religious text's claims? Because the internal and external tests need to be used together in historiography, I think it's best to intermingle their results and present them as a single unit.

Despite our modern binding of the Gospels, Acts, the Epistles, and Revelation into one work called the New Testament, they are in fact twenty-seven books and should properly be considered independent sources. Whatever testimony Paul might share concerning Peter and his epistles should be considered as external evidence that affirms or denies the reliability of Peter's testimony and instruction. However, we'll take the New Testament as a whole, apply the internal test to it, and work with documents outside of the Bible for the external tests.

One of the first questions to be addressed in the internal test is, who were the authors of the New Testament? Scholars believe there were likely nine. What was their relationship to the events they described? What we find within the text of the New Testament are the authors' claims that they were eyewitnesses of Jesus or that their writings are based on eyewitness testimony. The following are some verses that illustrate this internal evidence:

John concludes his gospel by saying, "This is the disciple who testifies to these things and who wrote them down. We know that his testimony is true. Jesus did many other things as well. If every one of them were written down, I suppose that even the whole world would not have room for the books that would be written" (John 21:24–25).

John also claims to be an eyewitness at the start of one of his first epistles, saying, "We proclaim to you what we have seen and heard, so that you also may have fellowship with us. And our fellowship is with the Father and with his Son, Jesus Christ" (1 John 1:3).

Peter echoes John's words, claiming that the apostles' accounts are not fabricated tales: "For we did not follow cleverly devised stories when we told you about the coming of our Lord Jesus Christ in power, but we were eyewitnesses of his majesty" (2 Peter 1:16).

Luke provides no eyewitness claim for himself but assures his reader that he is relaying testimony that he received directly from eyewitnesses: "Many have undertaken to draw up an account of the things that have been fulfilled among us, just as they were handed down to us by those who from the first were eyewitnesses and servants of the word. With this in mind, since I myself have carefully investigated everything from the beginning, I too decided to write an orderly account for you, most excellent Theophilus, so that you may know the certainty of the things you have been taught" (Luke 1:1–4).

Luke records Paul's account of seeing the resurrected Christ on the road to Damascus: "He fell to the ground and heard a voice say to him, "Saul, Saul, why do you persecute me?" "Who are you, Lord?" Saul asked. "I am Jesus, whom you are persecuting," he replied. "Now get up and go into the city, and you will be told what you must do." The men traveling with Saul stood there speechless; they heard the sound but did not see anyone. Saul got up from the ground, but when he opened his eyes he could see nothing. So they led him by the hand into Damascus. For three days he was blind, and did not eat or drink anything" (Acts 9:4–9).

Paul, according to many Bible scholars, claims in the third person to have been called up to heaven to hear and see unspeakable revelations from God: "I know a man in Christ who fourteen years ago was caught up to the third heaven. Whether it was in the body or out of the body I do not know—God knows. And I know that this man—whether in the body or apart from the body I do not know, but God knows—was caught up to paradise and heard inexpressible things, things that no one is permitted to tell" (2 Corinthians 12:2–4).

Paul's first letter to the Corinthians contains an early Christian creed that lists eyewitnesses of the resurrected Jesus, of whom Paul is one: "For what I received I passed on to you as of first importance: that Christ died for our sins according to the Scriptures, that he was buried, that he was raised on the third day according to the Scriptures, and that he appeared to Cephas, and then to the Twelve. After that, he appeared to more than five hundred of the brothers and sisters at the same time, most of whom are still living, though some have fallen asleep. Then he appeared to James, then to all the apostles, and last of all he appeared to me also, as to one abnormally born" (1 Corinthians 15:3–8).

You'll notice that the Gospels of Mark and Matthew do not have a verse cited in the above list. That doesn't automatically mean that their gospels don't relay eyewitness accounts. Matthew was one of the twelve apostles and is referred to as Levi in Mark and Luke's gospels. Although nowhere in the gospel of Matthew does the author claim to be an eyewitness or state his name, there is unanimous agreement among the early church fathers that Matthew is the author of the gospel attributed to him. In addition, all of the earliest copies of the gospel of Matthew have his name affixed to them. We would expect to see various names associated with the same text if apostles' names were attributed later to add authority to a text written by an unknown author.

Mark's gospel has similar support, in that there is unanimous agreement among leaders of the early church that Mark was the author, but Mark was not an eyewitness. According to Acts, he was a missionary companion of Paul and Barnabas (Acts 13:5), but had a falling out with Paul on that journey and was not accepted on a second journey (Acts 15:36–39). We see mention of Mark again in a few of Paul's epistles, and from these references it appears Mark regained favor with Paul (Colossians 4:10; 2 Timothy 4:11). Mark's gospel is believed to convey the eyewitness testimony of Peter. The order of the gospel presentation fits well with the chronology present in Peter's address in Acts 10. Externally, the early church recognized that Mark recorded his gospel based on Peter's testimony, and that Mark was in fact a close companion and interpreter for Peter.

The following two quotations are from early external sources that confirm the Gospels' authors are Matthew, the tax-collector turned apostle; Mark, the companion of Peter; Luke, the companion of Paul; and John, the apostle who received special affection from Jesus:

> Papias, a disciple of the apostle John, stated that Mark was dedicated to accurately recording Peter's testimony. Papias' words are preserved by Eusebius in his *Church History*, book 3, chapter 39:14–15.

> Papias gives also in his own work other accounts of the words of the Lord on the authority of Aristion who was mentioned above, and traditions as handed down by the presbyter John; to which we refer those who are fond of learning. But now we

must add to the words of his which we have already quoted the tradition which he gives in regard to Mark, the author of the Gospel.

"This also the presbyter said: Mark, having become the interpreter of Peter, wrote down accurately, though not in order, whatsoever he remembered of the things said or done by Christ. For he neither heard the Lord nor followed him, but afterward, as I said, he followed Peter, who adapted his teaching to the needs of his hearers, but with no intention of giving a connected account of the Lord's discourses, so that Mark committed no error while he thus wrote some things as he remembered them. For he was careful of one thing, not to omit any of the things which he had heard, and not to state any of them falsely." These things are related by Papias concerning Mark.[13]

Irenaeus, Bishop of Lyon, a disciple of Polycarp, a disciple of John the Apostle, states the apostles publicly proclaimed their message before writing down the Scripture. The authorship Irenaues provides for all four gospels in his work, *Against Heresies*, book 3, chapter 1:1 are exactly as we currently have them attributed.

We have learned from none others the plan of our salvation, than from those through whom the Gospel has come down to us, which they did at one time proclaim in public, and, at a later period, by the will of God, handed down to us in the Scriptures, to be the ground and pillar of our faith. For it is unlawful to assert that they preached before they possessed perfect knowledge, as some do even venture to say, boasting themselves as improvers of the apostles. For, after our Lord rose from the dead, [the apostles] were invested with power from on high when the Holy Spirit came down [upon them], were filled from all [His gifts], and had perfect knowledge: they departed to the ends of the earth, preaching the glad tidings of the good things [sent] from God to us, and proclaiming the peace of heaven to men, who indeed do all equally and individually possess the Gospel of God. Matthew also issued a written Gospel among the Hebrews in their own dialect, while Peter and Paul were preaching at Rome, and laying the foundations of the Church. After their departure, Mark, the disciple and interpreter of Peter, did also hand down to us in writing what had been preached by Peter. Luke also, the companion of Paul, recorded in a book the Gospel preached by him. Afterwards, John, the disciple of the Lord, who also had leaned upon His breast, did himself publish a Gospel during his residence at Ephesus in Asia.[14]

The evidence within the New Testament documents, as well as the statements found in reliable external sources, weighs in favor that eyewitnesses, or people associated with eyewitnesses, wrote the gospel biographies and the Epistles. Irenaeus considered it fitting that, just as there are four corners of the world and four winds, so there should be four pillars (gospels) that give men life anew.[15]

Tatian, a disciple of Justin Martyr in the late second century, took the Gospels and made a harmony of them, splicing and rearranging them to form one account to the best of his abilities. This harmony was called the *Diatessaron*, which means "through four" in Greek.

On such early evidence that positively affirms that there are four gospels, with no indication there could be more or less, and with no contradicting testimony from this period concerning who wrote them, we can safely conclude that we have at our disposal primary sources that accurately represent the original testimonies of their authors.

It's time to examine what these eyewitnesses claim concerning Jesus of Nazareth.

Examining the Gospels' Claims

I hope you haven't forgotten the aim of our historical testing. We're on the case to test the likelihood that Jesus of Nazareth was raised from the grave after being crucified. His resurrection, as the apostle Paul claimed in 1 Corinthians 15, proves the truthfulness of the Christian faith. The resurrection affirms the apostles' claims that Jesus is the Savior of the world. If Christ was not raised, their claims are lies or the words of crazy men who should be pitied for wasting their lives on a fabrication.

Jesus' resurrection is directly linked to his claims to be divine. The resurrection proves his deity as the second person of the Trinity. It affirms his teachings that his death would serve as an atoning sacrifice for the sins of mankind.

Apart from such claims, even if the resurrection occurred, it would not have any relevance to anyone. It would just be the most mysterious, improbable event in history. If his resurrection actually happened as the Gospels and Epistles claim it did, and he actually claimed to be God in the flesh, sent by the Father to die so we might have life after our deaths too—then that truly is good news!

Some readers might laugh at the perceived need to show from the primary sources that Jesus claimed to be God, as they have heard this taught their entire lives. Others might be highly skeptical. As we already saw in chapters 2 and 3, Muslims would deny that Jesus ever claimed to be God. They would say that the Gospels were corrupted and changed since their initial writing, and that he never said he was divine, merely a servant of Allah. For this argument, we can move back to the bibliographic test to show that the gospel copies can be trusted to accurately represent the original authors' works.

Others argue that Jesus never actually said, "I am God." He only claimed to be a "Son of God." Still others might say that he claimed to be God, but in the Hindu sense of the term, believing that we all are divine through Brahman.

With Jesus' claims to divinity providing meaning to the claimed resurrection of Jesus, we should first see what Jesus claimed of himself according to the eyewitness accounts we have to examine.

Did Jesus Claim to Be God?

In the gospel biographies, it is obvious that Jesus claimed to be God without actually saying the words, "I am God." One chapter that shows this is John 14. Jesus equated himself so closely with the Father as to claim that he too is divine. He said, "Trust in God, trust also in me" (John 14:1). He said, "I am the way and the truth and the life. No one comes to the Father except through me" (John 14:6). He said, "If you really knew me, you would know my Father" (John 14:7). He said, "Anyone who has seen me has seen the Father" (John 14:9). He said, "I am in the Father, and the Father is in me" (John 14:10). He also indirectly said that if a person loves and obeys him, that person will also love and obey the Father (John 14:23–24). This all comes from one chapter of John. In the next chapter, Jesus says, "He who hates me hates my Father as well" (John 15:23).

In this short section of one of the Gospels, we see that Jesus teaches that to trust him is to trust God; to know him is to know God; to see him is to see God; to love him is to love God; and to hate him is to hate God. In fact, we can't know the Father apart from him.

In our day and age, we might be able to find some interpretative loophole to circumvent this language, but such mental gymnastics are not in keeping with first-century Judaic understanding of who God is and who we are as humans.

John 5 records the healing of a paralytic man at a pool. This healing took place on the Sabbath, and the man Jesus healed picked up his mat and walked, just as Jesus had ordered him to do. However, Jews considered carrying a mat on the Sabbath unlawful; the Sabbath was a day of rest unto the Lord, and carrying a mat was work.

So the Jewish leaders questioned this man as to what he was doing. He explained that the man who healed him told him to carry the mat and walk, so he did. When the Jews learned that Jesus was the man who had ordered this, they were furious with him. Jesus should have known better as a rabbi, a teacher of God's Word.

When confronted with breaking the Sabbath rules, Jesus said to them, "My Father is always at work to this very day, and I, too, am working" (John 5:17). According to John, it is "for this reason the Jews tried all the harder to kill him; not only was he breaking the Sabbath, but he was even calling God his own Father, making himself equal with God" (John 5:18).

We may not recognize such talk as being "I am God" talk in the twenty-first century, but we have to trust the understanding that the Jews of Jesus' day displayed, especially since we have no record of Jesus saying, "That's not what I meant, guys; don't stone me!"

Jesus claimed to be divine in various ways, at numerous times, and among different audiences. He allowed others to worship him and taught that we can pray to him and ask for anything in his name. He forgave people's sins, an act that was recognized as something only God could do. He referred to himself as the "Son of Man," which was a weighty title for the Jews.

This title comes from a vision recorded by the prophet Daniel. Daniel saw "one like a son of man coming with the clouds of heaven" (Daniel 7:13). The Son of Man was able to enter directly into the presence of the Ancient of Days with no fear of death; he could see God and live! He was given authority to rule over all the earth, over every nation, and be worshipped by every tongue. His rule would never end. When we read the scriptural context of who the Son of Man is and what he can do, we see that it is very much a divine title. Who could ride the clouds, be in the presence of the Ancient of Days without dying, and rule, reign, and be worshipped forever by all men, except for one who is divine?

Such examples should be enough to illustrate that Jesus claimed to be divine. He did so in a Jewish context, as a Jewish rabbi, and the Jews of his day clearly recognized that he was making himself equal to the Father. For the pantheist to conclude that Jesus claimed to be God just as all of us are God, requires ignoring the fact that Jesus made no reference to any Hindu philosophy or thought. He affirmed Jewish Scripture and teachings and practiced Jewish ceremonial customs, such as Passover and Pentecost (Shavuot). He didn't quote from the Vedas, he never mentioned Brahmin or any of the Hindu deities, nor did he practice any form of Hindu yoga.

Some might ask, why didn't he make it clearer? Why didn't he directly say, "I am God"? I speculate that Jesus never said those three direct words because, when he said "God" and when the apostles wrote "God" in their letters, they were almost always referring to the Father, not the Trinity. If Jesus had said that he was God, it might have been construed to mean that he and the Father were the same person, that he was the Father, which he is not. Within Christ's theology and the theology of his apostles, God exists in three distinct persons, the Father, the Son, and the Holy Spirit, all of whom share in the same divine essence.

An aspect of Jesus' role as Savior of the world was to reveal the Father to us, and I think his use of Trinitarian language does just that. In John 10:30–33, Jesus says that He and the Father are one. The Greek language used indicates that he and the Father are one, not in person, but in deity. The translation might be read in English as "I and the Father, we are one."

The word used for "one," *hen*, is neuter in gender. In the Greek language, most words have gender. Using the neuter, asexual "one" instead of the masculine "one" indicates that Jesus is saying that he and the Father are one in nature, not personhood. This statement in John 10 was again a public statement in front of the Jews in the temple area, in response to the Jews pressing him to declare plainly whether he is the Messiah. When he said, "I and the Father are one," they responded by picking up stones to stone him, because they knew that he had just claimed to be God (John 10:22–33).

The following is an abridged and slightly rearranged list of verses taken from Kenneth Samples' book, *Without a Doubt*, that show various ways that Jesus and others claimed and attributed divinity to Jesus through titles, actions, and words:[17]

Divine titles proclaimed by or attributed to Jesus Christ:

God (John 1:1; John 20:28; Romans 9:5; Titus 2:13; Hebrews 1:8; 2 Peter 1:1)

Lord (Mark 12:35–37; John 20:28; Romans 10:9–13; 1 Corinthians 8:5–6; 12:3; Philippians 2:11)

Messiah (Matthew 16:16; Mark 14:61; John 20:31)

Son of God (Matthew 11:27; Mark 15:39; John 1:18; Romans 1:4; Galatians 4:4; Hebrews 1:2)

Son of Man (Matthew 16:28, 24:30; Mark 8:38; 14:62–64; Acts 7:56; Daniel 7:13–14)

Divine names, actions, or roles proclaimed by or attributed to Jesus Christ:

Creator (John 1:3; Colossians 1:16; Hebrews 1:2,10–12)

Sustainer (1 Corinthians 8:6; Colossians 1:17; Hebrews 1:3)

Forgiver of sins (Mark 2:5–7; Luke 24:47; Acts 5:31; Colossians 3:13)

Object of prayer (John 14:14; Acts 1:24; 1 Corinthians 1:2)

Object of worship (Matthew 28:16–17; Philippians 2:10–11; Hebrews 1:6)

Object of saving faith (John 14:1; Acts 10:43; Romans 10:8–13)

Divine attributes proclaimed by or attributed to Jesus Christ:

Eternal existence (John 1:1; John 8:58; John 17:5; Hebrews 13:8)

Self-existence (John 1:3; John 5:26; Colossians 1:16)

Omnipresence (Matthew 18:20; Ephesians 1:23, 4:10; Colossians 3:11)

Omniscience (Mark 2:8; Luke 9:47; John 2:25, 4:18; Colossians 2:3)

Omnipotence (John 2:19; Colossians 1:16–17)

Jesus made direct claims that many Jewish religious leaders considered to blasphemous:

"My Father is always at his work to this very day, and I, too, am working." (John 5:17)

"I tell you the truth, before Abraham was born, I am!" (John 8:58)

"I and the Father are one." (John 10:30)

"I am. And you will see the Son of Man sitting on the right hand of the Mighty One and coming on the clouds of heaven." (Mark 14:62)

Who Is This Man?

We can see that Jesus made a bold claim to be divine again and again through his words and actions, and the words and actions of others that he permitted without correction.

We could all make such a bold claim, and we could go about trying to persuade others that we are transcendently divine, the creators and masters of the universe, but we don't. What prompted Jesus to maintain his assertion to be God, even while on trial for blasphemy, even all the way down the crucifixion trail?

We should do our best to address all the possible explanations of who Jesus could have been, based on these claims. No stone should be left unturned. In historical testing, we deal in the realm of probability: what is the most likely explanation based on the evidence? Here we look at the claims of Christ to be God in the flesh. We evaluate the internal testimony of Scripture and the external evidence available to answer the question, "Who is this man?"

Could Jesus Be Mythological?

- The gospel biographies should not be rejected on the presupposition that miracles, the supernatural realm, and the existence of God are simply myths.
- The gospel accounts don't read as myths. They were written in a way that indicates the authors aimed to convey historical facts. For instance, Luke is very attentive in providing dates by referencing rulers, leaders, years, and months, as well specific location descriptions. See Luke 1:5, 26; 2:1–4, 41–42; 3:1–3; 23:1–26 for examples.
- The Gospels were written too close to the events they record, among other witnesses. The Jews and the Romans both had the means and the motive to prove the claims of the Gospels to be in error, but they could not. We see within Scripture and without that all they could do was persecute the early church to discredit the disciples' message of Christ. Under such persecution, the early church did not fold, as likely their assailants anticipated. The apostles also would have had to contend with Jesus' other disciples if their accounts of their rabbi were false.
- Pliny the Younger, a Roman governor, writing to Emperor Trajan, records in AD 112 the tenacity of the early Christians, saying, "I asked them whether they were Christians or not? If they confessed that they were Christians, I asked them again, and a third time,

intermixing threatenings with the questions. If they persevered in their confession, I ordered them to be executed; for I did not doubt but, let their confession be of any sort whatsoever, this positiveness and inflexible obstinacy deserved to be punished."

Pliny goes on to explain the rapid spread of Christianity and its apparent resilience: "Hereupon I have put off any further examinations, and have recourse to you, for the affair seems to be well worth consultation, especially on account of the number of those that are in danger; for there are many of every age, of every rank, and of both sexes, who are now and hereafter likely to be called to account, and to be in danger; for this superstition is spread like a contagion, not only into cities and towns, but into country villages also, which yet there is reason to hope may be stopped and corrected."[18]

These quotations, though written after the death of the apostles, still indicate that the second-generation disciples were fully persuaded by the apostles' eyewitness testimony and refused to recant their faith, even in the face of execution. It also indicates that emperors and rulers wanted to disprove the Christian "superstition," but they could not because Jesus was a true historical figure who was crucified under Pontius Pilate, as the Jewish historian Josephus and the Roman historian Tacitus confirm in their writings.

Could Jesus Have Lied about Being God?

- What would be Jesus' motivation to lie?
- The Jews had the expectation that the messiah would come as a mighty warrior-king who would free them from Roman rule and oppression. Josephus records an Egyptian prophet who attempted to lead four thousand men to revolt. The apostle Paul is actually mistaken as this prophet in Acts 21:38. Josephus records other false messiahs seeking rebellion, like the prophet Theudas and the weaver Jonathan. They all begin their "ministries" in the wilderness, in parallel with the way Israel's history began in the wilderness.[19] It's possible that Jesus was lying about being the Messiah in an attempt to rally the Jews behind him for revolt

against the Romans. This would be in line with Jewish messianic expectations, and fits with Jesus beginning his ministry in the wilderness, fasting.

- There is no indication that Jesus sought to physically overthrow the Romans or to possess worldly authority. On trial before Pontius Pilate, John records Jesus as having said, "My kingdom is not of this world. If it were, my servants would fight to prevent my arrest by the Jews. But now my kingdom is from another place" (John 18:36).

- Jesus was a carpenter by trade, without a fortune, and in his teaching ministry he did not seek wealth or gain it. He plainly stated his poverty when he said, "Foxes have holes and birds of the air have nests, but the Son of Man has no place to lay his head" (Matthew 8:20).

- He showed no animosity toward the Roman rulers, their laws, or their taxes. When asked about paying taxes to Caesar, his reply was simply, "Whose face is on the coin? Then give to Caesar what is Caesar's, and to God what is God's" (Matthew 22:21) At his arrest, one of his disciples pulled a sword and cut off the ear of the servant of the high priest. "'Put your sword back in its place,' Jesus said to him, 'for all who draw the sword will die by the sword'" (Matthew 26:52).

- Nothing in his character indicates that Jesus was a grandiose liar. In fact, his moral teachings are well revered and respected by many who are not Christians. His teaching ministry was accompanied by "healing every disease and sickness" and "compassion" on the crowds, "because they were harassed and helpless, like sheep without a shepherd" (Matthew 9:35–36). Pilate found no fault in Jesus and knew that it was because of envy that the Jewish leaders turned him over for crucifixion (Matthew 27:11–26). Herod was even "greatly pleased" to get to meet Jesus, expecting to see a miracle and not a traitorous criminal, based on the known reputation of the Jewish rabbi.

- If Jesus were lying, if all of his miracles were the product of deception, he would have profited financially from them, or he would have used them to instigate revolt against the Romans, but he didn't. If Jesus were lying, he wouldn't have persisted in the lie while on trial for execution before the Jews, Pilate, or Herod. Who would die in such a manner for a claim he knew was fabricated?

Could Jesus Have Been Mentally Sick?

- It's possible for people to think they are telling the truth, but in fact they are not. Someone could genuinely believe that the sun revolves around the earth, but he'd be dead wrong about it. Jesus could have honestly thought he was God, unaware that he was just a man. If someone were to claim to have existed before Abraham, to have a kingdom not of this world, and to be the Son of God, and to be able to do so in the face of execution, that person would have to be diagnosed as insane.

- Others have claimed to be divine, such as emperors and kings, and they were not insane. Still others, such as cult leaders, have claimed to be the returned Christ, or God. They have garnered followers who believe them, and yet we don't automatically label them insane. All this is true, yet there is no evidence these figures believed with complete certainty that they were in fact God. Were any of them put to the test of their claims as Jesus was, placed on trial for execution? Would they have stuck to their claims? Would they have admitted their claims were lies? Would they have committed suicide before arrest, or taken worse actions such as forcing a "revolutionary suicide," leading all their followers to commit suicide like Jim Jones? No cult figures or rulers who have claimed divinity compare to Jesus in their moral characters, teachings, or motives. None of them have resurrection claims by their followers after their deaths to support their claims to divinity either.

- There are no signs of mental instability in Jesus' life. His message was consistent; he did not add to, change, or contradict his teachings. He regularly had the audience of educated Jewish teachers of the Law, who actively tried to trap him or force him to contradict himself or Scripture. They were never successful in their endeavors. On all accounts, Jesus appears to have been mentally lucid and coherent.

- Some people are schizophrenic and manifest mental instability periodically. It's possible that Jesus was brilliant and had great moral teachings, and at times switched to an alternate personality that claimed to be divine. Such a scenario is unlikely because the gospel biographies indicate that Jesus' disciples were in close communication with him—in fact living with him. Surely over a period of three years, at least one of them would have recognized his mental illness, or a physician in one of his many audiences would have recognized his lunacy.

- Psychiatrist J. T. Fisher puts a nail in the coffin of the hypothesis that Jesus was psychotic by explaining just how profound the teachings of Jesus of Nazareth are; so profound, in fact, that it is highly implausible they could be the product of a madman.

> If you were to take the sum total of all authoritative articles ever written by the most qualified of psychologists and psychiatrists on the subject of mental hygiene—if you were to combine them and refine them and cleave out the excess verbiage—if you were to take the whole of the meat and none of the parsley, and if you were to have these unadulterated bits of pure scientific knowledge concisely expressed by the most capable of living poets, you would have an awkward and incomplete summation of the Sermon on the Mount. And it would suffer immeasurably through comparison. For nearly two thousand years, the Christian world has been holding in its hands the complete answer to its restless and fruitless yearnings.[20]

Could Jesus Have Been a Pantheist?

- If you go to Amazon and search on the term "Jesus went to India," you will find books that suggest that Jesus traveled to India in his youth. The theory is that in India, Jesus learned about the Hindu belief that all things are divine. The Gospels are mute concerning Jesus' life from twelve years old until he began his public ministry at about thirty years of age. That would have provided an eighteen-year gap for Jesus to have gallivanted around India, becoming well equipped to bring about a great spiritual awakening when he returned to Jerusalem. This explanation indicates that Jesus claimed to be God in the Hindu-Brahman sense of the meaning of divinity, and thus we all are as much a part of God as Jesus.

- There is no indication that Jesus left the Jerusalem countryside for India. As indicated earlier, people recognized Jesus and knew his family (Matthew 13:53–56). If he had been tramping around India for the majority of his life, he wouldn't have been recognized and so easily associated with his family, who likely would have gone with him, considering that a twelve-year-old wouldn't have been able to travel like that on his own.

- Jesus was a Jewish rabbi. He was not a Hindu Brahmin (priest).

- Jesus quoted Hebrew Scripture. He didn't quote the Vedic scriptures or the Upanishads.

- Jesus observed Jewish ceremonial laws. He did not perform puja services or practice yoga.

- Jesus spoke of God in the Jewish understanding of a transcendent God, and he equated himself to that divine Father. He never put any other human on the same plane, and he never gave any indication that we could rise up to it. He never spoke of any Hindu deities. Jesus was a Jew. Not a Hindu.

- If a person claims to have read the Gospels and walked away with the interpretation that Jesus was a pantheist, I don't believe that person actually read the texts. We must allow the texts to speak for themselves. The pantheist must bring his or her presupposition that everything is one and divine into the gospel reading to arrive at such a conclusion, which is not being honest to the text or the grammatical-historical rules of interpretation.

These four explanations are the most commonly considered alternatives to Jesus being the divine Son of God. Without even addressing the evidence for Jesus' divinity, the option that Jesus is divine is already sounding the most plausible. However, all possible explanations need to be measured before staking our final claim as to the most probable answer.

While the previous inquiries were natural explanations, the following possibilities move into the realm of the supernatural, extraterrestrial, or yet-undiscovered technology. To some readers, these explanations may seem so extremely implausible as to be laughable. Yet, these explanations do embrace the broader scope of Jesus' life—that is, his miracles, and maybe even the resurrection that his disciples claimed after his death—in a way that the previous explanations tend to completely ignore.

The following investigations consider whether Jesus could have been from another planet, a Buddhist Bodhisattva, an avatar of the Hindu god, Vishnu, a time traveler, an extraordinary prophet of God, a demon incarnate, or the promised messiah.

Could Jesus Have Been an Alien from Another Planet?

- Anything is possible. If Jesus was from another planet, he would be more technologically advanced than we are and more evolved. He would have to be in order to accomplish such interplanetary travel. His advanced knowledge would explain his ability to walk on water, heal people, have supernatural insights into people's lives, raise people from the dead, and even raise himself from the dead.

- Jesus was born of a woman named Mary. He is known to be her son. Shepherds didn't witness his birth, but they witnessed a baby in a manger with Joseph and Mary right after his birth (Luke 2:8–16). Those shepherds were in the fields near Bethlehem, prominent for the Jews since it was there that sheep were raised for temple sacrifice, including the lambs for Passover. After they witnessed Jesus in a manger, just as angels had told them they would, they "spread the word" and people "were amazed" (Luke 2:17–18). Someone in the first century would have been able to locate this special field and investigate the story. If this story recorded by Luke were not true, such a simple investigation could have corroborated or denied Luke's accounts.

- The biographies show that people knew Jesus was from Nazareth: they knew it was his hometown, they knew his mother was Mary, they knew he was the "carpenter's son," and they knew his brothers and sisters (Matthew 13:53–56). There is no evidence that Jesus of Nazareth came to our planet via a spacecraft.

- If Jesus were unaware of being an alien, then he might consider himself a demigod of sorts, but why would he consider himself to be equal with the transcendent God of the Israelites? Joseph and

Mary would have known the truth, and they would have corrected his public teachings in private.

- If Jesus were an alien, why would he die for a planet and species that were not his own?

Could Jesus Have Been a Bodhisattva?

- The gospel biographies do not contain any trace of Jesus mentioning Buddha, reincarnation, the eightfold path, or any Buddhist scriptures. Jesus was a Jewish rabbi, teaching in a Jewish context, using Jewish vocabulary, and speaking in parables that fit the culture of the Israelites under Roman rule. His fundamental claims to be divine and the only way to salvation, in fact, contradict the teachings of all branches of Buddhism, not just those Buddhists who believe in bodhisattvas.
- Bodhisattvas are enlightened beings who are reincarnated to guide others into nirvana. Jesus did not speak of nirvana or the afterlife in the sense that would be expected in Buddhist teachings. Instead, Jesus elaborated on a final judgment that would be made not by God, the Father, but by himself. It would separate people to eternal life with him, or eternal perishing in hell.
- Jesus was a Jew, not a Buddhist.

Could Jesus Have Been an Avatar of Vishnu?

- The gospel biographies never mention Jesus being an incarnation of Vishnu, or even uttering the name Vishnu, much less mentioning any other Hindu deities.
- Krishna, a previous incarnation of Vishnu, advocated the practice of numerous yogas (spiritual paths) as ways to obtain oneness with Brahman (the divine essence at the heart of all things) and release from reincarnation. Jesus instead advocates not adherence to specific spiritual actions, but repentance and trust in him for salvation from eternal death, a concept that is directly contrary to the fundamental teachings of Hinduism.
- If Jesus were an avatar of Vishnu, he would have followed the practice of not killing animals; he would have been a vegan. Jesus,

however, helped fishermen catch fish (Luke 5:1–11; John 21:3–7) and served people fish to eat (Mark 6:28–44; John 21:9–14). It was also a command of God for the Jews to eat lamb every year at Passover (Exodus 12:3–14), and Jesus is recorded as having observed Passover (Luke 2:39–43; John 2:23). Therefore, Jesus ate lamb and allowed others to eat lamb too. Jesus' eating of meat is inconsistent with Hindu teachings of ahimsa. An incarnation of Vishnu certainly wouldn't have eaten meat or served others meat due to the Hindu teaching that all things are divine. In Judaism, the consumption of meat is not forbidden, just restricted (Numbers 11). After the flood, Noah and his family were told that they could eat any living thing that moves as long as the blood no longer remains in it (Genesis 9:3–4). Restrictions were given on what types of animals were permissible to eat after the Exodus from Egypt (Numbers 11), while the ritualistic slaughter of animals was part of God's system of sacrificial atonement for the forgiveness of sins (Numbers 11). Jesus' death is interpreted as the fulfillment of that system's requirements.

- Jesus was crucified for claiming to be the Son of God, the Creator of the universe, not the son of a god. Hinduism has no doctrine of sin or the penalty of sin. Instead there are laws of karma that direct the flow of reincarnation. Hindu beliefs do not have a place for vicarious atonement or propitiation, so there is no good reason why an incarnation of Vishnu would suffer the excruciating and humiliating death of Roman crucifixion.
- Jesus was a Jew, not a Hindu.

Could Jesus Have Been from the Future?

- If, in the future, time travel is invented, why would a person travel back in time to die an agonizing death?
- Would there be a time machine?
- Why would Jesus not have used his knowledge of history for his personal gain?
- This explanation fails to recognize that Jesus was born at the time of Caesar Augustus (Luke 2:1), has a recorded history of being presented at the temple forty days after his birth, as God's Law

commands (Luke 2:22), that he amazed the teachers at the temple courts when he was twelve years old (Luke 2:46–47), and that the people of his hometown recognized him as being from Nazareth (Matthew 13:55–56). None of this would be possible if he was from the future, unless Mary was also from the future. But we know Mary's lineage from Luke's gospel, which he traces all the way back to Adam.

- Assuming that the technological advancements that would give rise to time travel are what allowed Jesus to perform miracles, why don't we see more people in the past or present who can perform such miracles at will?

- As implausible as time travel is, it's even more implausible that in the future people will have the ability to resuscitate themselves from the dead!

Could Jesus Have Been a Prophet, but Not God?

- Prophets such as Moses and Elijah are recorded to have performed miracles through the power God granted them. It's possible that Jesus' miracles were done in this manner. Even Jesus' disciples are recorded as having performed miracles. The Bible also records that there were sorcerers, magicians, diviners, witches, and false prophets who could perform miracles and work in the realm of the supernatural (Exodus 7:11; Numbers 22:5–7; 1 Samuel 28:7–19; Acts 8:9–25; 13:6, 8). Just because he performed miracles, Jesus did not have to be divine, and there are plenty of examples in the Bible to support this.

- Christians acknowledge that Jesus was a prophet, as do other religions such as Islam and Mormonism. Those who argue that Jesus was a prophet, but just a man or not fully God, tend to argue that the verses that demonstrate Jesus claiming to be divine have been corrupted through copying of the manuscripts, through errors in translation, or by intentional modifications on the part of the early church. The problem with this argument is revealed through the bibliographic test shared at the beginning of this chapter; the copies we have now can be trusted to accurately relay the message of the originals. If a person remains skeptical of this, that person would have to jettison all documents of ancient history, because none of them are as well attested bibliographically as the New Testament manuscripts.

- Within Judaism, the religion that gave birth to Christianity, a person is a prophet if he relays God's words to humanity. If his words are found to be false or his visions and dreams untrue, or if his words contradict the words of other known prophets, then that person ought to be labeled a false prophet (Jeremiah 14:14; 1 Corinthians 14:27–33). The context of Jesus' words must be considered. His words were spoken as a Jewish rabbi to a Jewish audience who recognized that Jesus was claiming to be divine. Since they recognized his words as such, they had him crucified for blasphemy. If Jesus is a prophet, he must either be telling the truth and be God, or he was a false prophet who was a deceiver and blasphemer. If Jesus were lying, why would he have stuck to his claims to divinity when he was arrested and on trial to be crucified? He was given the opportunity to recant or explain himself, but he remained silent in front of his accusers. Why would he do that unless he was telling the truth? Pontius Pilate is recorded in every gospel to have tried to convince Jesus to defend himself or the Jews to change their minds, because he could find no fault in Jesus. Mark even records that Pontius knew that "it was out of envy that the chief priests had handed Jesus over to him" (Mark 15:10). If envy is what motivated the Jewish leaders, then that doesn't sit well with Jesus being a false prophet.

- The opinion has been expressed that Jesus was a prophet, just as all the great religious leaders were prophets to mankind. Jesus is one of God's spokesmen, in company with Krishna, Buddha, Moses, and Muhammad. If this were the case, why draw the line with these? We could just as likely add Mahavira, the Bab, Guru Nanak, Mary Baker Eddy, Joseph Smith, Charles Taze Russell, and L. Ron Hubbard. And what would keep us from including the likes of Nostradamus, Jeane Dixon, Gerald Gardner, Aleister Crowley, Sun Myung Moon, Jim Jones, David Koresh, and others who have claimed to be the returned Christ? If you believe that Jesus is one of many of God's prophets, then God has intentionally revealed himself to mankind in contradictory ways. Why would the Maker of all things do that, unless he was a liar and intentional deceiver?

Could Jesus Have Been a Demon?

- Angels, as recorded in the Old Testament, have manifested themselves in the likeness of humans, so much so that people couldn't tell they were angels (Genesis 18–19; Judges 6 and 13). Angels are shown to have direct influence in our world in mighty ways, such as bringing judgment down upon entire nations (Daniel 4:17,23), wiping out an entire army (2 Kings 19:35), sending blindness upon the men of Sodom (Genesis 19:11), protecting God's people in times of impending death (Daniel 3:24–28; 6:19–22), and delivering messages from the Lord. Demons are angels that have sinned and are no longer servants of God. Just as God's angels are capable of physically manifesting themselves as humans with miraculous abilities, would it also be possible for a demon to manifest as a human and perform miracles to deceive God's people away from the Lord? Could Jesus have been a demon, performing miracles to deceive God's people into following a false messiah?
- The Old Testament doesn't provide any instances in which demons have manifested themselves in human likeness. This doesn't mean that they can't, but there are no recorded instances of this occurring. Some Christians believe that Genesis 6:1–4 refers to angels, likely demons, who manifested themselves physically and had sexual intercourse with women. The word "angels" is not used in this passage, but "the sons of God." While "the sons of God" can be interpreted to refer to angels, as in Job 1:6 and 2:1, here it is most likely referring to male believers who chose to marry female unbelievers. What is clear in Scripture, at least in the New Testament accounts, is that demons can possess and afflict individuals. In such cases, it was obvious to the witnesses that the person was possessed due to the symptoms of erratic behavior, restricted behavior, or superhuman power.
- The gospel biographies record that the Jewish rabbis claimed that Jesus was casting out demons by the power of Beelzebub (i.e.,

Satan), or through possession by him (Matthew 12:24; Mark 3:22; Luke 11:15). Jesus' reply, of course, was that Satan wouldn't drive out demons, because if he did, his kingdom would be divided and fall. Jesus then asks the leaders by whose power they drive out demons. He suggests that they should examine the fruit of his work to see if his life reflects God or the Devil (Matthew 12:25–37; Mark 3:23–39; Luke 11:17–20). The Jewish teachers of the Law have no comeback recorded in the Gospels, but certainly they must have agreed with his argument or found that he was observing God's Law. Otherwise they would have arrested him earlier than they did.

- If Jesus were a demon, how would he have been tempted in the desert by Satan? Why would Jesus have resisted those temptations? (Matthew 4:1–11; Mark 1:9–11; Luke 4:1–13).

- Even if demons can manifest physically into human likeness, there is no indication within the historical accounts of the Bible that angels or demons can be born as humans. Even assuming they could, why would a demon live an entire human life, observing the laws of God, to die a horrible death that involved much bloodshed (another questionable event for angels or demons to be able to experience), and then reappear later to fake a resurrection? The only motive based on Satan's character as a liar is that he would be deceiving people to trust in a false messiah, and thus turn from God. There would be much easier ways for Satan to deceive mass populations, like appearing to a man alone in the desert and claim to be an angel of God with a new message from the Lord.

Could Jesus Have Been the Messiah, the Son of the Living God?

- Jesus' disciples could have lied about his claims, but that's not likely. Many of the claims they attribute to him were said to have been spoken in front of others, both friend and foe. If such claims weren't spoken, the disciples' accounts would have been discredited before the church even began.

- His miracles were public and often impromptu and personal, which indicates that he couldn't have staged them. If they were staged, he would have used them for financial gain and popularity, like Simon the Sorcerer (Acts 8). Without the luxury of the many technological advances that modern-day magicians have, it's not likely that all the miracles could have been illusory. The people who witnessed Jesus' feats recognized them as miracles or signs from God.

- In the tractate *Sanhedrin*, part of the Jewish Talmud, it is recorded that Jesus was crucified because he "practiced sorcery and led Israel astray and enticed them into apostasy."[21] This is an important quotation because it indicates that we have records outside of Christian sources that acknowledge that Jesus was known for performing acts that could not be explained away without entering into the supernatural realm. The Jews didn't want to recognize his claims to be divine, so they explained his miracles as sorcery. If we admit that a supernatural explanation is needed, then God is more likely than sorcery, based on the words and motives of Jesus.

- Jesus proclaimed that he would suffer many things (Mark 8:31) and that he would in fact be handed over to be crucified (Matthew 26:2). He predicted this fate for himself, but he did nothing to change his course. The best explanation for why he didn't was because Jesus also believed and vocally professed that he would rise from the grave, with the additional detail that it would be three days later (Matthew 17:22; Mark 8:31; Luke 9:22). In these passages, he speaks this prediction clearly. At other times he made this prophecy more cryptic, saying, "For as Jonah was three days and three nights in the heart of a huge fish, so the Son of Man will be three days and three nights in the heart of the earth" (Matthew 12:40). Another time, he said, "Destroy this temple, and I will raise it again in three days" (John 2:19). In Jesus' mind, it was certain; crucifixion would not be his end game.

- It's one thing to predict you'll die a criminal's death. Anyone could predict that and follow through with it, but there'd be no reason to do so, unless you were an anarchist, thought you could reap personal benefit, were insane, or wanted to somehow gain fame postmortem, to live on in infamy for your crimes. It's a completely different prediction to claim that you'll rise from the grave after a public execution. Yet this is exactly what the disciples claimed Jesus did, and they preached this quite convincingly. They never recanted their testimony even in the face of a similar fate as their rabbi.

When the evidence is considered as a whole, with a willingness to accept the possibility of miracles and the existence of God, Jesus being the incarnate Son of God appears to be the best explanation.

Before we make this final conclusion, we need to examine the internal and external evidence for the resurrection. The resurrection, after all, is the single event that could discredit Christianity and the claims of Christ to be divine. If the proof of the resurrection isn't substantial, or if there is a natural explanation for the evidence that is as satisfactory as the resurrection explanation, then we might be able to put a nail in the coffin of one of the world's religions (or a boulder in front of the tomb).

Where is the Body of Jesus of Nazareth?

If a person in the first several decades after Jesus' death had wanted to investigate claims that Jesus rose from the grave, what would be his first move? The claims would probably come to his ears in substantially similar form: Jesus of Nazareth was crucified under Pontius Pilate, three days later his tomb was found empty, people are now claiming to have seen him raised from the dead, and no one can get his disciples to shut up about his resurrection. The person investigating might have met Jesus before his crucifixion, or heard him preach publicly, or witnessed one of his miracles, or heard the rumors about how special this Jewish rabbi was. Maybe this person would have been a highly motivated Jewish priest who wanted to disprove the resurrection, or maybe this person was working directly for a Roman governor such as Pilate to get to the root of all the commotion.

Whatever the case, a good number of people in the first century should have had the motive and the means to conduct a thorough investigation of the Christians' claims of Jesus' resurrection. It should be trusted that the information within the New Testament would have been accessible to an investigator, since the disciples began their public preaching and ministries fifty days after the Passover of Jesus' death, and were often arrested and questioned by court authorities. Luke's gospel affirms that this was in fact the case. Luke wrote that "many" did take up the task "to draw up an account of the things that have fulfilled among us" (Luke 1:1). He claims that he too "investigated everything from the beginning" (Luke 1:3).

If I were investigating the resurrection, as Luke and many others did, I'd want to ensure that Jesus of Nazareth actually died under Pontius Pilate by Roman crucifixion, that he was buried, and that his tomb was empty with no other, more plausible explanations for how the body went missing. I'd then want to interrogate individuals who declared they had seen the risen Jesus and evaluate their testimony, comparing their accounts for contradictions. It'd be a difficult process without a car, cell phone, photography, or the Internet, but it'd be doable. Otherwise Luke wouldn't have been able to claim to have done so in the first century. Luke didn't just investigate the death and resurrection; he even investigated the birth and youth of Jesus, which was what he meant when he said he investigated everything from the beginning.

Did Jesus Die on a Cross?

The gospel accounts record that darkness fell over all the land for a three-hour span as Jesus hung on the cross (Matthew 27:45; Mark 15:33; and Luke 23:44–45). This darkness is confirmed by the words of Thallus, a Samaritan historian who wrote about twenty years after Jesus' death, as well as by the Greek historian Phlegon. Their accounts of the darkness are preserved by the second- and third-century historian, Julius Africanus, who recorded both accounts. Julius says that Thallus tried to explain the darkness as an eclipse of the sun. Julius doesn't buy this argument because "The Jews celebrate their Passover on the 14th day according to the moon, and the death of our Savior falls on the day before the Passover. But an eclipse of the sun can only take place when the moon comes under the sun, how then could an eclipse have occurred when the moon is directly opposite the sun?"[22]

Concerning Phlegon's account, Julius records, "It is evident that he did not know of any such events in previous years."[23] This darkness is even recorded in Chinese history: "Summer, fourth month, on the day of Ren Wu, the imperial edict reads, 'Yin and Yang have mistakenly switched, and the sun and moon were eclipsed. The sins of all the people are now on one man. [The emperor] proclaims pardon to all under heaven.'"[24]

The time of this eclipse recorded during the Han Dynasty was AD 31. If the darkening of the sun occurred from noon to three o'clock in Jerusalem, that would correspond to five to eight o'clock in the capital of China at that time, Luo Yang. This would explain why the Chinese records claim not just a darkening of the sun, but also the moon.[25]

With such internal and external evidence connecting an unprecedented and unexplainable extinguishing of the sun to the time of Jesus' crucifixion, coupled with accounts of a subsequent bodily resurrection, it's likely that such news reached even the ears of the Roman emperor. He could have sent an investigator. Many other investigators of lesser political or financial status could have made inquiries about Jesus' death. It wasn't as if Pontius Pilate was completely inaccessible. The Jewish Sanhedrin clearly had no problem bringing Jesus before Pilate and Herod to be tried for insurrection (Luke 23:1–25). Without a doubt, many Jews and Romans in the region would have wanted to investigate Jesus' death and would have had the means of verifying if Jesus did die by crucifixion under Pontius Pilate. Even if they couldn't speak with Pilate in person, there were plenty of witnesses who saw Jesus sentenced to death, since a riotous crowd shouting for Jesus to be crucified forced Pilate to condemn Jesus to the cross (Matthew 27:15–24; Mark 15:9–15; Luke 23:20–25). Surely an eyewitness from this scene could have been found rather easily in the months and years following Jesus' sentence.

Both Matthew and Mark record that after Jesus' death sentence, he was taken to the Praetorium, the governor's residence, where the entire company of soldiers stationed there stripped him, put a scarlet robe on him, gave him a crown of thorns, mocked him, spit on him, beat him, and had him flogged (Matthew 27:27–31; Mark 15:16–20). After this treatment, the Gospels record that the soldiers led Jesus away to his crucifixion. Many of these men would have been able to serve as witnesses to Jesus' death. If they didn't see the execution through until the end, they would have been able to point an investigator to the centurion and soldiers who oversaw Jesus' final hours.

Another witness who could have been found was a man from Cyrene named Simon. The Synoptic Gospels record that the soldiers forced him to carry Jesus' cross. Mark records that this man was the father of Alexander and Rufus (Mark 15:21). He writes these names as if his audience would have known who they were. Surely a man named Simon from Cyrene, who had two sons named Alexander and Rufus, could have been found and interrogated in the early first century. He would have been able to answer the following questions with ease: Were you forced to carry a cross at the time of the Passover? Was the man whose cross you carried Jesus of Nazareth? Did he say anything to you? What was his condition when you carried his cross? Was he crucified at Golgotha, the Place of the Skull, as Jesus' disciples claim? Is it true that a sign was placed over his head that read, "This is Jesus, the king of the Jews"? Did you see Jesus nailed to the cross? What about his death? Did you stay to witness it? Could you tell if any of his followers or family were there for his execution? What did you think about the sky going dark at his crucifixion? Or the earthquake at his death? Do you think they are linked?

The Gospels make mention that many women followers of Jesus were watching his crucifixion: Mary Magdalene, Mary the mother of James and Joses, the mother of Zebedee's sons, Salome, Mary the wife of Clopas, and Jesus' mother and her sister. Any of these women could have been interviewed to confirm the death of Jesus. Likewise the apostle John, who claims in his gospel to have witnessed the crucifixion, even receiving instructions from Jesus to take care of his mother, could also be interrogated.

Already we have compiled a large list of alleged witnesses who could have been located and examined to verify the gospel accounts that Jesus did in fact die. The greatest witnesses of them all, though, would have been the centurion who oversaw the crucifixion and the soldier who stuck Jesus in the side with a spear (possibly the same centurion). The following is what John records of the death that he witnessed:

> Now it was the day of Preparation, and the next day was to be a special Sabbath. Because the Jews did not want the bodies left on the crosses during the Sabbath, they asked Pilate to have the legs broken and the bodies taken down. The soldiers therefore came and broke the legs of the first man who had been crucified with Jesus, and then those of the other. But when they came to Jesus and found that he was already dead,

they did not break his legs. Instead, one of the soldiers pierced Jesus' side with a spear, bringing a sudden flow of blood and water. (John 19:31–35)

If Jesus had not been sentenced to death by Pontius Pilate, surely Pontius would have publicly squelched that rumor, if not Pilate, then Herod or the Sanhedrin. If someone other than Jesus was nailed to the cross, then the mob who demanded his crucifixion, the women disciples who stayed until his final breaths, or his closest disciple, John, should have been able to confirm that Jesus did not die on a cross.

If anyone questioned whether Jesus could somehow have survived the crucifixion, the executioners would certainly have been able to affirm if he was dead or not. The man who thrust the spear into Jesus' breathless body would have been able to confirm if Jesus died on the cross. The Gospels record that the centurion in charge of Jesus' execution, after seeing how Jesus died, said, "Surely this man was the Son of God" (Mark 15:39). The first-century inquirer would have sought the centurion for confirmation of Jesus' death and would have learned if the centurion truly did believe Jesus was the Son of God based on the way he died.

If any of the gospel accounts misrepresented how Jesus died, these witnesses would have denied them. Living in the twenty-first century, we have no record that they ever did.

Was Jesus' Tomb Empty?

> Early on the first day of the week, while it was still dark, Mary Magdalene went to the tomb and saw that the stone had been removed from the entrance. So she came running to Simon Peter and the other disciple, the one Jesus loved, and said, "They have taken the Lord out of the tomb, and we don't know where they put him!" So Peter and the other disciple started for the tomb. Both were running, but the other disciple outran Peter and reached the tomb first. He bent over and looked in at the strips of linen lying there but did not go in. Then Simon Peter, who was behind him, arrived and went into the tomb. He saw the strips of linen lying there, as well as the burial cloth that had been around Jesus' head. The cloth was folded up by itself, separate from the linen. (John 20:1–7)

The answer, according to John's account, was, "No, it wasn't empty; there were burial linens and a burial cloth in the tomb."

The key is that there wasn't a body in the tomb. There are plenty of questions that need to be answered before jumping to the conclusion that an empty tomb means a dead person came back to life. Jesus was crucified; he was a criminal. Did executed criminals even receive proper burials and nice, private tombs, or were the bodies left to rot on the crosses for all to see, for all to be reminded of the penalty for insurrection against the Roman Empire? Jesus' chosen twelve disciples had deserted him at his arrest, with one of them, Judas, being the one to turn him over to the chief priests. Who would have cared enough to bury him? If the disciples fled at Jesus' arrest for fear of their own lives, and Peter denied Jesus three times, how can we be certain that they even knew what tomb he was supposedly buried in? Weren't Jewish burial practices to let a body decompose for a year, then collect the bones and store them in a box for the future resurrection of all the dead? Is it be possible that they went to the wrong tomb, and the linens were from a previous burial?

All of these are great questions that could very easily have been answered by one man, Joseph of Arimathea. Matthew, Mark, Luke, and John all record that Joseph was the one who buried Jesus. Matthew says that he was a rich man who was a disciple of Jesus (Matthew 27:57). Mark and Luke record that Joseph was a member of the "council," or the Sanhedrin (Mark 15:43; Luke 23:50). Luke adds that Joseph did not agree with the Sanhedrin's decision to crucify Jesus (Luke 23:51), and John adds the detail that Nicodemus, a Pharisee who was also a member of the Sanhedrin (John 3:1), who privately met with Jesus (John 3:1–21) and who publicly defended him at one point (John 7:50–51), aided Joseph with the burial. Every gospel records that Joseph asked Pilate for the body and permission to bury it, and Mark says that he did so with boldness (Matthew 27:58; Mark 15:43; Luke 23:52; John 19:38).

Matthew says that the burial took place in Joseph's tomb (Matthew 27:60). Mark and Luke say that it was a tomb cut out of rock (Mark 15:46; Luke 23:53). Luke and John both say that no one had been laid in this tomb before (Luke 23:53; John 19:41). John gives the most details about the location of the tomb, saying that it was in a garden near Golgotha, where Jesus was crucified (John 19:41). Women disciples from Galilee followed Joseph and Nicodemus to the tomb, and two of the women are listed by name: Mary Magdalene and Mary the mother of Joses (Matthew 27:61; Mark 15:47; Luke 23:55). When the burial was complete, a large stone was rolled in front of the tomb, sealing it shut (Matthew 27:60; Mark 15:46).

Such details could not be fabricated in the first century. The Sanhedrin was the judicial arm of the Jews in Judea, consisting of seventy-one men, including the high priest, former high priests, Sadducees, Pharisees, and prominent scholars of the Jewish Law. If a Joseph from the village of Arimathea did not exist and was not a member of the Sanhedrin, the Jews would have swiftly squelched the disciples' claims. The same applies for Nicodemus. As for Joseph and Nicodemus themselves, if they did not do what the disciples claimed, they would have actively put a stop to the rumors that painted them as supporters of the blasphemous insurrectionist, Jesus of Nazareth. Pilate would also have been able to deny the burial accounts if he did not relinquish the body to Joseph.

Despite having the authority, power, means, and motive to deny their roles in Jesus' burial and prove the Gospels' accounts false, we have no record of anyone denying that Jesus was buried in the manner that the gospel writers claim. Furthermore, we have no contrary claims regarding Jesus' empty tomb on Sunday morning.

A first-century investigator would have been able to locate a rich member of the Sanhedrin from a village near Jerusalem. He also would have been able to locate the burial site by looking for a new tomb cut into rock in a garden near Golgotha. Locals would have been able to guide him there; I'm sure they guided many people who were investigating this peculiar news. In addition to the disciples who were the first witnesses of the empty tomb, Matthew records that there were guards posted at the tomb. He records that the Pharisees remembered Jesus' claims that he would rise from the dead after three days. They wanted to ensure that the disciples wouldn't steal the body, so they asked Pilate to give them a guard of soldiers, which he granted. These men would have also witnessed the empty tomb, which Matthew records was opened with a violent earthquake as an angel of the Lord came down from heaven, rolled away the stone, and sat on it (Matthew 28:2–3). Matthew says, "The guards were so afraid that they shook and became like dead men" (Matthew 28:4).

These soldiers would also have served as good witnesses in corroborating the disciples' claims. Of course, Matthew records that the high priests paid the soldiers off to tell everyone that the disciples had stolen the body as they slept, but I'm sure an intensive interview with the soldiers would have revealed holes in their stories. The disciples stealing the body doesn't make sense. There's no way the disciples could have rolled away the stone, unwrapped the body of Jesus, and carried it off without waking the guards. And there is no way that the disciples could have expected to pull off such a heist without having to kill the guards to get the body. What point would stealing the body serve for them, especially since they were already in danger for their close association with Jesus? With their miracle-performing leader dead, what could they have really hoped to gain by stealing the body? Jesus had already failed to meet their expectations of a messiah who would overthrow the Roman Empire. Jesus died, and they were too afraid to stick with him until the end. Why would they think stealing his body would help them accomplish taking Jerusalem back from the Romans or that a fabricated resurrection would in some way usher in the real Messiah?

The disciples certainly had no motive to steal the body. If they did, why would they lie about him rising from the grave? Why would they share their hoax throughout the Roman Empire in the face of widespread persecution? The Jews wouldn't steal the body, since they wanted Pilate to post guards, and Jewish ceremonial laws were very strict about handling the dead. Pilate and any other Roman definitely had nothing to gain from stealing the corpse of an executed criminal. Grave robbers wouldn't have taken the body; grave robbers took treasure, and Jesus wasn't buried with valuables. Grave robbers would have taken the valuable linens and not the worthless body.

Once the first-century investigator had confirmed that Jesus did in fact die, Jesus' body was buried in a tomb, and that his corpse vanished with no explanation, he would have turned to investigating the disciples' claims that they saw Jesus back from the dead.

Was Jesus Seen Alive after Being Dead and Buried?

The New Testament documents give us numerous accounts of people witnessing Jesus alive after his public crucifixion. In the twenty-first century, we might recall stories of people witnessing Elvis alive after he died. You might also know someone who has claimed to see someone he knew who had died, usually referring to this as the *ghost* or *spirit* of that person. My aunt and uncle have both claimed to have seen their mother after her death. Tall tales could run wild, and the imaginations of superstitious people could generate all sorts of hallucinations or paranormal expectations.

This, of course, is speculation; I'm not aware of the phenomenon of ghosts being verifiable in any way. But we still have occurrences of people experiencing ghosts or seeing strange lights in the sky that sometimes can't be easily dismissed or explained. It seems reasonable to think that the people living during the first century might have become so accustomed to explaining aspects of the world through supernatural means that their minds in times of deep loss or expectation could produce false images or experiences to help them cope.

Mark records a time when the disciples were crossing the Sea of Galilee toward Bethsaida, but were struggling as they paddled against the wind. Jesus knew of their struggle, and at about three in the morning, he walked out on the water to them. Mark says that "when they saw him walking on the lake, they thought he was a ghost" (Mark 6:49). I reference this gospel story because it reveals that the disciples did have an understanding of ghosts, and it was in fact their initial explanation of what they saw on the lake that night.

I have read the footnotes in study Bibles on this verse and a few other, similarly themed verses. The Jews had beliefs in spirits or ghosts, and superstitions accompanied ghosts' presence and involvement in the world. This is important to know because the occasions when the disciples claim to have interacted with Jesus after his crucifixion are never explained as an encounter with the "ghost" of Jesus, although in one of the accounts they initially thought this due to his spontaneous entrance into a locked room. They recognized that their encounters did not categorically fit the description of a spirit encounter.

The following is a chronological listing of the postmortem appearances recorded in the New Testament with brief explanations of each of them:

- **John 20:10–18**—Jesus first appears to Mary Magdalene as she is alone, crying at his tomb. At first she does not recognize him, thinking he is the gardener, but once he says her name, she recognizes that he is Jesus. He then gives her instructions to share with his brothers.

- **Matthew 28:8–10**—Jesus appears to the other women. They clasp his feet and worship him. Jesus gives them the instructions to tell his brothers to go to Galilee, where they will see him.

- **Luke 24:13–32**—Two disciples, one of whom is named Cleopas, are walking to Emmaus, about seven miles from Jerusalem. Jesus begins to walk with them, but they don't recognize him. Jesus explains to them, citing all the prophets beginning with Moses, why the Messiah had to die. The disciples invite him to stay with them for the night, since it is getting late. He eats dinner with them. When he breaks bread and gives thanks, they recognize him to be Jesus. He then disappears.

- **Luke 24:33–35**—The two disciples who saw Jesus on the road to Emmaus meet with the Eleven (the apostles, minus Judas after his suicide), and confirm Simon Peter's account of having seen the risen Jesus. There are no details given about when exactly Peter saw Jesus, or what transpired during that appearance.

- **Luke 24:36–49**—The Eleven and other disciples gather. Jesus appears to them and scares them. They think they are seeing a ghost, but Jesus encourages them to look at his hands and feet, and to touch him; ghosts don't have flesh and bones, he explains. He eats fish in their presence and they are amazed. Jesus explains from the prophets why he had to die for the forgiveness of sins.

- **John 20:19–23** – Ten of the Eleven are gathered behind locked doors because they are afraid of the Jews and are in hiding. Thomas is the missing disciple. Jesus comes and stands among them. He shows them his hands and feet and speaks with them.

- **John 20:24–29**—Thomas has heard about the appearance to the Ten, and he refuses to believe them unless he can see the nail marks in Jesus' hands and touch his side that was pierced. A week after the Ten saw him, Jesus appears to them again while they are hiding behind locked doors. This time Thomas is present, and he believes that it is Jesus after seeing and touching him.

- **Mark 16:9–14**—I question if I should list this passage, since Mark 16:9–20 is not found in the earliest manuscripts, nor is it confirmed by other earlier witnesses. It does, however, serve as a good summary of the previously cited appearances. Jesus appears first to Mary Magdalene, then to two disciples walking in the country. The Eleven do not believe the testimony of these disciples, and it isn't until Jesus appears to them too that they believe. This addition to the end of Mark's gospel includes a detail that the others lack. It records that Jesus rebuked all of the Eleven for not believing the testimony of the disciples who had already seen him raised from the dead. Apparently, it wasn't just Thomas who was chastised for believing only after he saw him alive and had touched him.

- **John 21:1–24**—Simon Peter, Nathanael, James, John, and two other disciples are fishing in the Sea of Tiberias, also known as the Sea of Galilee. They fish all night and catch nothing. In the morning, Jesus stands on the shore, but the disciples don't realize it is Jesus. He tells them they should throw their nets on the other side of the boat and they'll find fish. They do as he says, and they catch many fish. Peter recognizes that it is Jesus. He jumps into the water to meet him. When the other disciples meet them on shore, they find there is already a fire of burning coals with a fish and some bread. They cook some of the fish they have caught and Jesus feeds them. They know it is Jesus; this is the third time they have seen him since the crucifixion. After they finish eating breakfast, Jesus speaks privately with Peter as John follows behind them.

- **Matthew 28:16–20; Luke 24:50–53; Acts 1:4–9**—Jesus shares a departing message with the Eleven before ascending bodily into the sky out of their sight. Matthew describes this event as occurring on a mountain; Luke says it took place in the vicinity of Bethany, which was a village on the Mount of Olives. Luke's account in Acts doesn't provide any details of the location, but all the accounts are similar enough that they are likely the same event. Matthew adds an interesting detail, saying that before Jesus' ascension, they worshiped him, but some doubted.

- **Acts 9:1–9; 22:6–11**—Saul of Tarsus is traveling to Damascus in search of Christians to imprison when he encounters a flash of light from heaven that knocks him to the ground and blinds him. Because he was blinded by the light, this encounter can't be considered a "sighting" of the risen Jesus, but Saul claims to have heard a voice say to him, "I am Jesus of Nazareth, whom you are persecuting." He is blind for three days until a Christian named Ananias comes to him and restores his sight through the power of God.

In addition to these accounts, there are two summaries of these detailed appearances and others that are mentioned elsewhere:

- **Acts 1:3**—"After his suffering, he [Jesus] showed himself to these men and gave many convincing proofs that he was alive. He appeared to them over a period of forty days and spoke about the kingdom of God."
- **1 Corinthians 15:3–8**—"For what I received I passed on to you as of first importance: that Christ died for our sins according to the Scriptures, that he was buried, that he was raised on the third day according to the Scriptures, and that he appeared to Peter, and then to the Twelve. After that, he appeared to more than five hundred of the brothers at the same time, most of whom are still living, though some have fallen asleep. Then he appeared to James, then to all the apostles, and last of all he appeared to me also, as to one abnormally born."

When I read through the New Testament to find these accounts, I began to wonder why the disciples on many of these occasions did not initially recognize who Jesus was. Mary Magdalene at first thought he was the gardener. Cleopas and the other disciple walked with Jesus, maybe for as many as seven miles depending on when Jesus joined them, but they didn't recognize him the entire time. The disciples fishing in the boat with Peter didn't recognize him either—but they were a hundred yards offshore according to John, and maybe it was a misty day. To the disciples' benefit, Jesus was crucified and he had just been buried. If I had a teacher who was executed and buried, and that teacher came back to the life, I wonder if my mind would recognize my teacher. Maybe I would have serious doubts about the reality of what my senses were telling me.

In the case of the disciples on the road to Emmaus, Luke writes that "they were kept from recognizing him" (Luke 24:16). At least in the Emmaus appearance, the impression is given that it was divine intervention that prevented them from recognizing Jesus.

If they were in fact divinely blocked from recognizing him, I speculate that it was so Jesus could share with them how all the prophets had spoken about him, uninterrupted by the disciples' inevitable shock and excitement at learning that he was alive. If any of you are teachers, you understand firsthand that excited students can't pay attention very well. The days leading up to Christmas and summer breaks are always borderline wastes of time, as the students have their minds on anything but listening to their teachers. To keep his pupils focused on his instruction, Jesus probably restricted their recognition of him until after his lesson plan was completed.

Even if the New Testament documents don't explain why the disciples didn't recognize him, the simple inclusion of their failures shows honesty and integrity in reporting. Too many of the disciples' flaws are revealed; these accounts reek of truthfulness. For example, members of the Sanhedrin were bold enough to ask Pilate for the body to bury, and women disciples weren't afraid of going to the tomb to anoint the body with spices, but his closest male disciples had deserted him. That's quite embarrassing. Joseph and Nicodemus would have been seen by their fellow councilmen as crossing over to the dark side! The women would have needed to ask for help from the guards to move the stone away from the tomb's entrance, at which point it would have been clear that they held allegiance to an executed insurrectionist.

And what were the inner Eleven doing? We know that Peter had denied Jesus three times already, and John records that they were hiding behind locked doors in fear of the Jews. If these resurrection accounts were fabricated, we would expect to see that John was bold enough to bury Jesus' body and that Peter would stay strong, never denying Jesus. The fact that the gospel writers list women as the first witnesses of the empty tomb and the resurrected Jesus is phenomenal, because in the early first century, women weren't considered reliable witnesses in a court of law. If Jesus rose bodily from the grave, the disciples wouldn't be required to divulge such damaging details against themselves within their accounts.

Everything about the accounts of these events smacks of truthfulness, which helps me set aside some of the more questionable or unclear details, such as why the disciples didn't always recognize Jesus, or didn't recognize him immediately even on the second or third appearances.

Can We Be Sure the Disciples Saw a Walking, Talking, Postmortem Jesus?

The disciples knew the difference between a ghost and a flesh-and-bones human body. They made this clear in their accounts. They understood that others would ask the same question about their experiences, so they included that at one point they thought he was a ghost, but then they touched him. Next they saw him eat a piece of fish, and it didn't drop through his body as it would have with Casper the Friendly Ghost. Then their minds were blown!

Not only did he materialize among them within a locked room, he also reenacted a previous miraculous catch of fish that he had demonstrated for Peter and Andrew when he first called them to be his disciples (Luke 5:1–11; John 21:1–14) He appeared to them in the early morning and in the evening. He walked with them and spoke in lengthy conversations. He shared several meals with them. He appeared to them multiple times over a period of forty days, providing many convincing proofs of his resurrection.

Their encounters with the resurrected Christ were rarely solo. The first appearance to Mary Magdalene, recorded by John, and the Damascus road appearance to Saul are the only solo encounters that are detailed by the disciples. Peter is referenced in Luke as having encountered Jesus individually after his crucifixion, but that encounter isn't given any specific details. The appearance to Peter is also mentioned in 1 Corinthians 15, as well as a solo appearance to James, the half-brother of Jesus (half, of course, if Jesus is the incarnate Son of God).

Because these appearances are attributed to multiple witnesses at multiple times, it becomes incredible to think that they could have been hallucinating. The disciples' temperament at the time was one of fear, anxiety, and sorrow, which might produce a hallucination in extreme cases, but other than these emotional dispositions, there were no physical indications such as dehydration, overexposure to sun, or poisoned food or water that would have created an ongoing state of hallucination. Also, hallucinations don't fit the experiences that they had. People can't share the same hallucination, since hallucinations are mental projections and not objective realities. But the disciples all saw Jesus in the same way and heard the same words spoken by and shared with him. Their accounts admit that they initially considered him a ghost, but they do not record ever considering a mass hallucination as an explanation of their experiences.

When it comes to the appearances listed in the New Testament, the hardest to refute is the one that Paul shares in 1 Corinthians 15:6, when Jesus "appeared to more than five hundred of the brothers at the same time, most of whom are still living, though some have fallen asleep." I could possibly see the inner Eleven fabricating a story in which they all saw Jesus privately behind locked doors one night, but I don't see how Paul could claim Jesus appeared to over five hundred people at once if it were not true (1 Corinthians 15:3). The gathering must have been in a public location to accommodate that many witnesses. The way Paul exhorts his audience to investigate the claims themselves by referring them to the many witnesses who were still alive speaks volumes to the fact that there actually were that many people who observed Jesus at one specific location after his death. Our first-century investigator could easily have ascertained the validity of that claim. All he'd have to do was find Paul, who was prone to be very public and open with his teachings of Jesus Christ, or any of the other apostles or prominent disciples, find out when and where this happened, and request some names of the people who saw Jesus that day.

In addition to the evidence of these appearances, when it comes to the Eleven and the additional apostle, Matthias, who replaced Judas, and Paul, the "abnormally born apostle" as he calls himself in 1 Corinthians 15, there are aspects of their lives that make it incredibly difficult to think that they created a resurrection hoax.

If the disciples were still gung-ho about overthrowing the Romans after their Messiah hopeful had been brutally executed, faking the resurrection could have served as a way to rally the troops and supporters of Jesus who had declared him to be their king when he entered into Jerusalem (Matthew 21:4–9). The palm branches they brought with them (John

12:13) symbolized victory and triumph and were associated with Judas Maccabeus and the reclaiming of the Jewish temple from Antiochus IV. The Jews all anticipated the Messiah would overthrow the Romans, so this motive for falsifying the resurrection fits Messianic expectations, but it doesn't fit the mold of how the Messiah would set God's people free from their oppressors. No one foresaw the Messiah dying and rising to disappear as the way for the Second Exodus from slavery to occur, and it is clear that the apostles weren't orchestrating a rebellious overthrow of the Romans. Instead, they became like Jesus, living, and dying for a kingdom that was not of this world. Therefore, there is no probable explanation as to why the disciples would have engineered a false resurrection.

Time and time again throughout Acts, we see that the apostles were persecuted, put on trial, thrown in prison, and even martyred. They wouldn't have suffered those trials if they were doing so for a hoax they had manufactured.

- **Acts 4:1–31**—Peter and John stood trial before the Sanhedrin, which was headed by Annas and Caiaphas, the same priests who presided over the trial against Jesus. They were on trial for healing a man who had been crippled from birth by using the name of Jesus Christ of Nazareth. Luke records that "since they could see the man who had been healed standing there with them, there was nothing they could say" (Acts 4:14). The Sanhedrin demanded that they no longer speak the name of Jesus, to keep such healings from spreading, but Peter and John refused, saying, "Judge for yourselves whether it is right in God's sight to obey you rather than God. For we cannot help speaking about what we have seen and heard" (Acts 4:19–20). After further threats they were released. Set free, what was the first thing they did? They prayed that God would help them share the gospel of Jesus despite the threats, and then they went right back out into the world, speaking the Word of God boldly.
- **Acts 5:12–42**—The apostles performed many public miracles and met in the outer court of the temple. As they continued to perform miracles, more and more people came to them for healing of the sick, crippled, and demon possessed. This made the Jewish

leaders jealous, so they had all the apostles arrested to be put on trial. But an angel is recorded to have broken them out of jail, and the apostles went back to the temple courts to publicly preach. The Jews and guards were completely confused about how the apostles could have escaped the jail, because the doors were still locked! The captain of the guard and his officers then brought the apostles to the Sanhedrin, which the apostles voluntarily did without the need for any physical coercion. Peter explained to the Sanhedrin that they were witnesses to Jesus being raised from the dead and that they "must obey God rather than men!" (Acts 5:29). Instead of putting them to death for their claims, the Sanhedrin were persuaded by a Pharisee named Gamaliel to just flog them, which they did. This flogging, which people could potentially die from, did not deter the apostles from continuing to preach in Jesus' name.

- **Acts 6–7**—Stephen was a Christian man who was not an apostle, but nevertheless spoke boldly the message of Jesus in public and performed miraculous signs. The Synagogue of the Freedmen would argue with Stephen, but could never win a debate with him. So they rallied some people to accuse Stephen of committing blasphemy against Moses and against God. Stephen was brought before the Sanhedrin, where he gave an account of the life of Moses and the receiving of the covenant that gave the Israelites the tabernacle. David wanted to replace the tabernacle with a temple that his son Solomon built. However, Stephen quoted Isaiah 66:1–2 to his jury, reminding them that the prophet taught that God does not live in houses made by men. He then harshly rebuked them, saying, "Was there ever a prophet your fathers did not persecute? They even killed those who predicted the coming of the Righteous One [John the Baptist]. And now you have betrayed and murdered him [Jesus]" (Acts 7:52). At this, they dragged Stephen out of the city and stoned him to death as Saul gave his approval.

- **Acts 8:1–4**—The church was persecuted and scattered, and as they scattered, they continued to preach the good news about Jesus.

- **Acts 12:2**—James, the brother of John and the son of Zebedee, was put to death by the sword by King Herod. James was the first apostle to be martyred for the faith.
- **Acts 12:3–19**—When King Herod saw that the death of James pleased the Jews, he arrested Peter. He intended to have him publicly tried and killed, but an angel of the Lord appeared to Peter and helped him miraculously escape. Herod had the guards executed. Did any of this keep Peter from preaching God's Word? No.
- **Acts 14:1–7**—In Iconium, Paul and Barnabas spoke at the Jewish synagogue, and many of the Jews and Gentiles believed their words. The Jews who refused their message stirred up dissension against them. Paul and Barnabas were unfazed and continued to work there, preaching God's message boldly while also performing miracles. The city became divided, and the Jews and Gentiles who were against them planned to mistreat them and stone them. Paul and Barnabas found out about this plot, fled to Lyconia, and continued to preach.

The bold proclamations of Jesus' resurrection in the face of persecution did not end here. The rest of Acts traces Paul's relentless preaching journeys, despite being thrown in prison and undergoing judicial trials (Acts 16:16–28; 18:12–17; 21:33; 24; 25). He survived plots and riots against his life (Acts 17:5; 19:23–31; 21:27–32; 23:12–22) that eventually brought him under house arrest in Rome, where he still proclaimed Jesus' resurrection to anyone who would visit him (Acts 28:30–31).

From Luke's recorded accounts in Acts *alone*, the first-century investigator would have had enough details to conduct an inquiry to affirm or deny that the apostles and their Christian brethren were adamant that they were witnesses of the resurrected Jesus, and that as a collective body they boldly refused to cease proclaiming this fact. After all, the apostles were flogged at once by the Sanhedrin, and one of the Twelve, James, had his head cut off by King Herod. Yet they still publicly proclaimed their message.

There is also evidence outside the Bible of widespread persecution against the Christian church. One such piece of evidence has survived in the writings of the Roman senator and historian Tacitus, who lived through the middle of the first century and died in the first part of the second century. He records details about a destructive fire, the Conflagration, which occurred in Rome under Emperor Nero's reign in AD 64. Many people thought that Nero ordered the fire to be set. To squelch that rumor, Nero had to find a scapegoat.

> Consequently, to get rid of the report, Nero fastened the guilt and inflicted the most exquisite tortures on a class hated for their abominations, called Christians by the populace. Christus, from whom the name had its origin, suffered the extreme penalty during the reign of Tiberius at the hands of one of our procurators, Pontius Pilatus, and a most mischievous superstition, thus checked for the moment, again broke out not only in Judaea, the first source of the evil, but even in Rome, where all things hideous and shameful from every part of the world find their centre and become popular. Accordingly, an arrest was first made of all who pleaded guilty; then, upon their information, an immense multitude was convicted, not so much of the crime of firing the city, as of hatred against mankind. Mockery of every sort was added to their deaths. Covered with the skins of beasts, they were torn by dogs and perished, or were nailed to crosses, or were doomed to the flames and burnt, to serve as a nightly illumination, when daylight had expired. Nero offered his gardens for the spectacle, and was exhibiting a show in the circus, while he mingled with the people in the dress of a charioteer or stood aloft on a car. Hence, even for criminals who deserved extreme and exemplary punishment, there arose a feeling of compassion; for it was not, as it seemed, for the public good, but to glut one man's cruelty, that they were being destroyed.[26]

With such widespread persecution in the Roman Empire as recorded by Tacitus, Luke, and others, it is highly implausible that the early church would have emerged as it did unless there was real, physical evidence to back up the apostles' claims.

The fact that the apostles, the originators of the resurrection accounts, were willing to die because they wouldn't recant their claims speaks volumes to the validity of their testimonies. In Acts we see the martyrdom of one apostle, James, but church tradition holds that all the apostles except John died martyr's deaths because of their testimonies concerning Jesus. These deaths are considered tradition because it's not until the late second to fourth centuries that accounts of them emerge in written history. But it's undeniable that there are no competing traditions, such as tales of their survival and lives of luxury.

Traditions, though often embellished and lacking credibility, tend to stem from actual events. Historically we can't say with certainty that all the apostles besides John were executed as a result of their proselytizing efforts, but we have no credible evidence to make us believe that they weren't. We do have every reason, based on the evidence at hand, to trust that they proclaimed their message without fear before highly antagonistic audiences of authority and power. The apostles' lives indicate that they believed with certainty that they saw Jesus alive after he was publicly crucified and buried.

Test Results

Bibliographic Test: The New Testament is the best attested ancient manuscript in terms of its total number of preserved copies; the short time span that elapsed between the date of their original writings and the date of surviving copies, and the accuracy of the copying. If the accurate transmission of the New Testament documents is in doubt, then no other ancient document should be considered reliable either, since no other document of antiquity comes close to the New Testament's bibliographic marks.

Internal Test: The gospel biographies report that they were written by eyewitnesses, or by people who used eyewitness testimony. This also means the authors were writing too close to the death and resurrection of Jesus for myths to have crept into the accounts. They report that Jesus claimed to be divine, performed public miracles, was crucified under Pontius Pilate, died and was buried, and then rose from the grave.

External Test: Authors outside of the Bible affirm the gospel authors were Matthew, Mark, Luke, and John, and that they wrote as eyewitnesses or based on eyewitness testimony. Other witnesses, both friend and foe, would have known if the gospel writers were telling lies. They would have revealed the testimonies to be false. However, we have no such competing accounts from contemporaries. We do, on the other hand, have non-Christian authors writing in the first and second centuries who affirm the claims of the Gospels. No one in the first century was ever able to produce the bones of Jesus to disprove his empty tomb or resurrection. The Jewish and Roman leaders and authorities had the motives and the means to disprove the resurrection, but they could not. The best they could do was to persecute Christians as an attempt to stop the spread of the gospel of Jesus Christ. The apostolic circle in which the claim of Jesus' resurrection originated never recanted their testimony, even in the face of martyrdom. They continued to proclaim the risen Christ all the way to their deaths.

The empty tomb, the postcrucifixion appearances, and the apostles' willingness to share their testimony at the risk of martyrdom are three solid pieces of evidence that point to Jesus' physical resurrection. After exploring the possibility that the apostles had the wrong tomb, or that they were mistaken about witnessing Christ alive again, or that the resurrection was a hoax created by the apostles, we are hard-pressed not to come to the conclusion that Jesus did rise from the grave, verifying his claims to be God.

If Jesus rose from the grave, then the Christian faith that stands or falls on Jesus' resurrection is true. The exclusive nature of Jesus' claims and the teachings of his apostles make no allowance for there to be salvation from sin and death apart from faith in Christ. According to the law of noncontradiction, if Christianity is true, then all other contradictory religious truth-claims must be false.

The realization of this historical evidence and the resultant conclusion are not easily received. Encountering this evidence has plagued many atheists, some of whom were brought into the kingdom of God "kicking and struggling." This is how atheists turned Christian apologists, John Warwick Montgomery and C. S. Lewis, described their conversions to Christianity.[27]

The next chapter delves deeper into evaluating the truthfulness of the Christian faith by examining whether the truth of Christian Scripture extends beyond the resurrection evidence.

6

THE RING OF TRUTH

The Chinese consider Dr. Sun Yat-sen to be the "Father of the Country." He led a revolution against the Qing Dynasty. Despite the fact that he advocated for democracy and not communism, his mausoleum, located in mainland, communist China, draws droves of Chinese tourists every year.

One Chinese tour company refers to this site as a "Holy Land for Chinese People," that boasts "deep historical significance, magnificent architecture, and beautiful scenery."

I've had the privilege of climbing the almost half-mile-long staircase ascending a section of Zhong Mountain to see the sarcophagus of Dr. Sun Yat-sen. The scenery is amazing, and I recommend the experience if you are ever in Nanjing, China. I was most impressed that the architect designed the mausoleum in the shape of a bell to represent Dr. Sun Yat-sen's ever vigilant ringing alarm for the Chinese masses to "wake up" and fight against oppression and tyranny, to take back their country from the feudal monarchy. I couldn't help but think of America's Liberty Bell, and how bells are used to arouse, to alert, and even declare. Dr. Sun Yat-sen rang the bell of democracy for most of his life, calling for freedom, and I'm curious if that is why so many Chinese visit the tomb. Perhaps they are longing for the free democracy that Dr. Sun Yat-Sen dedicated his life to.

Just as Dr. Sun Yat-sen called for freedom and human rights, I recognize the tolling bells of the New Testament documents and their claims concerning Jesus of Nazareth, ringing out the call for repentance.

When you listen to bells after they have been rung, there is a resonance that hangs in the air that resists the sound of silence. This lingering sound is referred to as the tail of a bell. It's in these moments in a bell choir's performance, when their song is finished and their final chord hangs, that the listening audience nods their heads and acknowledges, "That was good."

In this chapter, I want to share the tail of the gospel bells. After hearing the historical claims of the Gospels and evaluating them under the accepted tests that are applied to every other historical claim, what is left to linger? What stands out in your mind? What resonates in your heart? Is it the ring of truth?

The Details Ring of Truth

If a person provides specific details about an event that he was directly involved in or witnessed, especially freely given details that could lead to personal endangerment, then likely he is telling the truth. A blatant lack of details, or the avoidance of details upon inquiry, leads to the opposite conclusion.

For example, if I were to tell one of my high school classes that I got green tea frozen yogurt from the Yogurtland at the intersection of Jeffrey and Walnut in Irvine, California, last night at seven o'clock with my wife, and they were offering a 50 percent off sale for the night in honor of their fifth anniversary, the students probably would believe me. If I were lying, I wouldn't give this much information.

One of the students might have worked a shift at that store that night and would know if I had been there, if they were serving green tea frozen yogurt this week, and if it was the five-year anniversary. If that student didn't corroborate my details, I'd definitely be caught. If I was there, but not until eight o'clock, someone might say, "Oh yeah, I saw you eating dinner at seven last night, so you couldn't have been at Yogurtland at seven." If my wife wasn't with me, someone might say, "No; I saw your wife last night at the Edward's movie theater in Portola Hills. You must be mistaken." Also, the Yogurtland at Jeffrey and Walnut is located in an Asian supermarket, where a Caucasian with a very distinguishable white patch of hair such as myself would stick out like a sore thumb. I wouldn't pick that Yogurtland if I were making up this account.

If I simply said, "I got frozen yogurt last night," they'd probably believe me too, because it seems very reasonable that I might get frozen yogurt. But maybe one of them would ask a question like, "Where?" If I were lying, I could simply throw out the name of one of the many frozen yogurt chains in Orange County. Maybe I'd say, "Yogurtland." A student could then ask, "Which one? I work at Yogurtland." I would ask, "Which store do you work at?" Maybe she would say, "The one at Diamond Back shopping center off Alton." I would counter, "Oh, no. I went to the one on Jeffrey and Walnut."

At this point, the students still wouldn't suspect that I was lying, but you can tell that I'm not providing much information willfully. When I found out a student worked at Yogurtland, I made sure I knew which store before answering.

But then another student might ask me, "Hey, I live by that Yogurtland. What flavors are they serving this week?" If I were lying, I'd say, "I'm not sure, I forget." At that point, I might be asked, "Well, what flavors did you get last night?" If I make up some flavors, I could be trapped in a lie if I guess incorrectly. This is why liars do their best to avoid giving details, even when directly asked about the specifics of their whereabouts and doings.

Police detectives listen to the details when interrogating a suspect or witness. If a person provides very precise dates, times, locations, measurements, colors, and names without being asked for them, then he is likely telling the truth, or he'll easily be caught in a lie when his account is checked or other witnesses come forward. When it comes to ancient documents, historians take a similar approach.

The authors of the New Testament documents voluntarily provided many specific details in their testimonies. They dated events in reference to the reigning years of emperors, governors, and major historical events. They listed specific times of day and not only supplied city names, but described the locations within the cities where their recorded events occurred. They eagerly provided names of other witnesses too, even names of prominent figures in the Jewish community or Roman government. The presence of these details indicates that the disciples were not afraid of cross-examination or being found in error, even when their accounts would likely lead to personal injury at the mere telling. This provides a ring of truth to their testimonies, considering they had little or nothing to gain from them in this life.

The healing of Dorcas recorded in Acts 10 is an example of details with the ring of truthfulness. Dorcas, a Greek name, was also known as Tabitha in Aramaic. She lived in Joppa. She became sick and died, and her body was placed in an upstairs room. The believers in Joppa sent two men to Lydda, because they heard that Peter was there. Peter came to see Tabitha and was greeted by many widows, who showed him many clothes that Tabitha had made, presumably for the needy, since Luke records that she was always doing good and helping the poor. Peter sent them out of the room and then healed Tabitha. She was presented to all the believers. News of this healing became known all over Joppa, and many became followers of Christ. Peter didn't leave, but instead stayed in Joppa for some time with a man named Simon, who was a tanner.

While this account may not have all the fine points we desire in our Internet age, these details don't match what one would expect from a fabricated miracle report. Two cities are mentioned by name, Lydda and Joppa. If the account were fictitious, one would expect regional names to be provided, not specific city names. The specific name of the woman healed is given, and it is indicated that she was well-known in Joppa. Many people knew that she had died, according to the references to several widows and at least two men who were sent to get Peter. After she was brought back to life, Luke claims that everyone in Joppa knew about this event and that many became believers because of it.

Most revealing of honesty in the reporting is the detail that Peter chose to stay in Joppa at a specific tanner's home. It's not just because of the ease with which one could affirm whether a leading member of the Jesus movement stayed in Joppa at the home of a tanner named Simon, but because this detail shows Peter's decisive break from Jewish culture and practice. He chose to stay at the home of a man who broke Jewish cleanliness laws concerning the handling of dead animals.

With the information Luke provides, this miracle report could easily have been verified, especially since everyone in Joppa supposedly knew about it and many then believed in Christ. If a first-century investigator rolled in to Joppa and no one knew anything about a miraculous return to life involving a lady named Tabitha; if there wasn't a tanner named Simon in the city; if people had no recollection of a leading member of the Jesus movement staying in town; then likely this account could be thrown aside as false.

In our current situation, we can't go back in time to verify this account. But since we have no evidence to the contrary from Luke's contemporaries, and archeological data affirms that Joppa was a real place, we have to hear the ring of truthfulness in Luke's reporting. If Luke were lying, he wouldn't have provided these details.

Skim through the Gospels and Acts, the first five books of the New Testament, and you'll find that many exact details fill virtually every account, just like Luke's record of Tabitha's healing in Acts 10. I'll end this section with one of the most precise location descriptions found in the New Testament: "Some time later, Jesus went up to Jerusalem for a feast of the Jews. Now there is in Jerusalem near the Sheep Gate a pool, which in Aramaic is called Bethesda and which is surrounded by five covered colonnades. Here a great number of disabled people used to lie—the blind, the lame, and the paralyzed" (John 5:1–3).

Before continuing to read, take a moment to go online and conduct an image search for "pool at Bethesda." Images of the excavated pool will appear in the search results, and John's description fits the bill. You'll even see the remnant of the five covered colonnades in the images.

One Unified Message Rings of Truth

I met a college student who claimed that the Bible was a book written a long time ago by "some guy," just as J. K. Rowling wrote the Harry Potter series, except that thousands of years after he wrote it, people believed it. The student concluded that the same could happen with Harry Potter.

Despite the fact that the internal and external tests would fail concerning Harry Potter, I chose to correct this student on the basis of his larger error in thinking that the Bible was written by "some guy." The Bible, although it appears to be one book, is actually comprised of numerous books, written by many people of various walks of human existence across multiple generations. Henrietta Mears provides the numbers in her introductory book, *What the Bible Is All About*: "The Bible contains 66 books, written by 40 authors, covering a period of approximately 1,600 years."[1] These books come to us written in Hebrew and Greek, with sprinklings of Aramaic at times. Together these sixty-six books comprise one, consistent, noncontradictory message.

The books of the Bible might appear to be contradictory, since Judaism rejects the New Testament books, but Christians consider the New Testament books to be a fulfillment of the long-awaited Messiah promised to God's people time and time again in the Old Testament. To the skeptical Jews, Jesus says, "You diligently study the Scriptures because you think that by them you possess eternal life. These are the Scriptures that testify about me, yet you refuse to come to me to have life" (John 5:39–40).

With this understanding, one doesn't stumble on interpretive contradictions between the two testaments, but instead discovers foreshadowing and fulfillment. Christians study the Bible seeking Jesus in all of Scripture, finding many typologies that point to Jesus as the promised Messiah (the Christ). Jesus is the son that will crush the serpent's head (Genesis 3). Jesus is the way to the Father, just as Jacob's stairway connects heaven and earth (Genesis 28). Jesus is the slain lamb whose blood covers and shields us from death, just as the blood of the Passover lamb covered the door frames of the Israelites before the great escape from Egypt (Exodus 12). Jesus was lifted up to save everyone from the sting of death, just as Moses lifted up the bronze snake to heal venomous snakebites in the desert (Numbers 21). Jesus rose from the grave in three days, which is strikingly similar to the way Jonah was vomited out of the belly of a big fish after residing there for three days (Jonah 2). Jesus is firmly established as king on the throne of his Father, just as Solomon was securely established on the throne of his father David (1 Kings 2).

This consistency throughout generations concerning divinely revealed texts is unprecedented. In Hinduism, the Upanishads seem to do more than just explain what was revealed in the Vedas; they seem to add entirely new teachings, though the Upanishads aren't considered to have been divinely revealed. Buddhism emerges from Hinduism, rejecting key components of its predecessor, such as the divinity of all things and the individual soul. Islam arises almost six hundred years after Christianity, and although it claims the Bible is from God, it directly contradicts the Bible's teachings in many ways, first and foremost in its rejection of the Christian teaching of the Trinity. Mormonism emerges years after Islam, and like Islam, it claims that the Old and New Testaments are from God, but that Joseph Smith received "Another Testament of Jesus Christ," the Book of Mormon. Yet the Book of Mormon contradicts clear teachings within the Bible, such as the Mormon teaching that God the Father, Elohim, was at one point human just like us.

In these examples, it only took one man—Siddhartha, Muhammad, or Joseph Smith—to contradict the firmly established beliefs of their preceding religions. How incredible is it to have forty authors of sixty-six books over a span of sixteen hundred years write one, consistent, noncontradictory message concerning the most controversial topic of humanity, God?

Of course, some will argue that there are contradictions in the Bible, many of them. A contradiction that is commonly raised is the conflicting genealogies of Jesus found in the gospels of Matthew (1:1–17) and Luke (3:23–38). Matthew begins Jesus' genealogy with Abraham and works forward. Luke works backward from Jesus to Adam. The names given between King David and Joseph, the stepfather of Jesus, are completely different between the genealogies—none of the names are the same!

Skeptics point to this and say, "If they can't get the genealogy right at the start of the Gospels, then why trust anything else the Gospels have to say?"

For historical purposes, no historian would jettison all four gospels because of an apparent contradiction in two genealogy records. This doesn't mean that everything in those two gospels is wrong. It simply means that Matthew and Luke recorded different genealogies. What about the other material that Matthew and Luke agreed upon and that is also confirmed by Mark and John? And just because Matthew and Luke appear to contradict each other, that shouldn't also invalidate the witnesses of the other two gospels, Mark and John, who don't list genealogies.

No historian would trash all the material of an ancient manuscript on account of one obvious discrepancy, and in fact this inconsistency doesn't automatically mandate a contradiction. Matthew likely was following the lineage of David to Joseph, whereas Luke traced the lineage of Mary to David. One is recognizing Joseph's legal position as Jesus' father, and the other is acknowledging Jesus' actual bloodline via his only earthly parent, Mary. Luke even gives an indication of this approach in the introduction to his genealogy, saying, "He was the son, so it was thought, of Joseph" (Luke 3:23).

Theological contradictions seem to emerge in the Bible too. One of the most famous examples, which actually divides the Christian church, is the way a man is justified according to Paul and James:

> **Romans 3:28**—"For we maintain that a man is justified by faith apart from observing the law."

> **James 2:24**—"You see that a person is justified by what he does and not by faith alone."

So which is it? Is a man justified by faith alone, or by faith plus works? These two verses must be contradictory!

At face value, if these two verses were all that we had to answer the question of how a man is justified, we'd have to say that both of these can't be true.

In context, we can see that Paul and James have different meanings in their use of the word *faith*. James is addressing a misunderstanding that was arising in Christianity concerning the relationship between faith and works. Some were saying that all they needed was faith to be saved, and others were saying that all they needed were works to be saved.

James in his epistle was pointing out that "saving faith" is accompanied by works. James quotes Genesis 15:6, which says, "Abram believed the Lord, and he credited it to him as righteousness." He says that this verse was fulfilled when Abraham was "considered righteous for what he did when he offered his son Isaac on the altar" (James 2:21). James says that this illustrates how Abraham's "faith and his actions were working together, and his faith was made complete by what he did" (James 2:22). For those who thought that faith and works could be divorced from one another and a person still be saved, they were dead wrong; works are a sign of faith.

For those to claim to have faith apart from works, James is indicating that their faith isn't actually faith; it's knowledge. To the crowd that says, "I have faith [meaning knowledge]," James says, "You believe [know] that there is one God. Good! Even the demons believe that—and shudder" (James 2:19). If salvation is based on a faith that only "knows" there is a God, then even Lucifer and his horde of demons are saved.

When Paul writes that "a man is justified by faith apart from observing the law," he is building a case against those who think that their works apart from faith will justify them and earn them salvation. He too uses the example of Genesis 15:6 to indicate that Abraham was justified long before the observance of the command to be circumcised, before the trust in God that he and his wife Sarah would bear a child together when they were about hundred years old, and definitely before he offered his son, Isaac, on the altar as a sacrifice. Paul says that Abraham "received the sign of circumcision, a seal of the righteousness that he had by faith while he was still uncircumcised" (Romans 4:11).

For both James and Paul, Abraham's works were signs, seals, and fulfillments of the righteousness that was *already* credited to him on account of his faith. Faith produces works. The message is that simple. It is one that Jesus taught before them (John 15:6–7), but to see the harmony between James and Paul, both of their epistles need to be read in context.

There are many more examples of apparent contradictions in the Bible that I could share, but entire books have been dedicated to addressing these inconsistencies. For this investigation, I think it's enough to show a commonly raised objection to the biblical texts in the categories of historical reporting and theological teaching, and show that they can be harmonized. When apparent contradictions are discovered, they are usually just that—apparent. They are often the result of verses being removed from their context; not just their literary context, but also their historical, cultural, grammatical, and linguistic context. We can all easily check the literary context by reading the verses that precede and succeed the verses in question, but to find the other contexts demands a lot of knowledge and study on our part.

To give an example of the difficulty of understanding a text when we don't know the context of its writing, I want to share an e-mail I received from a friend (copied exactly as it came to me in my inbox):

> i'm glad to hear you r good at home, it must be great to do thing the same way you always do, haha.

> yeah,7.5 is quite a tragedy, a lot of people died that day. I was quite angry when i heard news. One of my friends is a soldier there, and he told me that our GOVERmNT sent about 100.000 soldiers to XINJIANG, to get things back to normal and to stop the revange, cus you know, lot of people who have family been killed at 7.5 take revenge during the following days. anyway, if i was them, i'll do the same thing.

> thx for the tips, i really need some exercise, i'm getting fat now. haha

> here is an article wirtten by DANIU, he is talking about you, haha. he thought you rock. i'll give you the link, but it's in chinese, probably i can translate it to you later

From the improper capitalization, lack of articles, and improper subject/verb agreement, you can likely guess that this author isn't a native English speaker. From his reference to "Chinese," you likely suspect he is from China, especially if you know enough about the Chinese language to recognize Xinjiang and Daniu as Chinese names.

I completely understand this e-mail because I know the historical context of this e-mail. I know that 7.5 refers to a July 5, 2009, incident that occurred in Xinjiang, China, and I know what that incident was. I also know who Daniu is. I know that Daniu is a nickname, and I know what it means and why he is called it. You might be wondering why this author thinks everything is so funny. I know it's a common Chinese practice to write "haha" multiple times in almost any message, so I just ignore the laughter.

Now imagine that you are alive in the year AD 4000 and you are reading this e-mail. How hard would it be for you to understand it? Has English changed so much that this e-mail reads like a foreign language? Is English even spoken anymore? Would any of these changes make any of his grammar errors that much harder to recognize? Does Xinjiang still exist in name, shape, or form? Did 7.5 get preserved in the annals of history? Is being fat considered popular and viewed as a sign of wealth? Do people even exercise anymore?

Now consider how much we are missing from the biblical text as we sit two thousand years removed, not knowing every detail concerning the language, customs, history, idioms, culture, geography, grammar, author, audience, or previous correspondence and shared experience between the two parties. This lack of understanding on our part explains most of the apparent contradictions—not all of them, but most of them.

It becomes plain when reading Scripture that the forty authors of sixty-six books across sixteen hundred years are progressively revealing more intimate details concerning God and his interaction with humanity. As a unit, their message forms one overarching story of God's direct interaction with mankind that, despite apparent contradictions, can be consistently harmonized. Such unity cannot be demonstrated in any other religion.

Accurate Predictions Ring of Truth

Read the following text, and ask yourself who the text is describing and why.

> See, my servant will act wisely; he will be raised and lifted up and highly exalted. Just as there were many who were appalled at him—his appearance was so disfigured beyond that of any man and his form marred beyond human likeness—so he will sprinkle many nations, and kings will shut their mouths because of him. For what they were not told, they will see, and what they have not heard, they will understand.

Who has believed our message and to whom has the arm of the LORD been revealed? He grew up before him like a tender shoot, and like a root out of dry ground. He had no beauty or majesty to attract us to him, nothing in his appearance that we should desire him. He was despised and rejected by men, a man of sorrows, and familiar with suffering. Like one from whom men hide their faces he was despised, and we esteemed him not.

Surely he took up our infirmities and carried our sorrows, yet we considered him stricken by God, smitten by him, and afflicted. But he was pierced for our transgressions, he was crushed for our iniquities; the punishment that brought us peace was upon him, and by his wounds we are healed. We all, like sheep, have gone astray, each of us has turned to our own way; and the LORD has laid on him the iniquity of us all.

He was oppressed and afflicted, yet he did not open his mouth; he was led like a lamb to the slaughter, and as a sheep before her shearers is silent, so he did not open his mouth. By oppression and judgment he was taken away. And who can speak of his descendants? For he was cut off from the land of the living; for the transgression of my people he was stricken. He was assigned a grave with the wicked, and with the rich in his death, though he had done no violence, nor was any deceit in his mouth.

Yet it was the LORD's will to crush him and cause him to suffer, and though the LORD makes his life a guilt offering, he will see his offspring and prolong his days, and the will of the LORD will prosper in his hand. After the suffering of his soul, he will see the light of life and be satisfied; by his knowledge my righteous servant will justify many, and he will bear their iniquities. Therefore I will give him a portion among the great, and he will divide the spoils with the strong, because he poured out his life unto death, and was numbered with the transgressors. For he bore the sin of many, and made intercession for the transgressors.[2]

As you read this passage, who did you think it was describing? My guess is that you thought it was referring to Jesus. I know that, since I've been presenting the historical testing for the resurrection of Jesus Christ, you might have been predisposed to think of Jesus. But consider what conclusion you would arrive at if you were going about your daily affairs, maybe entering a shopping center, and someone gave you a piece of paper with this text on it. If he asked you, "Who is this describing?" would you have answered any other way? Could anyone else in history fit the description in this text? Could anyone else even come close?

There are many reasons to draw connections to Jesus from this text. Here are some of the connections that came to mind as I read it:

- Jesus had "no beauty or majesty to attract us to him." He was born in a stable and placed in a feeding trough. His hometown was Nazareth, and "can anything good come from there?" (John 1:46).

- Jesus was "despised and rejected by men." His brothers didn't believe him (John 7:5). His friends deserted him at his arrest, fleeing for their own lives (Mark 14:50). Peter, who swore to even die with Jesus if need be, denied him three times before the rooster crowed twice (Mark 14:72). The people who praised him, waving palm branches, later called for his crucifixion (Mark 15:13). Not only was Jesus rejected by men; as he hung dying on the cross, Jesus cried, "My God, My God, why have you forsaken me?" (Mark 15:34).

- Jesus was a "man of sorrows." He had no place to call his home (Matthew 8:20).

- Jesus was "oppressed and afflicted, yet he did not open his mouth; he was led like a lamb to the slaughter, and as a sheep before her shearers is silent, so he did not open his mouth." This directly describes the demeanor that Jesus had before the Jewish council, Pilate, Herod, his executioners, and his mockers while on the cross.

- Jesus was "pierced" through his hands and feet during his crucifixion, and finally through his side with a spear.

- Jesus was "assigned a grave with the wicked and with the rich in his death." He died a criminal's death, with criminals on either side of him. Yet he was buried in a rich man's grave, the tomb of Joseph of Arimathea.

- After his suffering, Jesus saw the "light of life." Jesus was dead, buried, and raised.

These comparisons are of a *historical* nature, and certainly more can be drawn between the "servant" described in this text and Jesus than the ones that I have listed. Maybe someone else in history can fit many of these descriptions also, but certainly not all of them.

Turning to the descriptions that are of a *theological* nature, no one else comes to mind, and it's likely the theological descriptions that made you first think of Jesus. No religion besides Christianity has a single man bearing the sins of all of mankind. No other religion has at its center, as its core teaching, a person suffering for others and making peace for all of mankind through that suffering.

Now, for the shocker ...

This text is Isaiah 52:13–53:12, and it was written about seven hundred years before Jesus of Nazareth.

Isaiah's description of the "Suffering Servant" is an example of fulfilled prophecy concerning Jesus. There are numerous other prophecies written centuries before Jesus that he fulfills. Since Matthew wrote his gospel for a Jewish audience, to present Jesus as the long-awaited Messiah, he highlights many of the Old Testament's prophecies throughout his gospel record. The following is a table charting some of the most important prophecies connected by Matthew to Jesus' fulfillment:

OT Prophecy	Jesus' Fulfillment
Virgin with child—Isaiah 7:14	Mary is the virgin—Matthew 1:23
Bethlehem is the birthplace—Micah 5:2	Jesus is born in Bethlehem—Matthew 2:6
God calls his son out of Egypt—Hosea 11:1	Jesus is called back from Egypt—Matthew 2:15
Rachel weeps in Ramah over the loss of her children—Jeremiah 31:15	Herod kills the infant males of Bethlehem, a town that Rachel was heading toward when she died in childbirth in Ramah—Matthew 2:18
The righteous king of salvation comes to Jerusalem riding, humbly riding on a donkey—Zechariah 9:9	Jesus enters Jerusalem to shouts of praise as he rides on a donkey—Matthew 21:5

From the mouths of infants and babes I have ordained praise— Psalm 8:2	Children dance and praise Jesus— Matthew 21:16
Strike the shepherd and the sheep shall scatter—Zechariah 13:7	Jesus says that the Scriptures must be fulfilled, and as he is arrested all of his disciples scatter— Matthew 26:54
For turning the flock over for destruction Zechariah was given 30 pieces of silver at which he threw it into the temple of the Lord to the potter—Zechariah 11:12–13	Judas receives thirty pieces of silver for turning Jesus over for destruction. In guilt, he throws the silver down in the temple and hangs himself. The priests take the money and buy the potter's field as a place to bury strangers—Matthew 27:10
The Lord says that he will make the sun go down at noon, making the land go dark in broad daylight— Amos 8:9	From the sixth hour (noon) to the ninth hour there was darkness over all the land as Jesus hung on the cross—Matthew 27:45

These are just a few examples of Old Testament prophecies that Jesus has fulfilled. Many more remain. He's from the tribe of Judah (Genesis 49:10), the line of Jesse (Isaiah 11:1), and the house of David (Jeremiah 23:5). The line of David makes him a king, as the Jewish people recognized when they declared him to be the "Son of David" as he rode into Jerusalem (Matthew 21:9). Jesus is also a priest from the line of Melchizedek (Psalms 110:4; Hebrews 5:5–6). And he is a prophet, just as the multitudes of his day recognized him to be (Deuteronomy 18:18; Matthew 21:11).

In ancient Israel, prophets (1 Kings 19:16), priests (Exodus 40:13), and kings (2 Kings 9:3) were all anointed with oil as a sign of God setting them apart for their particular offices of service. *Messiah* is the Hebrew word that means "anointed one," and *Messiah* in Greek is Christ. To call Jesus the Christ is to call him the Anointed One, and as the prophesied Messiah, he fulfills all three anointed offices. It is here in these fulfilled prophecies of Jesus, and the many other prophecies of the Bible, that the ring of truth permeates the air the longest.

Uniqueness Rings of Truth

Christianity stands out among the world's religions because of its uniqueness. It does have the largest number of adherents, and it has transcended race, culture, and language in a way that no other religion has come close to matching. The Bible is by far the world's best-selling book. These qualities certainly make Christianity unique, and many people might interpret Christianity's high ranking numbers as signs of its truthfulness, but popular belief shouldn't serve as the gauge of truth.

Christianity does stand out in two ways that are both so unique that they give off a ring of truthfulness. Christianity alone stands as the only "saved by grace" religion, and the only religion whose founder is God incarnate.

First, Christianity is the only *paid* religion. It is not a way of life; it is life given to you. In other words, Christianity is not a system of moral rules that must be followed or an arrangement of obligatory rituals. At its heart is mankind's utter inability to adhere to God's standard, and our universal need of God's grace, which comes to us through the work of Jesus Christ. It is often said that Christianity is the only free religion, or that it is the only religion in which salvation comes through faith apart from works, but that's only partially true. For humanity's part, Christianity does teach that salvation is freely given through faith in Jesus apart from works, but for God's part, our salvation was not free; it came at a great cost. Jesus paid dearly for our salvation. That is why the acrostic for *grace* is "God's riches at Christ's expense."

All other religions can be classified as *not paid*. Humanity must work to rectify our ultimate problem, which varies from religion to religion. In Hinduism, we all must practice yoga as the means of seeking union with Brahman. Our karma dictates how well we are doing in that process, affecting the direction of our rebirth. In Buddhism, our desires lead to pain and suffering. To escape our suffering, we must follow the eightfold path. In Islam, we must all submit to Allah and his coming judgment. Our good works must outweigh our bad, and the best way of ensuring we end up on the right side of the scales is to strictly adhere to the five pillars of Islam and the teachings of the Qur'an. In Jainism, killing anything, even a fly, restricts the hope of escaping reincarnation. In Scientology, we must partake in auditing sessions to detect engrams. Through many, many audits, we can clear our engrams and scale the operating thetan ladder to eventually reach our full potential of godlike status. The beat goes on; it's the same pattern for all other religions. Humanity has a problem (ultimately death) and we can overcome it through our dedication to hard work.

Second, Christianity can set itself apart as the only paid religion because it is the only religion that is *from God*. It claims to be founded by God in the flesh. Christianity teaches that God exists in three persons, and that the second person of the divine Trinity assumed a human nature and was born in this world as Jesus of Nazareth. As the God-Man, Jesus was able to redeem mankind from its sinfulness. Being fully divine, he was able to fulfill God's standard of righteousness. Being fully man, he was able to be tempted and die in our place, suffering hell eternally on the cross. Now that may not make sense, but since Jesus is fully God, he could suffer hell eternally in a short time span; God can do all things. And since Jesus is fully God, he was able to die as a replacement for all of mankind. In Christ, the divine nature was put to death with his human nature. The death of God is valuable enough to serve as a vicarious atonement for all of mankind, past, present, and future. No other religion can claim such divine redemption, because no other religion was founded by God incarnate.

All other religions are *from man*. They were founded by people who were merely human teachers, prophets, enlightened beings, guides, or esoteric gurus. These men, and in some cases women, took the revelations, knowledge, and insights that they gleaned from their divine or spiritual source and shared it with others, to guide them out of mankind's ultimate problem and into the sole (soul) solution.

None of these founders could offer redemption free of charge. All they could provide was the bill that needed to be paid and the way humanity could pay it. Since these religions are the product of man, their presentations of salvation plans make sense in the system of our world from which they are derived, a system in which our self-worth is dependent upon our value to society. It's no wonder that the solution lies in earning your merit badge.

Religions are either *paid* or *not paid*. Christianity is the only paid religion. Religions are also either *from God* or *from man*. Again, Christianity stands alone. It is the only religion whose founder was God incarnate.

These two exclusive attributes of Christianity work together, giving a final ring of truth. If the only religion that claims to be from God, is also the only religion that offers paid salvation, then it seems reasonable that it actually is from God, since it is completely different from everything that has been founded from man.

Add to this that the religion that is from God adamantly refuses to borrow from the religions that are from man. However, all the religions that are from man tend to want to borrow from the only religion that is founded directly from God, by incorporating Jesus into their religion, either through claiming him as a prophet (Islam), a bodhisattva (some forms of Buddhism), an avatar (some adherents of Hinduism), or a good, moral teacher (basically everyone). The exceptions are religions that split off from Christianity or include Jesus centrally in another way—Rastafarianism for example. The ring of truth is hard to avoid.

Follow the Way

The fact that all religions can't be true due to their contradictions doesn't mean we have to hate others who adhere to differing religious paths; we simply have to recognize that they have chosen to follow a path that is irreconcilable with our own. This acceptance doesn't mean we can resign ourselves to saying it doesn't matter which religious path a person walks, because all roads, even the nonreligious road of atheism, will lead all travelers to the door of death, and what lies on the other side is of utmost importance for all who value and desire life.

To reiterate, the following is the intended objective stated at the close of the first chapter:

> The goal of this book is to evaluate the claims of religious pluralism in light of such apparent contradictions and to raise the level of true tolerance toward the world's religions by upholding and proclaiming what makes each religion unique and special to its adherents. If this can be accomplished, it swings wide the gates for interreligious dialogue among orthodox practitioners of contradicting worldviews. The end goal is to usher in the evaluation of religious truth-claims. Are any of them true? With what each religion claims about the purposes of life and the future of an individual after death, this

is the most important question a person can ask for the here and now and for his or her eternal future.

After evaluating the resurrection of Jesus Christ under the accepted methods of historiography, a preponderance of evidence indicates that Jesus rose from the dead. The occurrence of this event is the verification of the truthfulness of the Christian faith according to the apostle Paul in 1 Corinthians 15:14. He goes on to say that if Jesus was not raised from the dead, his preaching would be a lie, and that he and other Christians of his day who were receiving severe penalties of imprisonment, floggings, and even execution should be pitied.

No other religion has at its heart a historical event that can be evaluated objectively to determine the truthfulness of that religious belief system. Since Christianity meets the accepted standards of historical evaluation, I see no need to share or present the historical evaluation of other religions at this time.

Beyond this evidence, Christianity has the ring of truth with its detailed disclosure of facts, consistent message, fulfilled prophecy, and unique standing as the only religion that offers divine redemption through the work of its founder, who claimed to be God incarnate. This information concerning Jesus is not meant to merely serve as mental stimulation that prompts us to ponder the deep questions of life. Jesus intended his work and teachings to demand an implicit response.

The response that Jesus commanded again and again was straightforward: "Repent, for the kingdom of heaven is near" (Matthew 4:17). This single sentence serves as a summation of his public teaching, and it was accompanied by Jesus' offer to be his "disciple," which simply means being his student.

To be a disciple of Jesus, a person had to follow him. To his first disciples, whom he called while they were working at their profession of fishing, "'Come, follow me,' Jesus said, 'and I will make you fishers of men'" (Matthew 4:19). This was the same call to Levi, also known as Matthew: "Follow me" (Luke 5:27). Immediately, they left everything, and they followed Jesus.

The call is the same to all of us. Jesus has an open-door enrollment policy. To anyone desiring to be his disciple, Jesus gave this one stipulation:

"Anyone who does not carry his cross and follow me cannot be my disciple" (Luke 14:27). Referring to himself as a shepherd, Jesus said, "My sheep listen to my voice; I know them, and they follow me" (John 10:27).

When you read Matthew's account of Peter and his brother Andrew being called from their fishing job to follow Jesus, it comes as a shock that they left their nets and followed him. Down the shore, two more fishermen, James and John, were mending their nets, and they too left their boat, their nets, and even their father to follow Jesus. We ask, "Why would anyone ditch their profession, their belongings, and even their family to pursue a random stranger calling out for them to follow him?"

Of course, there is more to the story. In John's gospel, we discover that Andrew was one of John the Baptist's disciples, and that he had heard John the Baptist say that Jesus was the "Lamb of God," so Andrew followed Jesus and was invited to spend the day with him. In Luke's gospel, we learn that Jesus had already driven out many demons and healed many people, including healing Simon-Peter's mother-in-law (Luke 4:38). Luke also shares that before Jesus extended the invitation to be his disciple to Peter and Andrew, he performed a miracle in their boat, providing a catch of fish so large that the nets began to break after a night of catching nothing. James and John were Peter's partners, and they were astonished at the miraculous catch.

Peter's initial response was, "Go away from me, Lord; I am a sinful man" (Luke 5:8). In the moment of the miracle, Peter became tragically aware of his sinfulness and the awesome holiness of Jesus' divinity. Sin wants nothing to do with holiness, and in fact can having nothing to do with it, just as darkness cannot coexist with light. But Jesus still drew him near, saying, "Don't be afraid; from now on you will catch men" (Luke 5:10).

In this passage, the essence of Christ's command to repent is demonstrated. Repentance is twofold, or has two parts. *The Augsburg Confession*, written by Philip Melanchthon and presented to Emperor Charles V in the city of Augsburg in 1530, defines the two parts of repentance: "One is contrition or the terrors that strike the conscience when sin is recognized; the other is faith, which is brought to life by the gospel or absolution. This faith believes that sins are forgiven on account of Christ, consoles the conscience, and liberates it from terrors. Thereupon good works, which are the fruit of repentance, should follow."[3]

This is exactly what we see happen with Peter in his fishing boat with Jesus. He recognizes or becomes aware of his sinfulness, and he is in terror and wants to get out of God's presence. Jesus tells him not to be afraid and absolves Peter of his sin. Instead of jumping out of the boat, Peter trusts Jesus' words of absolution and follows Jesus. The fruit of his faith is made visible in his life devoted to Christ.

Peter received direct confirmation of Jesus' divinity through the sign of the miraculous catch on the day he was called to follow Jesus, and he was shown many signs afterward that culminated in the resurrection of Jesus of Nazareth, the man that Peter recognized to be the Christ. When Peter proclaimed his first sermon to a large crowd of skeptics, he appealed to their firsthand knowledge and experiences, saying, "Men of Israel, listen to this: Jesus of Nazareth was a man accredited by God to you by miracles, wonders and signs, which God did among you through him, as you yourselves know" (Acts 2:22). He proceeded to share prophecy from King David concerning Jesus' death and resurrection, before crushing them with the weight of what God and they had done, telling them, "Therefore let all Israel be assured of this: God has made this Jesus, whom you crucified, both Lord and Christ" (Acts 2:36).

At his declaration and admonition, Scripture says, "They were cut to their heart and said to Peter and the other apostles, 'Brothers, what shall we do?' Peter replied, 'Repent and be baptized, every one of you, in the name of Jesus Christ for the forgiveness of your sins. And you will receive the gift of the Holy Spirit. The promise is for you and your children and for all who are far off – for all whom the Lord our God will call'" (Acts 2:37-39).

You may not have had the miraculous experience that Peter had, or the wonders and signs that the contemporaries of Peter saw, but you do have Scripture, which testifies about Jesus, and you have seen how Scripture is historically reliable and carries the ring of truth.

The call is the same for you as it is for the first-century disciples: follow Jesus. Repent. Do you feel the weight of your sins, the sins that put Christ on the cross? Do you fear the terror of hell's gates on account of your evil deeds? If your answer is yes, then you have the first part of repentance, and rightfully so; you have reason to be afraid, because "when a man works, his wages are not credited to him as a gift, but as an obligation" (Romans 4:4), and all of our works fall short of God's righteous standard. However, the good news is that "to the man who does not work but trusts God who justifies the wicked, his faith is credited as righteousness" (Romans 4:5). That is the second part of repentance: faith in Jesus.

The *Apology of the Augsburg Confession* explains these two parts in detail from Scripture: "For Christ says in Matthew 11, 'Come to me, all you that are weary and are carrying heavy burdens, and I will give you rest.' There are two parts here: being weary and carrying heavy burdens refer to contrition, anxieties, and the terrors of sin and death; to come to Christ is to believe that on account of Christ sins are forgiven. When we believe, our hearts are made alive by the Holy Spirit through the Word of Christ."[4]

This book's goal has been to accurately uphold and claim what each religion teaches and what makes each religion unique and appealing to its adherents. I think that I have done this to the best of my abilities with the five major religions of the world, and in lesser detail with a good number of the minor religions. Their truth-claims have been presented.

Because of religion's nature of dealing with eternal principles, knowing which religion is true, if any, is of utmost importance to every individual. We need to know which one is the correct way to follow. Before Christians were called Christians, they were known as Followers of the Way (Acts 9:2 and Acts 24:14). Jesus claimed to be "the way" in John 14:6. His exact words were, "I am the way and the truth and the life. No one comes to the Father except through me."

Jesus' claim to be the only way to the Father is associated with Jacob's dream in which he saw a "stairway resting on the earth, with its top reaching to heaven, and the angels were ascending and descending on it" (Genesis 28:12). In John 1:51, Jesus says, "I tell you the truth, you shall see heaven open, and the angels of God ascending and descending on the Son of Man." Jesus commonly referred to himself with the Messianic title, "Son of Man," and in this verse, it is obvious that he is substituting himself into Jacob's dream as the stairway to heaven. As the stairway to heaven, Jesus alone bridges the gap between earth and heaven (the Father). There is no other way to God.

The image becomes clear: there is a separation between sinful man and holy God. Jesus descends from heaven to earth to connect us with God. He provides a way back into a right relationship with the Father.

Jesus said, "Whoever believes in him is not condemned, but whoever does not believe stands condemned already because he has not believed in the name of God's one and only Son" (John 3:18). Intellectually *knowing* the Word is far different from *believing* the Word. You might already believe Jesus is the stairway to heaven, and if so, according to the Bible, salvation is yours. If you do not believe and are not following the Way, there's still time to change the road you're following. You do not have to fear death or work your way to salvation any longer. Jesus has paid the debt in full, bearing the penalty of all your sins on the cross. If you are cut to the heart, as the Israelites in Acts 2 were, I give you the same words that Peter gave to them: "Repent and be baptized in the name of Jesus Christ for the forgiveness of your sins" (Acts 2:38).

What's Next?

One of Jesus' teaching parables speaks about a farmer sowing seeds. He sows them liberally, casting them all over his land. Some of the seeds of course land on soil that is not fit for vegetation. Some seeds fell on the open path and birds came and ate it. Some fell on rocky soil and experienced growth, but since the plants had no solid roots, the heat of the sun scorched them and they died. Some seeds fell in the thicket of thorns and were swallowed up. Some, however, landed on good soil and were able to grow and bear fruit.

Many did not understand this parable, so Jesus' twelve disciples asked him in private to explain its hidden meaning. His explanation is vital for everyone who has received the Word of God (the seed). The following is Jesus' explanation as recorded by Mark 4:13–20:

> Don't you understand this parable? How then will you understand any parable? The farmer sows the word. Some people are like seed along the path, where the word is sown. As soon as they hear it, Satan comes and takes away the word that was sown in them. Others, like seed sown on rocky places, hear the word and at once receive it with joy. But since they have no root, they last only a short time. When trouble or persecution comes because of the word, they quickly fall away. Still others, like seed sown among thorns, hear the word; but the worries of this life, the deceitfulness of wealth and the desires for other

things come in and choke the word, making it unfruitful. Others, like seed sown on good soil, hear the word, accept it, and produce a crop—thirty, sixty or even a hundred times what was sown.

The message is clear: we can receive the gospel, believe it, and then fall away from faith in Christ. Those who remain in faith will bear works that are evidence of the faith that they have. God the Father is the gardener and Jesus is the vine (John 15:1). We are the branches. If a branch doesn't bear fruit, God will cut it off. The branches that do bear fruit, he prunes, so that they might bear even more fruit (John 15:2).

We are not the judges of who is or isn't bearing fruit that is pleasing to God; he is the gardener, not us. How can we be sure if we are bearing fruit? Jesus answers this in John 15:5–6, 8: "I am the vine; you are the branches. If a man remains in me and I in him, he will bear much fruit; apart from me you can do nothing. If anyone does not remain in me, he is like a branch that is thrown away and withers; such branches are picked up, thrown into the fire and burned. ... This is my Father's glory, that you bear much fruit, showing yourselves to be my disciples."

Works are the sign of being a disciple; they do not make us a disciple. Faith in Christ makes a disciple, and in that faith we follow Jesus; we remain in Christ and we bear fruit; our hearts are good soil.

Some Christians will bear more fruit than others. As Jesus said, "Some will produce a crop—thirty, sixty or even a hundred times what was sown" (Mark 4:20). The amount we bear is for God to decide, and only God is the judge of the fruit. We must also remember that he is pruning us and caring for us. Those of us in Christ will grow at different rates and produce different amounts of fruit. What's important is that fruit, any kind and of any amount, is a sign of being in Christ. The command to us in this process of growing in holiness is to "remain in Christ."

If you have been a believer for a long time, or even a short time, remain in Christ. If you have just accepted God's gospel while reading this book, it's vital that you remain in Christ. We remain in Christ by drawing near to the ways in which Jesus comes to us. He comes to us through his Word, the Bible; through fellowship and prayer with other believers; and through baptism and communion. These are the means by which the Holy Spirit works to create faith in us and to sustain and nurture that faith.

The product of this faith in Christ is, first and foremost, salvation that comes to us by grace. If you just came to faith reading this book, and my prayer is that many people will, the next step for you is to get planted in a local church congregation, where you can grow deep roots. Faith also produces works. The last command that Jesus gave to his followers was to be his witnesses (Acts 1:8) and to make disciples of all nations (Matthew 28:19). Sharing Christ with others through our words and deeds is the work of the church—that is, all believers.

The remaining chapters of this book focus on sharing and addressing the many objections that arise when engaging in evangelistic conversations with non-Christians.

7

Using Contradict to Share the Gospel

I have been sharing the gospel using a Contradict logo comprised of different religious symbols. I've used it for about three years with several Christian brothers on multiple universities. There have been three different designs, and the one on the cover of this book is the latest version. I designed it with my graphic artist friend, Danny Martinez.

The majority of the time, our Contradict sign has been taped to a table in the Freedom of Speech Zone at the University California–Irvine (UCI). We have offered free coffee to anyone passing by. We started by brewing our own coffee, but the prep time was too cumbersome. So we broke down and started to order from the campus Starbucks, conveniently located around the corner from our table. For less than fifteen dollars, we are given ninety-six ounces of hot coffee in an insulated cardboard box with all the cups, creamer, sweeteners, napkins, and stir-sticks we need for a couple hours of sharing the gospel. It's hard for me to think of a more rewarding, adventurous, and entertaining way to spend fifteen dollars and a few hours of time each week.

At the offer of free Starbucks, many students and even campus visitors gladly stop for some brew, especially students on their way to the library to study all night. The community at UCI loves engaging in intellectually stimulating conversation and debate. Each night, several students stay for lengthy discussions about faith differences. Some students make multiple visits over an academic year, and others sometimes approach us simply to say, "I've seen you out here every week; I don't want any coffee, but I'm curious what this means," as they point to the Contradict sign. Similar approaches and responses have been received at Saddleback Community College, Chapman University, California State University, Fullerton, and even grocery stores.

We are often mistaken as atheists because many people interpret the sign to mean that we are against all religions. That isn't the case; we just recognize that the religions of the world contradict each other in their fundamental teachings and therefore can't all be true. We are Christians who believe Jesus' claim to be the way, the truth, and the life—the only true way to the Father (John 14:6). This usually creates an interested audience for further discussion, and why not? There is free coffee involved, and it's a personal conversation, not a bullhorn speech.

As of the time I wrote this book, I have taught World Religions and Christian Apologetics for four years at a private Christian high school in Southern California. I have found that before the class, most of my students know very little about any religion besides Christianity. The mainstream college students at UCI are also uninformed about many of the world's most prominent religions. Most students are very interested to know more.

If you can remember just a tenth of the information shared in the previous chapters, you will definitely know more than the average American, as the surveys cited in the first chapter attest. Starting a Christ-centered conversation from a starting position that demonstrates that you have a working knowledge in many of the world's religions instantly builds your credibility as a reliable source for religious information. It shows religious pluralists, adherents of other religions, atheists, agnostics, and various breeds of skeptics that you are not a close-minded, ignorant Christian.

The goal is to always present the gospel message because "it is the power of God for the salvation of everyone who believes" (Romans 1:16). From my experience and point of view, if the discussion is likely to be a one-time encounter, it's vital to share a short sentence or two presenting the gospel message that Jesus is God and that he died for the sins of the world. I combine this with the message that all religions can't be true due to their contradictory teachings.

The reason I love this approach is that, after this initial Contradict conversation starter, the direction of the dialogue, if you allow it, is entirely in the hands of the other person. Most gospel tracts are like railroad tracks, a mandatory route of biblical information that must be followed in a set order.

One of the most popular gospel tracts is "Have you Heard of the Four Spiritual Laws?" written in the 1950s by Bill Bright, the founder of Campus Crusade for Christ. The first law is that God loves you and has a plan for you. The second law is that, because you are a sinner, you can't know that love or plan. That leads to the third law, which states that Christ died for you so you can know God and have a relationship with him. The fourth law expresses the necessity for individual reception of Christ as Savior through faith.[1]

Another popular gospel tract, which to my knowledge doesn't have a specific author besides the apostle Paul, is "The Romans Road to Salvation." This popular method of sharing the gospel cherry-picks specific verses from the Book of Romans to introduce a systematic presentation of how a person can have eternal life. The first stops that most people use are Romans 3:23

and Romans 6:23, showing that all have sinned and that the penalty for sin is eternal death.

Way of the Master, an evangelism-training ministry led by Ray Comfort and Kirk Cameron, follows a similar route. Their approach first asks people if they would consider themselves good. They usually do. Then the authors ask, "Have you kept the Ten Commandments?" With some follow-up questions, they soon have individuals admitting that they are liars, thieves, adulterers, and blasphemers, and therefore not good in the eyes of God. They are guilty of breaking his laws and deserve hell. Then the gospel is presented, that Christ died as atonement for their sins, with a subsequent invitation to repent and be baptized. Most of *Way of the Master*'s gospel tracts follow this typical format, although in an entertaining, nonthreatening manner.[2]

Evangelistic endeavors, like most gospel tracts, typically start with the aim of convincing a person that he or she has sinned and deserves hell. This is a good move sequentially. People must first know their sins and their inability to save themselves from eternal damnation before acknowledging or accepting the work of the Savior.

I'll be honest: I agree with this process, and for the most part I followed it in my evangelical life. The change came when I met Brian, a Christian who converted to following Christ in his twenties. I had the privilege of spending time with Brian for a semester in college when he was still relatively new to the Christian faith. He became a believer after a long series of hard knocks due to poor decisions: drunk driving, drug use, drug dealing, a stint in military prison, and other experiences that most of us will only know through television and movies.

I have long lost connection with Brian (just hunted him down on Facebook though, so we'll see what happens), but he was the type of person who comes to faith in Christ and undergoes an immediate, drastic transformation. He stopped his drug use and started reading the Bible. He knew the Bible more intimately and lived it more radically than people who have grown up in Christian homes, reading the Bible and professing faith from their earliest years.

We came out of a chapel service on campus and Brian was frustrated with the homily for the day. The bulk of the message had focused on our sinfulness and our inability to earn our salvation, before a brief thanks in the wrap-up to Jesus Christ who has died for us. It wasn't just this message that set Brian off; it had been a slow boil over the course of the semester. He had been on some evangelism outings in the community and to other college campuses, and even on our own Christian campus with evangelism-centered Bible studies for international students learning English. He saw the sinner first, sinner first, sinner first method again and again. He couldn't grasp the point of focusing on our sin and pinpointing our total lack of involvement in salvation, especially in a chapel service geared for born-again believers.

The explanation finally came. "When I wasn't a Christian," he said, "I knew I was a sinner. I knew I had problems. I went to a random church one day seeking help, and all I got was a message like today's! The preacher told us how sinful we were and how much we deserved hell, and I was like, no joke, that's why I'm here! And I just tuned out. That was always the case when Christians came to me telling me I was an alcoholic and I needed help, or that I was going down a bad road. What I needed to hear was that God loved me just as I was. I knew I needed help. I didn't need to be told I was sinner again and again; what I needed was *help*! I never heard of God's grace through the words of condemnation."

Contradict is what I call an open gospel tract. The start is simple. All religions or worldviews can't be true, because they contradict each other. If a person disagrees with that premise, then you simply share a few of the contradictions present in the world's religions.

I like to share, "Jesus said in John 14:6 that he is the way, the truth, and the life, the only way to the Father. If this statement is true, then all other religions would have to be false. I believe there are good reasons for believing it to be true, namely that Jesus died for our sins and proved his divinity and our forgiveness through his subsequent resurrection from the dead."

If the person still stresses that all religions can be true, you have to address that issue more, but often the person will agree that religions do contradict each other and respond with a question that he or she has concerning the message that you just shared.

Since the proclamation that Jesus died for our sins already has the underpinning of sin and its consequences, people don't have to be confronted with the typical hammer on the head of their sinfulness that they are likely already accustomed to experiencing. The ball is in their court and they can ask any question or raise any complaint.

If a person instantly gets the meaning behind the Contradict design and agrees with it, you could ask, "Do you consider yourself religious, or do you have a religion?" The answer you receive will direct your response, but your next question will likely be, "Why do you think that religion (or view) is true?" After listening and learning more about a person's beliefs and understanding, you can ask questions to learn more about what he or she believes. You can even frame inquiries that require the person to defend or question the validity of those beliefs. You can then present the gospel message and ask what he or she thinks about the Bible's claims.

Since the direction of the conversation is very open-ended when using Contradict, you will need to be more prepared to share various aspects of the Christian faith than if you were using a more linear, scripted pattern of sharing the gospel. This is good! It will make you more dependent upon the help of the Holy Spirit and the presence of Jesus in your sharing of his Word, both of which are promised in Scripture.

It is also good because this means you will be meeting people individually with their concerns and questions about the gospel message. If a person is in the state that Brian was in before his conversion, knowing his sinfulness and already feeling the weight of guilt and the need for God's forgiveness and help, then you don't have to risk losing that person through an initial barrage of "sin talk," which could easily be interpreted as uncaring, unknowing, and judgmental no matter how loving or well-intentioned you are.

Of course, depending on the person's heart position with regard to his or her sinfulness, a healthy dose of God's Law might be the right prescription. Like any good doctor, you should let the patient share his or her condition and run some diagnostic tests before lobbing Romans 3:23 pills in their direction.

Twenty of the Most Commonly Encountered Questions and Objections

Just because Contradict is an open-ended, Christ-centered conversation starter, it doesn't mean that we have to be completely clueless about where the conversation will head. There are numerous Christian apologetics books on the market that address common objections to the Christian faith. Reading these will be helpful for your own nagging questions and doubts, as I'm sure we all have them from time to time, and they'll give you good answers to share with others.

Most books of this nature address similar questions, if not the exact same questions, but one author might use an analogy that fits your personality better than another, or one person might write in a voice that you relate to more than another's. There are also numerous Web sites dedicated strictly to answering challenging questions and objections raised in evangelistic conversation. I recommend spending some time browsing the *Christian Apologetics and Research Ministry* Web site. If you find an article or two that you really like and that you anticipate being helpful to share with others, print a few copies to keep on hand.

After sharing the gospel message using Contradict for a year at UCI, it became apparent that the same questions were being asked each week. As a resource to help prepare you for using Contradict to share the gospel, I have compiled twenty of the most commonly encountered questions, using the format of initiating the Christ-centered conversations that I have just shared. These questions are not listed in order of frequency or difficulty. I have grouped questions that are similar in their line of reasoning or doubt.

For most of the questions, I have categorized replies you might want to try using. The reply categories are Validation, Answer, Socratic Method, Scripture, and Back to the Gospel. Not every question contains answers from all of these categories and their order is not set in stone. I share these categorical answers in a sequence that I think provides the best flow of responses for grasping the numerous possible replies to each question. In a conversation I always strive to start an answer with a validation response and work towards connecting the answer to the Gospel.

Validation replies are responses that will show the person asking the question that you understand why he or she is asking the question. In some cases you may admit that Christians have asked these questions too. We've all heard that there are no stupid questions, but sometimes we do feel stupid when we ask questions. We don't want to create an atmosphere in which questioning the Christian faith is barred. This means we shouldn't immediately shoot down questions that nonbelievers ask us or make them feel as if they are stupid for asking. We want to encourage their questions, especially if they are honestly seeking answers from Scripture. Showing that we can relate to the reasoning and emotion behind the question will also help prepare the person for receiving a Scripture-based answer. Paul demonstrates this approach when speaking to the "men of Athens" in Acts 17. Instead of ridiculing them for their prolific polytheism, he praises them by saying, "I can see in every way that you are very religious." He then speaks to them where they are, addresses their shortcomings, and shows them Jesus.

Answer replies are just that, the straightforward answer to the question. It never fails. When these answers are given to nonbelievers, they truly are shocked. I can't count how many times I've heard an atheist, an agnostic, a religious pluralist, or an adherent of another religion say, "I've never heard this before. This is all new to me." That makes me sad. It makes me wonder, "Do other Christians not know this information?" "Does this person not know any Christians in his or her day-to day life who could have answered this question?" "Why am I, a stranger, the first Christian to have the opportunity to answer this person's question?" Trust me: these answers will be well received. If they aren't instantly embraced, don't worry. They will definitely provide food for thought for some time to come, and might even help kick-start a conversation with a Christian friend with whom that person has just never openly spoken about religious faith.

Socratic Method replies are often very helpful. Jesus taught this way all the time. He'd answer a question with a question. Good teachers can ask the right questions as guides to prompt their students to sift through the information they already know and pull out the answer to their own question. It might take a series of questions to get this to happen, but it's pretty magical when it works. At the end of the back and forth, the person has shared the truth of Scripture and has to admit, "I said it, not him. So what does that mean? Do I actually believe my own answer? Did I resolve my own objection? What now?" Or maybe the question is just scratching the surface, and you give a better question to ask. Even without getting an answer, this can blow a person's mind and leave him or her wanting to learn more.

Scripture replies are verses that demonstrate where the answers are found in the Bible. The Bereans were praised for checking all of Paul's words with Scripture. They never took anything Paul said as truth until they saw that God's Word confirmed Paul's teachings (Acts 17:11). The passages I provide in these answers are provided to aid you in checking my answers with Scripture. Often times, you will encounter people who might question the Scriptural validity of your answers, at which point; don't hesitate to open a Bible and conduct an impromptu Bible study. I have had the opportunity to do this with Jews and Muslims several times over the years. Questions that are directed towards Christian doctrine necessitate a Biblical answer, so don't be hesitant to use Scripture when the question at hand is a theological question thinking it's not an authoritative source for the nonbeliever.

The goal is to always end each answer with a *Back to the Gospel* reply. The word *evangelism* means "sharing the good news," so our goal as evangelists should always be to share the gospel, which also means good news. Sometimes the questions raised can get very far off the topic of Jesus Christ crucified and raised for the forgiveness of all our sins. Whenever possible, all objections and questions need to be steered back to Jesus. Who is he? What did he say? What did he do? Why did he do and say these things? Our conversations at all times should revolve around these questions, not the questions about how all the animals fit into the ark or did people and dinosaurs coexist? Those are good questions, but they aren't the most important ones. Those don't invalidate the Christian faith. The question that invalidates the Christian faith is did Jesus rise from the dead or didn't he? Paul is very clear in Romans 10; a person comes to faith through hearing the gospel message proclaimed. That is where we want to attempt to steer the conversation. Whenever possible, Christ's atoning work needs to be integrated into our answer.

I hope these questions give you an idea of what to expect to hear when sharing the gospel from the Contradict launch pad. I also hope to give you answers that you think are convincing, in case you have never considered these questions yourself.

If lack of knowledge is the hindrance to your evangelism, remember the honest response is always the best answer, even it means you have to say, "I don't know; that's a good question." It would be much worse not to evangelize at all due to fear of not being able to share an answer to a question or to make something up if the Holy Spirit doesn't bring an answer to your mind. Even though "I don't know" is actually a good answer, and an answer that could lead to further conversations if you ask to meet again after conducting some research, Scripture urges us to be prepared to give an answer to anyone who asks us about the hope that we have in Christ (1 Peter 3:16). To that end, I pray that these answers will help you prepare.

Finally, these answers aren't intended to be memorized word for word. Each conversation should be different. As I have already said, Contradict doesn't come packaged as a neatly scripted gospel tract. It's open ended to address people where they are in their current understanding of Christ. It serves as an open door to examine the truthfulness of the Christian message.

I hope the answers I provide will be integrated into the context in which you are sharing the gospel. Who is receiving the message? Is it someone who has been in the military? If so, they will likely relate to war analogies. Is the person wearing a T-shirt of a band or musician? Can any song lyrics from that band, musician, or genre of music be used when answering the person's questions? What ethnicity is the person? Are there any stories or practices from that cultural background that can be connected to the gospel message or serve as analogies for answering his or her questions? Does the individual use specific terms or phrases in reference to God, sin, heaven, hell, the afterlife, salvation, faith, or religion that you can adopt and use to present the gospel in words that he or she will more readily grasp and even appreciate?

I sincerely hope that what you are reading is exciting you to share the gospel, either with or without using Contradict in the process.

With no further delay, here are twenty of the most commonly asked questions I have encountered sharing the gospel by this method.

1. Why Are You Out Here?

Answer:

Option 1, the Relationship-Building Answer—We are Christians (or followers of Jesus) and we come here once a week to serve the student community. I know when I was in college, some dorms wouldn't allow coffeemakers, and I couldn't afford to buy coffee.

Option 2, the Contradict Invitation Answer—We're all former theology majors (the people whom I share this with are all theology majors, so this works for us, but you could say something different: Christians, theologians, followers of Jesus, studying religions) and we love to discuss religion, share what we have learned, and see what others believe. If people want to discuss their religious views, we love to talk and are out here every week at the same time. If not, we hope the free coffee is a blessing to you. We like to use this Contradict sign as a conversation starter.

Option 3, the Direct Contradict Answer—We're Christians, and we're here to discuss our faith with students on this campus while drinking coffee. We're using this Contradict sign as a starting point for conversation. When you look at all the religions, it becomes apparent that they can't all be true due to their contradictory teachings. They could all be false, but they can't all be true. We personally believe that the teachings of the Bible are true, that Jesus is God and died for the sins of the whole world so that we might have eternal life.

(The ball is in the questioner's court now. He or she can ask any question. If the person doesn't want to talk, or wants to just take the coffee and go, this is when you can give a handout with more information about what you believe. Let the person know that you'll be at the same spot next week at the same time with more coffee. Invite the person to ask some questions about what's on the handout. I'd suggest making sure the handout contains the gospel and some of the information about why we can trust the gospel to be true. Include contact information so the person can reach you later if he or she wants to discuss the handout.)

Socratic Method:

What do you think this sign means?

Do you believe its message is true?

Have you seen the coexist bumper stickers? What message about religions do you believe the people who put those stickers on their cars are trying to share with others?

Do you believe all religions can be true, or that all religions lead to God?

Do you believe religions contradict one another and can't all be true?

Do you believe we can know which religion is true, if any are true?

2. All Religions Teach the Same Thing

Validation:

I think many religions agree on certain points, such as is the existence of life after death, or that there is some sort of higher power or entity in the universe. And most religions have similar moral laws, so I can see where people can come to this conclusion. I think the real reason people come to this conclusion is because they don't want to exclude anyone from having the best existence possible after this life. We don't want to say anyone is wrong, and we want to avoid drawing lines of division that lead to segregation, elitism, and at times hate and violence. But the contradictions found among the world's religions forces the recognition of such distinctions.

Answer:

It might be possible to squeeze the world's religions into teaching the same thing on secondary or superficial levels, but on the primary or fundamental doctrines, they contradict each other. For instance, Christians believe that Jesus is God and the Savior of the world, whereas Muslims believe that Jesus is just a prophet who should not be worshipped, and Jews, at least conservative Jews, would say that Jesus was a false prophet. These are just the views of three religions concerning one person in history! Clearly, they don't all teach the same thing, and their contradictory teachings can't all be true.

Socratic Method:

How do they all teach the same thing?

On what doctrine do they all agree?

Do they all teach the same thing concerning the afterlife?

Do they all agree on what mankind's ultimate problem is and how that problem can be overcome?

Do they all agree on who, or what, God is? Do they all even believe in an eternal, transcendent God?

How do Christianity, Islam, and Hinduism teach the same thing?

Scripture:

1 Timothy 4:1—"The Spirit clearly says that in later times some will abandon the faith and follow deceiving spirits and things taught by demons."

Acts 4:12—"Salvation is found in no one else, for there is no other name [Jesus] under heaven given to men by which we must be saved."

Back to the Gospel:

Let's look at what Christianity teaches concerning the way of salvation. Romans 4:4–5 says, "Now when a man works, his wages are not credited to him as a gift, but as an obligation. However, to the man who does not work but trusts God who justifies the wicked, his faith is credited as righteousness." In Christianity, salvation is free for men. God steps in to redeem and rescue mankind through the work of Jesus Christ. None of us can save ourselves by our own work or merit, because we are all sinful people who do evil. In all other religions, people must work to earn a good afterlife. In Hinduism, a person must practice yoga and have good karma. In Buddhism, a person must follow the eightfold path. In Islam, a person must excel in the five pillars of the Islamic faith. In Judaism, Jews have rejected Jesus as their Messiah and have chosen to justify themselves through observance of the Law. All religions do not teach the same thing.

In Christianity, salvation is free. In all other religions, salvation, if they call it salvation, is not free and must be earned through personal works.

3. Why Does It Matter What You Believe?

Validation:

(This question can be validated in a comparable manner as the previous question because it likely originates from a similar heart position, but here is another possible validation.)

I think I understand where you are coming from. As Westerners, we value personal freedom of choice, and in America we have built it into our constitution that we all have the right to choose what religion we want to believe and follow.

Answer:

In many areas of our lives, our beliefs drastically matter. If a person believes one race or nationality is inferior and must be exterminated and follows through with that belief, it causes a serious problem for the race that is considered to be inferior and for any other race that believes acts of genocide should be stopped. (Many examples can be given similar to this in realms of morality, interpreting reality, or handling financial situations, and from any of these they'll likely clarify that some beliefs matter, but religious beliefs don't. They might move into arguing that when it comes to religions, the truth can't be known, which is the next question on this list. If they stick with the current question, I'd continue with …) It seems that you are treating religious faith as an inconsequential preference, similar to your choice of what movies to watch or what music you listen to. But religion pertains to matters after this life. If Islam is true, I'd better submit to Allah and follow all that's commanded in the Qur'an. If Hinduism is true, I'm in for a rough reincarnation. If Christianity is true, I'd better repent, turn away from my sins, and turn to Jesus for my righteousness and forgiveness. If atheism is true, then you're right: it doesn't really matter what you believe, since we're all destined to be worm food.

Socratic Method:

What if someone believed that rape was okay? Or incest?

What if someone believed that doctors and medicine should not be used, and thus denied their children medical care that could save their lives? This is a real scenario that has arisen in America among followers of Christian Science.

Are you afraid of death? Do you believe that there is life after death? What if religions teach contradictory ways to obtain life after death—would it matter which one you believed and followed?

Why do you think it doesn't matter what you believe in the realm of religion? Do you believe that all religions have the same core beliefs?

Scripture:

Mark 16:16—"Whoever believes and is baptized will be saved, but whoever does not believe will be condemned."

Romans 10:9–13—"That if you confess with your mouth, 'Jesus is Lord,' and believe in your heart that God raised him from the dead, you will be saved. For it is with your heart that you believe and are justified, and it is with your mouth that you confess and are saved. As the Scripture says, 'Anyone who trusts in him will never be put to shame.' For there is no difference between Jew and Gentile—the same Lord is Lord of all and richly blesses all who call on him, for, 'Everyone who calls on the name of the Lord will be saved.'"

Back to the Gospel:

Have you heard the verse John 3:16 from the Bible? It's a verse that is often quoted by Christians because it contains a summary of the gospel message, and *gospel* means "good news." John 3:16 says, "For God so loved the world that he gave his one and only Son, that whoever believes in him shall not perish but have eternal life." According to this verse, belief in

Jesus is necessary for salvation. Later in the same chapter, Jesus says about having faith in himself, "Whoever believes in the Son has eternal life, but whoever rejects the Son will not see life, for God's wrath remains on him" (John 3:36). If Christianity is true, then what you believe concerning religion does matter.

4. It Doesn't Matter What You Believe as Long as You Are Good

Socratic Method:

Do our beliefs provide the formation of our morals? What if you believe something is good that I believe is evil? What if I believe abortion is murder and someone else doesn't? What if I believe we shouldn't smoke pot because it is illegal, and someone else thinks it is okay even if it is illegal, and a third person says it's never okay even if it is legal? Is there an objective standard to decide if a person is good? What would that standard be, and how would we as humans decide and agree upon it?"

Do you think you are good?

What's the Golden Rule? Do you think you have loved your neighbor as yourself?

Let's consider Christianity and some of the Ten Commandments. Have you ever told a lie? What does that make you? (A liar) Have you ever looked with lust at someone? According to Jesus, if you have lusted with your eyes, you have committed adultery in your heart. Have you ever hated someone or wished someone harm in your heart? According to Jesus, if you have hated someone, you have committed murder in your heart. Have you ever stolen anything? What does that make you? (A thief) Have you ever used the Lord's name in vain? So by your own admission you are a liar, an adulterer, a murderer, a thief, and blasphemer. Do you think in God's eyes you are good? Do you think you would go to heaven if you were to die tonight?

Answer:

Option 1, the Extreme Atheism Answer—I believe morals and beliefs go hand in hand. If I were an atheist, what motivation would I have to do good for others unless there was some sort of personal benefit to myself? In a purely atheistic, Darwinian worldview, life is survival of the fittest. Only the strong survive. In a purely naturalistic worldview, when we die, we no longer exist. Why shouldn't I steal and cheat to get ahead? Why shouldn't I rob a bank and shoot myself if it looks like I'm going to get caught? Why shouldn't I have sex with thousands of people even if I have an STD? This life is all I have. There's no reason for me to do anything except what gives me the most pleasure in this short time that we have here on earth.

Option 2, God is the Objective Standard for Good Answer—In some religions, such as Hinduism and Jainism, people shouldn't kill animals. They believe everyone should be vegan. They would say that I am not good because I eat meat and support the use of animals for lab experiments. If it doesn't matter what you believe as long as you are good, whose view of what's good and what's evil should we choose to use? What if you think homosexual acts are perfectly okay when I think they are sinful? Who do we appeal to decide what's right and what's wrong? Is it the majority rule in a given nation, geographic region, or culture? What if the majority is racist? Would racism be considered good? We need to have an objective, unchanging standard that we can appeal to for discerning what is good. We need one, transcendent, eternal, unchanging, and good God in order to have an objective standard that can be appealed to throughout time. Otherwise, we only have subjective morality based on individual human opinion, which is always different. We need a God who has revealed his nature and will to us in order to discern what is good. We need one God we can appeal to in order to objectively say what's good and evil. How would you even go about saying Hitler was wrong without an absolute, objective standard of morality that can only come from God?

Option 3, No One is Good Answer—Your view that it doesn't matter what you believe as long as you are good could be true if all religions are wrong. One of the aspects common to all religions is their provision of a moral code of ethics for their adherents to follow. Even the Satanic Bible of the Church of Satan provides a moral code for all Satanists to adhere to. What's good varies from person to person based on what they believe constitutes being good. Christians believe that no one is good—no one except God. All of us, like sheep, have gone astray, each to our own way, away from God's perfect standard (Isaiah 53:6). If the Bible is true, then none of us are good in God's sight. And let's be honest: all of us have lied, cheated, stolen, hated, lusted, and put ourselves above others again and again. None of us are good even by the human standards that we expect each other to uphold.

Back to the Gospel:

It would matter what you believe if there is a God who has directly revealed himself to us, telling us what he considers to be good and what he expects from us. I believe God has revealed himself to us in the person of Jesus Christ. The Bible says that Jesus is the "image of the invisible God" (Colossians 1:15). If you want to know who God is, you simply have to look to Jesus, his words and actions. What you will find is that none of us are perfect, but Jesus was able to bring us back into a right relationship with God despite our evilness "by making peace through his blood, shed on the cross" (Colossians 1:20). I believe that there are good reasons to trust the Bible to be true, based on what God has revealed to us through it. It does matter what we believe, because none of us are good, and it is only through faith in Jesus Christ that we may have forgiveness for how we have broken God's perfect Law.

5. We Can't Know What Is True

Validation:

With all the competing worldviews, cultures, and religions that contradict each other in their claims to truth, it is hard to discern which is correct, if any of them, especially since we all have different experiences.

Answer:

Option 1, That's a Self-Contradictory Statement Answer—"We can't know what is true" is a truth statement. If your truth-claim is that we can't know what is true, then how do we know if your claim is true? It's a self-contradictory claim. It's the same as claiming that there is no truth. It's a truth statement that says it's not true.

Option 2, Truth Concerning God Answer—You can't mean we can't know what is true. I know it is true that if you wrote me a check for all the money in your bank account, your account would be empty. I know it is true that if I tried to derail a moving train with your body, you'd be dead. I know that if you thought a red light meant "go" when driving, you'd cause a wreck on your way home. (At this point, the person will likely clarify that he or she meant we can't know truth concerning God.) It could be true that we don't currently know truth about God. I think it's wrong to say that it's impossible to ever know truth concerning God. I believe you just mean that we don't as of right now have enough evidence to know for certain one way or the other what is true concerning who God is. But if God *has* revealed himself or *will* show himself to us, then we *can* know who he is.

Scripture:

Psalm 33:4—"For the word of the Lord is right and true; he is faithful in all he does."

Psalm 119:160—"All your words are true; all your righteous laws are eternal."

1 John 5:20—"We know also that the Son of God has come and has given us understanding, so that we may know him who is true. And we are in him who is true—even in his Son Jesus Christ. He is the true God and eternal life."

Socratic Method:

If we can't know truth, on what grounds can we say what is right and what is wrong, or what is good and what is evil?

If we can't know truth, on what grounds can we say the attacks on America on September 11, 2001, were wrong?

Do you really mean we can't know if anything is true? Or do you just mean that we can't know truth concerning God? Do you believe God exists, but we just can't know who he is? What if God directly revealed himself to us? Could we know who God is then? How do you know he hasn't revealed himself to us?

Is it true that we can't know truth?

6. There's No Way of Knowing God

Validation:

With all the competing views of who God is, it is difficult to know which view of God is true. If you mean that it's hard to relationally know God, I'd agree with that too. I mean, I know who the president of the United States is, but it'd be next to impossible for me to have relational knowledge of him. I can't just text him and meet up with him for coffee as I could with any of my friends, and he's just a human being. Now imagine an all-powerful, all-knowing, eternal God who happens to be everywhere at all times; oh, and he can't be seen.

Socratic Method:

Does this mean you believe there is a God, he's just not knowable? (if the answer is yes...) Why do you believe there is a God? What makes you believe you can't know God? Do you think it's possible that God has somehow revealed himself to us?

If there is a God and he created everything, why do you think he made us? Do you think he'd want us to know him? Do you think he would want to reveal himself to us if it was possible for us to know him?

If God was to reveal himself to us, how do you think he'd do it? The Bible teaches that Jesus was God incarnate, God in human flesh. Who do you think Jesus is? How much do you know about Jesus? Have you ever read the Gospels?

Answer:

I think you are partially correct. It's impossible for us to know who God is on our own. God is spirit, and in our four-dimensional existence of length, depth, width, and time, there is nothing *we* can do with our five senses to uncover or discover who God is. However, that doesn't mean God is incapable of revealing himself to us. God is God, and he can do anything he pleases. He has shown himself to us indirectly and directly. God has indirectly revealed himself to us through what he has created. When we look around and observe the universe, we see design, order, complexity, and beauty, all of which point to a Creator. When we consider the first cause of the universe, an eternal, all-powerful God who exists outside of time is the best explanation for the genesis, the beginning, of the universe. Nothing comes from nothing, and life does not come from nonlife, as the atheistic model of Darwinism projects. So simply from what he has created, God has made it plain that he exists. But God has also directly revealed himself to us through the person and work of Jesus Christ. In Jesus Christ, the fullness of God dwelled in human flesh, and he proved his divinity through his life, death, and resurrection.

Scripture:

Psalm 19:1–4—"The heavens declare the glory of God; the skies proclaim the work of his hands. Day after day they pour forth speech; night after night they display knowledge. There is no speech or language where their voice is not heard. Their voice goes out into all the earth, their words to the ends of the world."

Colossians 2:9—"For in Christ all the fullness of the Deity lives in bodily form."

7. Why Doesn't God Show Himself to Us?

Validation:

I agree. God, show yourself to us right now if you are real! You would think that if God wanted a relationship with us, that if he wanted us to actually know him, he would visibly show himself to us, or audibly shout with his God-megaphone to all of us in the whole world at the same time. Have you ever seen God? Have you ever heard God? Me neither.

Socratic Method:

If God showed himself to us right now, would you have faith in him and worship him for the rest of your life? How would you know that he is God and not possibly a pretender? Would you ever doubt your experience?

Do you only believe in things you have seen? Do you believe there are planets outside of our solar system? Have you seen them personally, not in photographs? Can you see the air you are breathing right now? If you already believe in things you can't see, why do you have to see God in order to believe in him?

"How do you know God hasn't directly revealed himself to us? Do you know what he looks like? Could he look like one of us? How do you know I'm not God? Can you think of any religions that are based on God directly revealing himself and making himself visible to people?

Answer:

Option 1, That's a Self-Contradictory Statement Answer—When you ask this question, you are actually saying that you only believe in what you can see. This belief is self-contradictory. You believe in a belief, but beliefs can't be seen. Neither can ideas, thoughts, or abstract realities such as zero. You can see the belief in written form, but you aren't actually seeing the belief; you are seeing written text that is a visual representation of the belief.

Option 2, You Believe Things All the Time that You Can't See Answer—If someone told me that he didn't bleed blood, he bled ketchup, I'd say I'd have to see it to believe it. I would cut the person with a knife and see if he bled ketchup! In most scenarios, however, I believe things all the time that I can't see. If someone who is almost always on time to meet me is late, and she says she was late because there was heavy traffic, I will believe that person without getting in my car and driving to find out for myself. But let's be honest, most of life's important realities can't be seen, such as the air we breathe, gravitational pull, and love. Why must you see God in order to believe in him?

Option 3, Theological Answer—Since your question is theological by nature, I want to share with you what the Bible says concerning this issue. You are not the first person to ask to see God. Moses had seen God before—in a burning bush, in a pillar of fire, and in a tent of meeting. Moses had felt God performing miracles through him and had heard God speak often. Yet Moses still asked to see God face-to-face, not behind any smoke and mirrors. God told Moses that no sinful man could see his face and live! In our sinful state, if we were to see God in his full, unadulterated glory, we would die. This is why God showed himself to Moses by masking himself in various ways. This is also partly why God showed himself to us by taking on flesh in the historical person of Jesus Christ. In Jesus, the fullness of the deity of God dwelled, but because that divine nature was masked in flesh, people could see, touch, and hear God directly without dying. So to answer your question, God has shown himself to mankind through Jesus Christ, and we can trust that Jesus was actually God through his miracle-filled life, death, and resurrection.

Back to the Gospel:

There are good reasons why God revealed himself in human likeness in the person of Jesus Christ and not through rending the heavens. God created humanity as morally responsible beings with free will who had an intimate relationship with him, knowing full well that we would choose to sin. God warned Adam and Eve, the first humans, that if they disobeyed him, they would die. This might seem like a harsh consequence, but it's a consequence that is first necessary since sinful beings can't survive in the presence of a holy and awesome God. That would mean that if we didn't die, we would never be able to have an intimate relationship with him again. Second, if God allowed us to live forever, we'd live forever in a sinful, evil world. God, who exists in a Trinity (three persons, the Father, the Son, and the Holy Spirit, who share in one divine nature), chose to redeem us from our sinful state. For this to occur and for God to remain just and holy, he could not simply overlook our sin. So he set in motion a divine plan of salvation, which means God the Father sent his one and only Son, Jesus Christ, into the world as a human. Jesus, being in very nature God, was born without sin and had the righteousness necessary to live up to God's perfect standard. He never sinned at all. As a sinless human, Jesus was not subject to the penalty of death that comes with sin. However, he chose to serve as a substitute for us, taking the penalty of our sin upon himself, dying the death we deserve to die. The Father received Christ's sacrifice and accepted it, granting us Christ's righteousness and holiness so we are forgiven for our trespasses. On account of Jesus' obedience, the Father had Jesus raised from the dead. Though we will still die physically for our sins, we won't suffer eternal death. We will be raised from the dead bodily at the end of the world, just as Jesus was raised from the dead. The Holy Spirit works faith in our hearts, leads us and guides us in this life, and keeps us in that one true faith. So you see, there are very good reasons why God doesn't just reveal himself visibly to everyone as you might expect him to, but he has revealed himself visibly in the person of Jesus Christ.

8. There Isn't One Correct Way to God

Validation:

I think we all wish this were true. Religions usually provide a path to a positive afterlife, and they usually teach that a negative afterlife awaits those who follow a different path. I think that none of us wish a negative eternal existence upon anyone, especially an existence such as the hell that is described in the Bible. Professing that there isn't just one correct way to God can definitely provide a sense of comfort when we think of the possibility of loved ones, or anyone for that matter, suffering eternally.

Socratic Method:

How do you know *for sure* that there isn't one correct way to God?

What do you think about a religion like Christianity that teaches that there is only one correct way to God? I'm a Christian, and I believe that faith in Christ is the only way to God. Do you believe that the path I am following is incorrect? How do you know that Jesus' exclusive claims to be the only way to God aren't true?

Answer:

Option 1, Following Directions Answer—If you were to enter an address in your smartphone and it told you to take I–5 northbound, but you took it southbound; if you never turned around; if you took the freeway all the way across the border into Mexico and still never rerouted, would you make it to your initially intended destination? No. The North Pole is not the South Pole, and China in the East is not America in the West. All roads don't lead to the destinations we want in life. Why do you think it will be different in regard to an afterlife with God? If I told you the directions to my house and you didn't follow them, you wouldn't end up at my house. If God has given us directions to his house and we don't follow them, we won't make it to his doorstep. The Bible is God's road map to salvation. It reveals that the only way to God is through faith in Jesus Christ. There are good reasons to believe that Jesus is our one and only, all-sufficient Savior.

Option 2, Show Me the Proof Answer—If I were to tell you that I saw Sasquatch hiking through Silverado Canyon, or that I bleed yellow mustard and not blood, you'd want some proof, right? If I were to tell you that I have no proof, you would likely not believe me. That's where I sit with your claim that all religions lead to God. Based strictly on the various religions' teachings about the divine and the afterlife, they contradict each other about who God is and what to expect after the end of this life. It's possible for them all to lead to a positive existence with the same God, but if that is the case, they'd all have to be wrong in what they actually confess. For me to turn away from what I believe as a Christian, and for followers of other religions to turn away from their faiths, you must offer some convincing proof. As it stands, I think there are really good reasons to believe that Jesus is the Son of God, who died for the sins of the world and rose from the grave. It might take some time to explain these reasons, but I'd love to share them if you have the time. (Then share the historical evidence from chapter 5.)

Scripture:

John 14:6—"Jesus answered, "I am the way and the truth and the life. No one comes to the Father except through me.""

1 John 5:12—"Whoever has the Son has life; whoever does not have the Son of God does not have life."

Matthew 7:13–14—"Enter through the narrow gate. For wide is the gate and broad is the road that leads to destruction, and many enter through it. But small is the gate and narrow the road that leads to life, and only a few find it."

9. Why Do You Believe Christianity Is True?

Answer:

I was taught the truths of the Bible from a young age, and my earliest memories are praying to God. I have always believed in Jesus, first because I trusted my parents and their words to me about Christ, but also because I have experienced his work in my life. I have seen answered prayer and I have felt the presence of God. But that's my experience, and that doesn't help you know that it is true. There is, however, good reason to believe that Jesus is God and that he died for the forgiveness of your sins. Jesus' life, death, and resurrection can be investigated and verified, just as any other historical event can be investigated and verified.

The good news for Christians and all of humanity is that the New Testament is the best attested ancient manuscript in terms of the number of early copies that exist, the dates of the copies as compared to their original writings, and the accuracy of the copies. In addition to this, the original Gospels were written by eyewitnesses, or written by people who used eyewitness testimony. This also means the authors were writing too close to the death and resurrection of Jesus for myths to have crept into the accounts. Other witnesses, both friend and foe, would have known if the gospel writers were telling lies, and they would have revealed the Gospels to be false. However, we have no such competing accounts from contemporaries. We do, on the other hand, have non-Christian authors writing in the first and second centuries who affirm the basic claims of the Gospels concerning Jesus. No one in the first century was ever able to produce the bones of Jesus to disprove the empty tomb. The Jewish and Roman authorities had the motive and the means to disprove the resurrection, but they could not. The best they could do was to persecute Christians in an attempt to stop the spread of the gospel of Jesus Christ. The apostolic circle in which the claim of Jesus' resurrection originated never recanted their testimony in the face of martyrdom. They continued to proclaim the risen Christ all the way to their deaths.

Socratic Method:

Can you think of any ways to prove or disprove Christianity?

If Jesus rose from the grave, what would that mean?

Is there any evidence that would actually make you reconsider your current beliefs?

What questions or objections do you have about Christianity that lead you to believe it's not true?

10. There's No Way of Knowing What Happens after Death

Validation:

You and I certainly haven't experienced death to know what is on the other side. I personally don't believe the narratives of people who have died and been resuscitated are reliable, especially since not everyone who has died and been brought back to life has had an experience to share. I think it is good that you are asking for evidence to back up Christianity's claims that there is an eternal existence after death, either in heaven or in hell.

Answer:

I believe we can know what happens after death because Jesus died and rose from the grave. Stop and think about it. Jesus foretold his death and his resurrection. He was dead for three days, violently slain by public execution, yet there was an empty tomb the Sunday morning after his crucifixion. Resurrection appearances were seen by numerous people at various times over a span of forty days. The evidence of Jesus' miracles, and his most impressive miracle of all, his foretold resurrection, affirm his claims to divinity. As all the evidence points to Jesus being God, I trust his testimony about heaven and hell and how he came to pave the way for all of us to have eternal life. If you want to have more details on the evidence of Jesus' resurrection, or to run any of your questions about how Jesus is our Savior by me, I'd love to share the answers that I have found helpful and convincing.

Scripture:

Matthew 20:17–19—"Now Jesus was going up to Jerusalem. On the way, he took the twelve disciples aside and said to them, 'We are going up to Jerusalem, and the Son of Man will be betrayed to the chief priests and the teachers of the law. They will condemn him to death and will turn him over to the Gentiles to be mocked and flogged and crucified. On the third day he will be raised to life!'"

Acts 1:3—"After his suffering, he showed himself to these men and gave many convincing proofs that he was alive. He appeared to them over a period of forty days and spoke about the kingdom of God."

11. I Believe If You Are Good, God Won't Send You to Hell

Validation:

You and I aren't in prison right now. We haven't robbed a bank, forged important documents, dealt drugs, or killed anyone. Well, I know I haven't. I'm assuming you haven't. People who commit such crimes go to jail, but often they get out for good behavior. So it seems that eternal punishment doesn't fit the crime for people like you and me who haven't done anything seriously wrong. I also know that a lot of people who are not Christians still serve the poor and the needy, physically and financially. By our standards of law and order, only the worst of the worst would deserve hell.

Answer:

Option 1, God is the Objective Standard for Good Answer—Refer to option 2 under question 4.

Option 2, No One is Good Answer—Refer to option 3 under question 4.

Option 3, the Punishment Must Fit the Crime Answer—We must admit that we all have lied, cheated, stolen, lusted, hated, coveted, disobeyed authority, and the like. To the degree that most of us have committed such acts, we don't deserve time in prison or exorbitant fines. I believe we all agree that punishments should fit the crimes. The problem I think you are raising with this question is that, for the degrees to which we have sinned against God, we don't deserve eternal punishment in hell. If we think about how we measure the degree of punishment for crimes in this life, I believe we can draw a parallel to see why eternal time in hell does fit the crime. If a person commits murder via a gunshot to the head, how long did the murder take? A second, but the punishment is life. This is considered an equal exchange: a life was taken, so a life must be taken in return. If a person takes part in illegal dog fighting and has dogs killed, his jail sentence won't be the same as a person who murdered another human being. Why? The life value of a dog is not as great as that of a human. In the case of God and hell, the crimes are being committed against God, and the crimes occur over the course of an entire life. The laws being broken, of course, are God's laws, and we must be tried by his standards, according to which all of us have fallen short. By his standard, hating someone in your heart is on par with actually murdering. In your heart, you have murdered that person. By rejecting God through hatred and open rebellion against his Word, existence, and provision, you have murdered God. God is eternal. The punishment, likewise, for the crime that occurred constantly over the course of your lifetime warrants an eternal sentence.

Scripture:

Romans 3:9–12—"What shall we conclude then? Are we any better? Not at all! We have already made the charge that Jews and Gentiles alike are all under sin. As it is written: "There is no one righteous, not even one; there is no one who understands, no one who seeks God. All have turned away, they have together become worthless; there is no one who does good, not even one.'"

James 2:10—"For whoever keeps the whole law and yet stumbles at just one point is guilty of breaking all of it."

Back to the Gospel:

Even though none of us are good in God's sight, God is good and gracious. He provided a substitute for us. Imagine if someone you loved was on death row, awaiting execution. You were innocent of those crimes, but the judge allowed you to take the place of your loved one and be put to death in his or her place. Most of us wouldn't make the exchange, but if the judge saw that the substitution still met the requirements of the law, a life for a life, the exchange could occur. God provided the substitute by sending his Son, Jesus Christ, into the world. Philippians 2:6–8 says that Jesus, "being in very nature God, did not consider equality with God something to be grasped, but made himself nothing, taking the very nature of a servant, being made in human likeness. And being found in appearance as a man, he humbled himself and became obedient to death—even death on a cross!" Jesus was innocent and took the place of sinful man, setting us free from the penalty of eternal death. We must remember that the laws we have broken are God's laws and the allowance for substitutionary atonement is built into *his* judicial system. As both the lawgiver and judge, God has from all time instituted a system of law that allows for such an extraordinary provision of both justice and love through the sacrifice of his *own* son, Jesus Christ.

12. Why Would an All-Loving God Send People to Hell?

Validation:

This is a difficult question for us to comprehend. We can't imagine allowing our worst enemies to suffer eternally, much less subjecting them to such inescapable torment. I think that this question and the problem of evil are the two most common rejections of Christianity offered in our day and age. I think they are the root of our other objections.

Answer:

Option 1, Hell is God's Monument to Human Freedom Answer—It's clear in Scripture that God does not desire for anyone to perish forever. Everyone may come to repentance and salvation. Again, God does not desire for any of us to suffer perpetual death! Hell is God giving individuals what they both desire and deserve: eternal separation from him. John 3:19–20 says, "This is the verdict: Light has come into the world, but men loved darkness instead of light because their deeds were evil. Everyone who does evil hates the light, and will not come into the light for fear that his deeds will be exposed." The Light is Jesus Christ, and men love darkness instead of Light. Those who reject Christ do not want to know God and have a relationship with him. In hell, God is giving them the desire of their hearts: to be forever separated from his grace, riches, and provision, forever awake and dying in the darkness of eternity.

Option 2, Who Are We? Answer—Based on our human understanding of love and hate, crime and punishment, we reject the notion that a loving God could possibly punish someone for eternity for matters that we feel are trivial. This is arrogance on our part. As God reminded Job, "Who has a claim against me that I must pay? Everything under heaven belongs to me" (Job 41:11). Have we not stopped to consider that God's ways are not our ways, and that in fact his ways are greater and better than ours? Is it not possible that in this situation, hell is the only possible consequence for sin that a good, loving, and just God can deliver?

Option 3, Share the Gospel Answer—Read "Back to the Gospel" within this question.

Scripture:

2 Peter 3:8–9—"But do not forget this one thing, dear friends: With the Lord a day is like a thousand years, and a thousand years are like a day. The Lord is not slow in keeping his promise, as some understand slowness. He is patient with you, not wanting anyone to perish, but everyone to come to repentance."

1 Timothy 2:1–6—"I urge, then, first of all, that requests, prayers, intercession and thanksgiving be made for everyone—for kings and all those in authority, that we may live peaceful and quiet lives in all godliness and holiness. This is good, and pleases God our Savior, who wants all men to be saved and to come to a knowledge of the truth. For there is one God and one mediator between God and men, the man Christ Jesus, who gave himself as a ransom for all men—the testimony given in its proper time."

Isaiah 55:9—"As the heavens are higher than the earth, so are my ways higher than your ways and my thoughts than your thoughts."

2 Corinthians 5:21—"God made him who had no sin to be sin for us, so that in him we might become the righteousness of God."

Back to the Gospel:

Thinking of the terrors of hell, we rationalize that a *loving* God who chooses to send people there could not exist. However, we have no grounds upon which to make this accusation because God himself has suffered the penalty of hell in the person of Jesus Christ. What greater love is there than for God to give his only, eternally begotten Son to die, who though he was sinless bore our sin and took the penalty of our guilt upon himself? We can't claim that God is not a loving God for sentencing people to hell, when God allowed his own innocent Son to suffer hell so we don't have to. God didn't have to send his Son to die for us, but he did so out of love for the world.

13. What about Those Born into Other Religions? Isn't God Playing Favorites?

Validation:

I know what you're thinking. You're thinking that I'm a Christian, because I grew up in a Christian family and in a Christian culture. If I grew up in Turkey, I'd likely be a Muslim, or if I grew up in India, I'd probably be a Hindu. I agree with you; it's not always the case, but more often than not we are a product of our environment. The apple doesn't fall far from the tree as the saying goes. It seems as if God is playing favorites, since some people are born into lives that appear to be more receptive to having a relationship with him.

Socratic Method:

How is it playing favorites, if Jesus died to take away the sins of all people?

Is it really playing favorites if we are all sinful and deserving of condemnation? For God to remain just and not overlook lawlessness, he had to send his one and only Son, Jesus Christ, to die as a substitutionary sacrifice. Does God have to go through such pain and suffering, considering we are all guilty of sin? Shouldn't we be fortunate that he has paved a way for us to have salvation?

Where do you stand in the so-called "favorites" ranking? Have you heard the good news of salvation through Jesus Christ?

Answer:

The Bible is very clear that God does not show favoritism. He is the savior of all men. Jesus' last words to his disciples before ascending to heaven were commands that they should make disciples of all nations (Matthew 28:18–20). He even promised that it would happen and that the disciples would receive power through the Holy Spirit to accomplish that feat (Acts 1:7–8). It is clear in Scripture that people from all races, nations, and tongues will have salvation and be with God in heaven. This is already evident if you look on a map that marks the spread of religions. Christianity is the only religion that has spread across the globe, breaking through all sorts of barriers of language, culture, ethnicity, and nationality. Jesus even promised that the end would not come until the gospel has been preached to all nations (Matthew 24:14). It is clear that Jesus does not show favorites due to place of birth.

Scripture:

Galatians 3:26–29—"You are all sons of God through faith in Christ Jesus, for all of you who were baptized into Christ have clothed yourselves with Christ. There is neither Jew nor Greek, slave nor free, male nor female, for you are all one in Christ Jesus. If you belong to Christ, then you are Abraham's seed, and heirs according to the promise."

Revelation 7:9—"After this I looked and there before me was a great multitude that no one could count, from every nation, tribe, people and language, standing before the throne and in front of the Lamb."

Acts 10:34—"Then Peter began to speak: 'I now realize how true it is that God does not show favoritism but accepts men from every nation who fear him and do what is right.'"

14. What Is the Fate of Those Who Never Hear about Jesus?

Validation:

I think this is one of the first questions I had about what is revealed in the Bible. Questions can run deep on this issue. For example, the ancient Chinese or Native Americans or African tribesmen never had a chance to hear about Jesus, so how can they be placed on the same scale with someone who rejected Jesus purposefully? Also, what about other cultures that existed during the time of the Israelites? They weren't God's *chosen* people? I believe that the Bible has an answer to these questions, but the answers might never fully satisfy us.

Socratic Method:

Have you heard the gospel? So this question doesn't apply to your eternal future, does it?

Is it possible for God to inadvertently and even directly reveal himself to mankind, apart from mankind? If so, how could he do that, and do you think he has?

Answer:

Option 1, God Has Revealed Himself to Everyone Answer—God has revealed himself to everyone, even those who have not heard the gospel message. God has revealed himself in two different ways: general revelation and special revelation. General revelation is what God has revealed about himself from what he has created. Romans 1:18–20 says, "The wrath of God is being revealed from heaven against all the godlessness and wickedness of men who suppress the truth by their wickedness, since what may be known about God is plain to them, because God has made it plain to them. For since the creation of the world God's invisible qualities—his eternal power and divine nature—have been clearly seen, being understood from what has been made, so that men are without excuse." If such people have suppressed the truth of what God has already revealed to them, what would ensure that they wouldn't do the same with the gospel? Ultimately, God's general revelation places everyone in a state of guilt. Everyone is left without excuse.

General revelation itself is not enough for salvation. Special revelation is God's direct communication of himself to mankind through his Word and through the person of Jesus Christ. Faith in Christ is explicitly required for salvation. Faith receives the benefits of grace. Scripture teaches that "it is by grace you have been saved, through faith—and this not from yourselves, it is the gift of God—not by works, so that no one can boast" (Ephesians 2:8–9). Jesus directly speaks this truth to Nicodemus in John 3:16, stating, "For God so loved the world that he gave his one and only Son, that whoever believes in him shall not perish but have eternal life." A person can only believe the good news of Christ's life, death, and resurrection, if he or she has heard the good news (Romans 10:12–15).

Option 2, We Deserve Damnation Answer—These questions seem to imply that the people who have not heard the gospel are going to perish and suffer hell, not because of their fault, but because of God's fault or the fault of the church for not sharing the gospel with them. This is totally and utterly not true. Those who have not heard the gospel are sinners. They still deserve eternal punishment for their sins, and general revelation leaves them without excuse. Sin is the cause of death. God did not create sin. He created the world, and it was good. God did not tempt Adam and Eve, and he has no blame for sin or its effects. Since he is a just God, he must punish sin.

Option 3, Check the Numbers Answer—The numbers tell us that there are more people living now than ever before. There are more Christians in this world than ever before too. We can travel to far-off lands and, because of the Internet, communicate with more people all over the globe without even leaving our houses. This means that in this period of time, more Christians can reach more people than ever before in history. This means it is time for Christians to quit asking why and what if about the unevangelized from the past, present, or future, and simply get to work sharing the gospel.

Option 4, God Can Reveal Himself to Anyone Answer—God is not limited to saving only people who have heard the gospel through a proclamation of the message of Jesus Christ via a human agent. God can and has stepped in to reveal himself directly to people through vehicles other than men. God can communicate the gospel directly to people through dreams, visions, angels, and even through burning bushes and talking animals. We have no guarantee that everyone *will* hear the gospel at least once during their lives, but we do know that it's possible for people to receive knowledge directly from God apart from a human intercessory, if God chooses to reveal himself in this way.

Option 5, We Must Trust God Answer—I know that these answers aren't satisfying, but in this case the unsatisfying answer must be trusted. When we look to the person of Jesus Christ, we see that he was a righteous man who upheld his own moral teachings. He established his divinity through his public miracles and especially his resurrection from the dead. In light of Jesus' demonstrated love for humanity and his power to overcome death, we must come to trust God in areas of his revelation that are unsettling to us. We might question the nature of God's judgments, but Jesus gives us the assurance that God is just.

Scripture:

God speaks through a dream—Matthew 2:1–23; Genesis 37:5–7.

God speaks through a vision—Daniel 2:19; Acts 10:9–17; Acts 9:10–14; Acts 16:6–10.

God speaks through an angel—Daniel 10–12; Luke 1:26–38; Judges 13.

God speaks through a burning bush—Exodus 3:1–4.

God speaks through an animal—Numbers 22:21–41.

Jesus directly reveals himself to Paul—Acts 9:1–9.

Back to the Gospel:

Because God is not at fault in our sin, he didn't need to give anyone a second chance. If God chose to damn everyone, he would still be holy and just. We must remember that God suffered dearly in the process of bringing about salvation for mankind. He sent his one and only Son, Jesus Christ, into the world to die as a ransom for the sins of all of mankind. When we see the price that God himself had to pay for there to be salvation for any of us, our response should be one of repentance, praise, and thanksgiving, not ridicule and disdain.

15. All Religions are Fallible Because They Come from Men

Validation:

This objection recognizes that all men are fallible. I doubt any of us can be 100 percent trustworthy in all of our words and deeds. I think you are correct in being skeptical about placing your full reliance in any religion that has its genesis in the work of men to see you through this life's pain, suffering, guilt, and eventual death.

Socratic Method:

Do you think it's possible for any religion to have been directly received from God or initiated through the direct guidance of God? How would you be able to ascertain if God has or hasn't directly revealed himself through men?

Christianity teaches that Jesus was not a mere man, but God in the flesh. If this is true, wouldn't that mean that Christianity originates from God? Who do you think Jesus was?

Answer:

We have to be careful to separate the message from the messenger. You are dismissing all religious claims due to mankind's propensity to fall into error, misconception, and misunderstanding, and even worse, our tendency to generate intentional deception for selfish gain. Just because everyone has an inclination toward these pitfalls, we shouldn't dismiss all religious truth-claims without first observing what the evidence indicates. Otherwise, we'd have to apply the same level of skepticism to all other truth-claims, not just religious ones. We must follow where the evidence leads us, and there is a lot of good historical evidence to support the message of the Bible concerning Jesus. One such piece of evidence is related to your objection of the errant character of humanity. That is, the Bible makes no effort to mask the shortcomings of Jesus' disciples. For instance, it shows Peter denying Jesus three times (Matthew 26:69–75). It also shows how Paul had to rebuke Peter for being a hypocrite—acting one way among the Gentiles, but differently when Jews were present (Galatians 2:11–21). If the New Testament documents were fabricated stories about Jesus and his work, the leaders would have painted themselves in better light. The fact that the New Testament authors intertwined their own sins into the narrative of their witness brings about a ring of truth.

Back to the Gospel:

You are right in thinking that mankind is not perfect. The way we come up short by God's standard of perfection is called "sin" in the Bible. Sin separates us from God and brings death to all men. To remedy this sin, God set in motion a plan of salvation that required his Son, Jesus, who is fully God, to assume a human nature and step into human history. The Old Testament documents follow the lineage of Jesus' human ancestry, illustrating God's preparation of mankind to understand and receive the crucifixion of his Son at the hands of Roman officials as an atoning sacrifice for the sins of the world. The life, death, and resurrection of Jesus are historically recorded for us inside the Bible and outside of the Bible, and verify that he is both God and Savior of us all. Jesus affirmed the Old Testament Scripture to be true and that they testified about him (Luke 24:27, 44 and John 5:39). He also put his seal of approval on the words that his disciples were to write, which are now referred to as the New Testament Scripture (John 14:26). We can trust that though men wrote the documents of the Bible, their origins and authority lie not in their human authors but in the power and witness of God who led the men to write.

Scripture:

2 Peter 1:16–21—"We did not follow cleverly invented stories when we told you about the power and coming of our Lord Jesus Christ, but we were eyewitnesses of his majesty. For he received honor and glory from God the Father when the voice came to him from the Majestic Glory, saying, 'This is my Son, whom I love; with him I am well pleased.' We ourselves heard this voice that came from heaven when we were with him on the sacred mountain. And we have the word of the prophets made more certain, and you will do well to pay attention to it, as to a light shining in a dark place, until the day dawns and the morning star rises in your hearts. Above all, you must understand that no prophecy of Scripture came about by the prophet's own interpretation. For prophecy never had its origin in the will of man, but men spoke from God as they were carried along by the Holy Spirit."

16. Religions Cause Evil

Validation:

The Crusades and the Inquisition are two accounts of evil and bloodshed often cited as a means to discredit religion. Islamic terrorists' attacks come to mind as well as Catholic versus Protestant fighting in Ireland. Religions or religious connections have also been used to spur racism, such as with the Klu Klux Klan; the oppression of females; and extreme hatred of others, as with the Westboro Baptist Church. It's also no longer a surprise to hear of pastors stealing money from their churches or being caught in affairs, or for Roman Catholic priests to be accused of child molestation. Eastern religions don't fare much better, with Hinduism creating a large population in India known as the untouchables, who are treated as not human, and lower than some animals. I can see where you can come to this conclusion, but I don't believe it is completely accurate.

Socratic Method:

How do you account for what is evil and what is good? Are there absolute morals across the board for all of humanity?

Do religions also lead people to do good acts? Do the good acts produced by religious adherents outweigh the evil acts?

Do the nonreligious members of society also cause evil? Have there been atheistic leaders who have led nations into wars for reasons stemming from their worldviews?

When evil has been done in the name of a religion, have such acts violated the code of ethics prescribed in the sacred texts of that religion, as interpreted by conservative and orthodox branches of that religion? Have others within that religion cried foul when such acts were performed?

Answer:

Option 1, God Is the Objective Standard for Good Answer—To even entertain this objection to religion, there must be a God! You must enter into the realm of theology to even initiate conversations about what is good or evil in *absolute* terms. (Refer to option 2 under question 4.)

Option 2, Violation of Religious Laws Answer—Most of the cases of religious adherents causing evil in the name of their religions can be shown to be violations of the explicit commands of those religions. If Christianity is being used to justify and advocate for oppression, suppression, deceit, theft, brutality, hatred, or racial discrimination, the legitimate teachings and example of Jesus of Nazareth are being violated. LaVeyan Satanism teaches that one can do anything he pleases as long as he doesn't harm someone else who doesn't deserve it or desire it, and there are detailed guidelines for when someone deserves to be harmed. Even Satanism as an organized religion has rules to curb evil!

Option 3, Atheists Cause More Evil Answer—Don't simply nail religions for the cause of evil. Here's a short list of atheist leaders you might have heard of who have killed millions upon millions of more innocent people than the church ever did during the Crusades or Inquisitions of centuries ago: Adolf Hitler, Joseph Stalin, Mao Zedong, Kim Jong-Il, and Pol Pot. This shows that atheists and religious adherents are all prone to and capable of evil. None of us are innocent. If anything, religions have been shown to curb evil and promote benevolence. For instance, Islam can be praised for stopping the practice of female infanticide that was rampant in the Saudi Arabian peninsula at the time of its inception. Islam gave more rights to women than they had previously had in that region.[3]

Scripture:

Matthew 5:43–47—"You have heard that it was said, 'Love your neighbor and hate your enemy.' But I tell you: Love your enemies and pray for those who persecute you, that you may be sons of your Father in heaven. He causes his sun to rise on the evil and the good, and sends rain on the righteous and the unrighteous. If you love those who love you, what reward will you get? Are not even the tax collectors doing that? And if you greet only your brothers, what are you doing more than others? Do not even pagans do that? Be perfect, therefore, as your heavenly Father is perfect."

Romans 5:8–11—"But God demonstrates his own love for us in this: While we were still sinners, Christ died for us. Since we have now been justified by his blood, how much more shall we be saved from God's wrath through him! For if, when we were God's enemies, we were reconciled to him through the death of his Son, how much more, having been reconciled, shall we be saved through his life! Not only is this so, but we also rejoice in God through our Lord Jesus Christ, through whom we have now received reconciliation."

Back to the Gospel:

Christ taught that we should love our enemies and pray for those who persecute us. When Christians have twisted God's Word to justify acts that go against orthodox reading of his commands, we are blatantly sinning. Sinning is disobeying God's Law; sin is lawlessness (1 John 3:4). God demonstrates this perfect love that we have not kept or shown toward others by offering his Son, Jesus Christ, as a sacrifice to reconcile us to himself, to bring us from being his enemies into his family as dearly loved children.

17. Why Does God Allow Evil?

Validation:

Scripture teaches that God is omnipotent, omniscient, and omnibenevolent. The occurrence of evil acts seems to not fit with a God who is all-powerful, all-knowing, and perfectly good! I understand what you are thinking. It appears that if God is good and all-powerful, he'd desire to stop evil—and he would! Therefore, he's either not good, or he's not capable of doing anything he pleases. The other option would be that he is all-powerful and good, but he's just not omniscient; he can't know everything that will happen in the future, so he can't stop all evil before it occurs.

Socratic Method:

Do you think an omnibenevolent God would settle for anything less than the absolute greatest scenario of good? Is it possible that God would allow evil for a time if it could produce a greater good?

Are there degrees of goodness? Is it feasible for there to be a good state of existence for God's creation and yet another achievable state of existence for us that is even better? Would an omnibenevolent God desire the greatest possible state of goodness for his creation? What if allowing evil for a time is necessary for such an environment to exist for eternity?

How does your worldview address the problem of evil? What are its origins? How can you even define what is good or evil objectively?

In the Christian worldview, God does punish evil, now and after death. What sense of justice does your worldview provide when humans commit heinous crimes for their entire lives and die without having suffered any penalty in this life?

Answer:

Option 1, the Problem of Good Answer—The question you are asking is usually referred to as the problem of evil, but that is if the objection is lobbied from your point of view to mine. Christians do struggle with this question, and we should be open to acknowledging the difficulty that this problem raises and do our best to answer it. If the Christian faith is true, our worldview should be able to account for the problem. If you are an atheist, your worldview has a different struggle: your worldview must account for the origin of good. How do you come to a conclusion about what is evil in comparison to what is good? Do you have an objective standard by which to make such a judgment? From the Christian worldview, we have such a standard: the moral character of God and his Law revealed to us by him in the Bible. If we are all the product of millions of years of random chance, there are no grounds upon which to form any determination of good or evil. We're still in the process of evolution. Since the material is all that exists, and after death we are no longer conscious, survival of the fittest is fully in play. The Darwinian/atheistic model of the universe is left with the problem of defining what is good and explaining why any of us should care.

Option 2, He'd Have to Terminate You Answer—You want God to eliminate evil? Then he'd have to eliminate you. I'm sure you have lied, cheated, stolen, hated, and hurt others emotionally and even physically, with no sign of ever being able to fully stop. I am sure that you don't love others as yourself, that you put your needs above others, and that you selfishly seek gain for yourself and those who are close to you rather than for the common good of all of mankind. If God restricted every thought, word, or action of yours that wasn't good, you would no longer exist consciously. If he were to just stop all evil while preserving our free will, he'd have to wipe all of humanity off the face of the earth. The root of the problem of evil lies within our nature as sinful people and pours out externally into the world, wreaking havoc on others and ourselves.

Option 3, Free Will Answer—When God created Adam and Eve, they were good, without any hint of evil within them. But they had the capacity to commit evil, to go against God's good and perfect will. Essentially, God created them as morally responsible beings with the ability to choose between good and evil and to act upon such decisions. They chose to go against God and fell into sin. Thus, they introduced all sorts of evil human actions into the world. All of their offspring have inherited a sinful nature. We all still have the ability to choose between being obedient to God's good will or breaking it and being lawless sinners, because his law has been written upon our hearts. But since we are born with a sinful nature, we are bound to commit evil, and we all do. God could stop us all. But if he did stop us, our decisions would have to be restricted to doing good acts. If our words and thoughts were restricted, how would we be any different from Mario, Sonic, Mega Man, Link, or any game character we control by mashing buttons? Would we even have conscious knowledge of our own existence in such a state? Mario doesn't know he's saving the princess.

Option 4, Love Answer—If God restricted our free will, thus eliminating our ability to do evil, he'd also be destroying love. Love has many definitions and types within the English language. Love can just be a feeling, but what about when the feeling wears off or the "love runs cold"? You have to make the decision to continue being affectionate, caring, and sacrificial toward the people you love. What if your spouse or kids don't reciprocate the love you have for them? If you love them, you have to decide to continue to love them despite their shortcomings. For a loving relationship to exist, both parties must decide to love one another. God desires to have such a relationship with us, but if he forced us to love him by removing our free will to commit evil, he'd also do away with our ability to love him. Allowing evil for a time is a consequence of God allowing love to persist.

Option 5, Greater Good Answer—You are correct that if God is all-powerful, he can stop evil; that if he is all-knowing, he knows in advance how and when evil will occur; that if he is all-good and all-loving, he would want to stop evil. However, you take these conclusions to mean that God would stop evil immediately or never allow it to happen in the first place. It is also true that if God seeks ultimate good, the best scenario for his creation, he could allow evil for a time if it meant a state of greater goodness could occur. This might seem unfathomable to us, but when we consider the previous answers concerning free will, we can begin to understand how this scenario is possible. When we read the Bible, we learn that this is God's actual plan.

God allowed Adam and Eve to sin, and thus lawlessness, death, and evil entered into the human experience along with separation from God. He wouldn't have allowed this unless he had a plan to save us. Through the work of Jesus Christ, God has made a way for us to have a restored relationship with him for eternity. At the end of this age, Christ will return, and all the dead will be raised. At this point, those who had faith in Christ will have new bodies, bodies without a sinful nature. Scripture also indicates that all of creation will be restored to the perfect state that existed in the garden of Eden. We'll have free will and get to see God face-to-face in heaven. We won't need to worry about falling into sin again, because we've been down that road before; we know where it leads. It's like touching a hot stove—you don't do it twice! Thus God's allowance of evil for a period of time will lead to a greater good for those who love him, a state in which we can maintain our freedom and our ability to choose to love and to be loved forever. We'll be in a relationship with our Creator that is not forced or coerced.

Option 6, You Got to Have a Little Patience Answer—We're not patient people. We live in a culture of instant gratification. We also live in a culture that seeks to reduce pain and difficulty, full of individual entitlement. Therefore we expect God to meet all of our needs and expectations. Wipe out evil, Lord; come on, get with it already! In our finite nature, we feel God is dragging his feet. However, God is outside of time. He's eternal. He's not slow, that's for certain. Instead of being slow as we see it, he is actually being patient. He doesn't want any of us to suffer and perish, so he is waiting to usher in the end of this world, waiting for more people to come to the knowledge of salvation that is found in Jesus Christ our Lord. When the day of the Lord arrives, it will happen in an instant. If that instant were to happen today, if Christ were to return now, everyone who is not found to be in him would be condemned forever. God doesn't want that (1 Peter 3:8–13). The end will come when the last person to be saved is saved. Jesus says that this end will come when the good news has gone out to all nations, and Peter writes that we can speed Christ's return

(Matthew 24:14). We speed his return by sharing the gospel message to the ends of the world. At that point, there will be an end to all sin, death, and sorrow for those who are found to be in Christ.

Scripture:

James 1:13–15—"When tempted, no one should say, 'God is tempting me.' For God cannot be tempted by evil, nor does he tempt anyone; but each one is tempted when, by his own evil desire, he is dragged away and enticed. Then, after desire has conceived, it gives birth to sin; and sin, when it is full-grown, gives birth to death."

Isaiah 65:17–25—"'Behold, I will create new heavens and a new earth. The former things will not be remembered, nor will they come to mind. But be glad and rejoice forever in what I will create, for I will create Jerusalem to be a delight and its people a joy. I will rejoice over Jerusalem and take delight in my people the sound of weeping and of crying will be heard in it no more."

Matthew 24:12–14—"Because of the increase of wickedness, the love of most will grow cold, but he who stands firm to the end will be saved. And this gospel of the kingdom will be preached in the whole world as a testimony to all nations, and then the end will come."

2 Peter 3:9–13—"But do not forget this one thing, dear friends: With the Lord a day is like a thousand years, and a thousand years are like a day. The Lord is not slow in keeping his promise, as some understand slowness. He is patient with you, not wanting anyone to perish, but everyone to come to repentance. But the day of the Lord will come like a thief. The heavens will disappear with a roar; the elements will be destroyed by fire, and the earth and everything in it will be laid bare. Since everything will be destroyed in this way, what kind of people ought you to be? You ought to live holy and godly lives as you look forward to the day of God and speed its coming. That day will bring about the destruction of the heavens by fire, and the elements will melt in the heat. But in keeping with his promise we are looking forward to a new heaven and a new earth, the home of righteousness."

Back to the Gospel:

The greatest act of evil that ever occurred in history has to be when Jesus, God in the flesh, innocent of any wrongdoing, was viciously beaten, whipped, and crucified at the hands of his sinful creation. Can anything more evil possibly happen than man killing God? But what we see from the greatest act of evil is that the greatest good was produced: the forgiveness of all of our sins, the salvation of mankind. With God, good eventually triumphs over evil. He makes beautiful things rise up out of the ashes. Just as Christ was raised from the dead, so too shall we be raised from the dead. Those who have faith in him will rise to eternal life; those who do not will have an eternity of perpetual perishing.

18. Why Does God Allow Suffering?

Validation:

This question is even more perplexing than the questions we have about why God allows evil. Suffering that is the result of birth defects, physical and mental handicaps, disease, old age, mistakes, accidents, and natural disasters can't be easily explained away. If God is really a loving Father, why wouldn't he stop such suffering within his creation? I'm not sure if any answer will ever fully satisfy us.

Socratic Method:

Can you think of any good reasons God would allow suffering?

Have you ever learned from your sufferings or become a better person because of them?

Were there times where your parents allowed you to suffer or struggle so that you could learn to do things on your own and to grow in maturity? Were they right to allow such suffering and trials? Where would you be right now if they always intervened to ensure you never had to struggle?

Is God the cause of all our suffering, or does much of our suffering come as the result of our personal decisions and the decisions of others? If God were to eliminate all suffering, would he have to also eliminate our free will?

Answer:

Option 1, You Live You Learn Answer—Alanis Morrisette, in her immensely popular debut album *Jagged Little Pill*, sang the song, "You Live, You Learn." In that song she encouraged her listeners to take risks, to not be afraid of being uncomfortable or having our hearts trampled upon, because troubles are a part of life, and we'll learn and grow from everything life has to offer, even our pain and suffering. I always heard from coaches in high school, "No pain, no gain." It seems that we commonly accept that from our pain and suffering, we can grow, learn, and become better equipped for future endeavors in life. The Bible affirms this principle, teaching that through suffering we grow in moral qualities, as well as hope and joy. I must admit, though, that this answer only seems satisfactory with mild forms of suffering. It becomes difficult to accept in extreme cases such as rape, cancer, the loss of a loved one, or natural disasters.

Option 2, God's Calling Answer—The late Cambridge professor C. S. Lewis is often quoted as saying, "God whispers to us in our pleasures, speaks in our conscience, but shouts in our pain: it is His megaphone to rouse a deaf world."[4] I don't necessarily agree with the distinction of volume, but I definitely agree with the progression of our attention to these methods of God's speaking to us. We are more likely to turn to God in earnest in times of trouble instead of in times of peace. Our sudden, intense acknowledgement of God when tragedy strikes shows the condition of our sinful hearts. Every good and perfect gift comes from God (James 1:17), but we don't often recognize this or give him thanks for what he has given us. We rebel against our consciousness that spurs us toward the better way, the right way, God's way. But when the crap hits the fan and our lives are spinning out of our control, we suddenly consider God, either to blame or for aid. We turn to him only when we desperately require his services, failing to realize that our very existence and preservation comes from him in the first place. If it weren't for suffering, would we even consider God and his calling, his invitation to have a relationship with him?

Option 3, Scripture Promises Suffering Answer—It's a misconception to think that just because God loves us, we will not suffer any pain or anguish. Many Christian preachers and evangelists give the false impression that the Christian life should always be peaches and roses, that if we are faithful to God we will prosper. Make no mistake: we will prosper, but not necessarily in the way the world gauges prosperity. We will be blessed in Christ, but that doesn't mean we won't suffer. Instead, Scripture promises that we will suffer, despite being faithful to Jesus. (Read the Scripture verses below to see a selection of passages that speak of the certainty of suffering and how such affliction fits into God's plan for us.)

Scripture:

Romans 5:1–5—"Therefore, since we have been justified through faith, we have peace with God through our Lord Jesus Christ, through whom we have gained access by faith into this grace in which we now stand. And we rejoice in the hope of the glory of God. Not only so, but we also rejoice in our sufferings, because we know that suffering produces perseverance; perseverance, character; and character, hope. And hope does not disappoint us, because God has poured out his love into our hearts by the Holy Spirit, whom he has given us."

1 Peter 4:12–19—"Dear friends, do not be surprised at the painful trial you are suffering, as though something strange were happening to you. But rejoice that you participate in the sufferings of Christ, so that you may be overjoyed when his glory is revealed. If you are insulted because of the name of Christ, you are blessed, for the Spirit of glory and of God rests on you. If you suffer, it should not be as a murderer or thief or any other kind of criminal, or even as a meddler. However, if you suffer as a Christian, do not be ashamed, but praise God that you bear that name. For it is time for judgment to begin with the family of God; and if it begins with us, what will the outcome be for those who do not obey the gospel of God? And, 'If it is hard for the righteous to be saved, what will become of the ungodly and the sinner?' So then, those who suffer according to God's will should commit themselves to their faithful Creator and continue to do good."

Hebrews 2:18—"Because he himself suffered when he was tempted, he is able to help those who are being tempted."

Hebrews 12:2–11—"Let us fix our eyes on Jesus, the author and perfecter of our faith, who for the joy set before him endured the cross, scorning its shame, and sat down at the right hand of the throne of God. Consider him who endured such opposition from sinful men, so that you will not grow weary and lose heart. In your struggle against sin, you have not yet resisted to the point of shedding your blood. And you have forgotten that word of encouragement that addresses you as sons: 'My son, do not make light of the Lord's discipline, and do not lose heart when he rebukes you, because the Lord disciplines those he loves, and he punishes everyone he accepts as a son.' Endure hardship as discipline; God is treating you as sons. For what son is not disciplined by his father? If you are not disciplined (and everyone undergoes discipline), then you are illegitimate children and not true sons. Moreover, we have all had human fathers who disciplined us and we respected them for it. How much more should we submit to the Father of our spirits and live! Our fathers disciplined us for a little while as they thought best; but God disciplines us for our good, that we may share in his holiness. No discipline seems pleasant at the time, but painful. Later on, however, it produces a harvest of righteousness and peace for those who have been trained by it. Therefore, strengthen your feeble arms and weak knees."

Romans 8:28—"And we know that in all things God works for the good of those who love him, who have been called according to his purpose."

Back to the Gospel:

When it comes to blaming God for our suffering ... there isn't a place for it when we consider that Jesus Christ suffered for us. In 1 Peter 3:18, the apostle says, "For Christ died for sins once for all, the righteous for the unrighteous, to bring you to God. He was put to death in the body but made alive by the Spirit." This quote comes from the New International

Version of the Bible, but some translations say that Christ "suffered for sins." He was innocent, and he didn't have to do that for us, but he did so out of love—the love he has for us.

19. What about Science and Darwinian Evolution?

Validation:

I know that the scientific enterprise has greatly blessed us with knowledge that has improved our lives in so many aspects that to enumerate all the ways would be a lifelong endeavor. I know that the Darwinian model of evolution is often presented as possessing a plethora of irrefutable proof. Since the existence of God doesn't gel with the naturalistic worldview that typically accompanies Darwin's theory, it likely appears to you as Christians are living on blind faith, ignoring the evidence, and derailing the advancement of scientific discovery.

Answer:

Option 1, Science and Christianity Are Not at Odds Answer—In the Jack Black movie *Nacho Libre*, there is a scene in which his wrestling monk character wants to pray with his partner before a tag-team match and his partner refuses, on the grounds that he "believes in science." I think this is a common sentiment: that if a person believes in God, he or she must then discard science, and vice versa. This simply is not the case! Early founding fathers of European science, such as Johannes Kepler, Galileo Galilei, Blaise Pascal, and Isaac Newton were Christians. Their study of the Bible and their faith in its teachings of the world and God propelled their research and ideas. Since Darwin, there have been many Christian scientists who have offered much in scientific theory, philosophy, and discovery, such as Charles Townes, who invented lasers and won the Nobel Prize in physics in 1964. A simple search online will reveal large lists of reputable, accomplished scientists who hold position in academia. Science and Christianity are only at odds when certain scientists claim that God has no place in science whatsoever.

Option 2, Science Depends on God Answer—It might appear as though God and science clash, and that Christianity and science are irreconcilable due to theories of Darwinism, but in fact, science depends on God to even function. For instance, the Christian worldview maintains that God created the world to be good and orderly and that he preserves his creation in such a way that there is uniformity and consistency across the entire universe. These beliefs are essential to the scientific enterprise that depends on the ability to repeat tests in the exact same manner again and again. This can only happen if we can trust that the laws of nature are the same today as they were yesterday, and that they'll be the same tomorrow and forever—not just where we are when we are conducting the tests, but anywhere in the universe. An atheistic worldview doesn't provide the basis for believing there are consistent, unchanging laws of nature.

Option 3, Naturalism Provides No Basis for Science Answer—If there is no God and nothing supernatural resides in the universe, then all that exists would have to be natural, purely physical material. This naturalistic model of the world reduces all things to constantly progressing, shifting, evolving matter. There is no purpose or design behind the universe or our lives, and any indication toward another conclusion is solely coincidental. Such a worldview cannot provide any basis for the uniform laws of nature that are necessary for the scientific method of repeatable testability. If our sensory organs are the product of chance, can their relayed observations and data be trusted? Such a worldview provides no reason to explore and pursue a deeper understanding of the world. We already know that the cosmos is purposeless and in constant flux. We're here today and gone tomorrow. What is now will no longer be. We might as well eat, drink, and be merry, enjoy our material possessions and freedom, and drink deep of the well of hedonism for as long as we have the means to do so. Naturalism must borrow from Christian theology to obtain the required presuppositions necessary to practice science.

Option 4, Show Me Answer—Darwin's theory, although labeled "the origin of species," is used to provide a model for the origin of life and even the origin of the universe. Such hypothetical models can never be proven via science, since none of them can be submitted to the necessary modes of testing required under the scientific method to verify a hypothesis. We have to admit that we can observe evolution today. People are gradually getting taller and stronger. Just look at the rise of concussions in American football! I can see that people who have ancestry closer to the equator are darker skinned, and that people with ancestry from Asia have dark hair and dark eyes. Such visible signs today support the notion of evolution within the human race, but there is no evidence that we are evolving into something more than human, such as Marvel's *X-Men* or the mutants with telekinetic abilities in the Bruce Willis movie *Looper*. As of yet, such degrees of evolution, one species changing into a new, different species, isn't observable except in the realm of science fiction.

Other problems also emerge with the model of Darwinian evolution and science. Has it ever once been observed that life can come from nonlife? Has it ever been observed that a random pile of scrap material can explode and form a city of skyscrapers, with an infrastructure of roads and utilities, complete with humans, pets, birds, and insects to populate it, and function? Can the Big Bang produce the world we see now? Has it ever been observed that something can come from nothing? Can the primordial soup that exploded in the Big Bang have popped into existence from nothing? If you can show me any observable evidence to fit any of these questions, then there might be some credibility to your worldview. Since there is none, I want you to consider the Christian worldview as it fits with what we have observed to be possible: the universe was created by a Creator, not nothing; life came from the highest form of life, God, not nonlife; universal order, design, and laws of nature came from a divine Orderer, not mindless chaos.

Option 5, Game On Answer—If you are correct—there is no God; everything is the product of purposeless, mindless, random chance; there is no objective basis for morality; when I die, I'm good and gone; survival of the fittest is truly what makes the world go round—then game on! I'll take whatever I want and do whatever I want, and the only way to stop me will be to kill me, at which point I will no longer exist to know my past or to have a cognitive future. I'll be worm food, nothing else, nothing more. However, I've believed in God and I've worshipped him since my earliest memories, and I like to think that he saved me at such a young age because he knew what I would do if I had a worldview like yours. You ought to be very thankful that I have a relationship with Jesus. If I truly believed what you *confess* to believe concerning Darwinian evolution, I'd be the world's worst nightmare.

Back to the Gospel:

The Darwinian worldview provides no purpose for life besides survival, and it offers no hope after death besides escape from pain and suffering, at the cost of annihilation. The Bible shows that God created humanity in his image, which sets us apart from the animal kingdom. It's the reason Scripture provides for why we are not to harm, curse, or murder our fellow humans. Being made in his image, we had eternal life, perfection, and the intellectual abilities for moral decision making, discovery, and creativity that the rest of creation lacked. We also had capability for intimate relationship with God that the animal kingdom was lacking.

When Adam and Eve sinned in the Garden of Eden, the image of God was tarnished; we became sinful, subject to death, and cut off from God. We retained aspects of the image of God, however, which is evident through our creation and use of the scientific enterprise. It is through Jesus that a way back to God has been established, and in him that the image of God is being restored within us. The word *repent* comes from a Greek word that actually means "to change one's mind." Repent—turn from your evil ways, and turn to Jesus for the cleansing of your sins and the renewal of your mind.

20. I Don't Think People Should Force Their Beliefs on Others

Validation:

I agree with you, especially when it comes to Christianity. The Christian faith shouldn't be forced upon someone. Jesus taught that we should make disciples through sharing his teachings, not at gunpoint with an ultimatum to convert or die. The example of Jesus and the early church is that the spreading of the gospel needs to be done through service to the community, coupled with dialogue, storytelling, Scripture proclamations, and reasoned arguments communicated in love. Submission holds with tap-out conversions aren't part of God's plan of proselytizing, and if you have experienced Christians sharing God's Word in an unloving manner, I apologize.

Socratic Method:

Is there a difference between sharing and forcing your beliefs upon others? How would you classify what I am doing right now with a table set up in a Freedom of Speech Zone, handing out free coffee, creating the atmosphere for religious dialogue like we are having? Would you consider what I am doing to be forceful?

Do you support the First Amendment rights provided to all citizens of the United States of America?

Can you think of any examples where it could be right to force your beliefs on others even if they don't want any part of what you confess to be true? Would it be okay if you were convinced that sharing your beliefs was a matter of life and death, the type of truth that could save someone's life or make society as a whole better?

What if your belief system involved a command to share your beliefs with others? Would you disobey the conviction to share what you believe to be true?

Answer:

I am simply sharing my beliefs with anyone who wants to listen to them and engage in dialogue with me. I offer coffee and a chair to create a relaxed, enjoyable environment for religious conversation on this public campus. If you don't want to stay and discuss the person and work of Jesus Christ with me, and how he stands out among the other religious founders by being the only one to die for the sins of the world and rise from the grave, then I don't want to force you to listen. I wish you a good night.

Scripture:

Ezekiel 33:7–9—"Son of man, I have made you a watchman for the people of Israel; so hear the word I speak and give them warning from me. When I say to the wicked, 'You wicked person, you will surely die,' and you do not speak out to dissuade them from their ways, that wicked person will die for their sin, and I will hold you accountable for their blood. But if you do warn the wicked person to turn from their ways and they do not do so, they will die for their sin, though you yourself will be saved."

Back to the Gospel:

The reason I am out here sharing my Christian faith is because I am convinced that Jesus is God and that he died to take away the sins of the world. I'm sure that you have heard this message before, living in America. I have strong convictions that the gospel is true, so much so that I come out here once a week to spend my evening sharing the gospel of Jesus Christ. I hope you understand that because I believe the life, death, and resurrection of Jesus is good news for the entire world, I must tell people. If I were to keep silent and not share what I believe to be the best news anyone could ever receive, that would mean I really hate you. If you have any questions about the Christian faith or why I believe it to be true, it'd be my pleasure to answer them to the best of my ability.

Joining the Contradict Movement

THEY CAN'T ALL BE TRUE–JOHN 14:6
WWW.CONTRADICTMOVEMENT.ORG

Why Is Contradict a Movement?

When I decided to begin sharing Contradict with a broader audience than tabletop evangelism, I chose to start a Web site with the name *Contradict Movement*. Calling trends, fads, and new tendencies "movements" seems to be a popular development of its own lately. I think that what I'd like to see happen is for Contradict to spread, classifying as a movement in the traditional sense of organizing and rallying the troops behind a cause of action or expression. In a way I was jumping on the movement-branding bandwagon, but I have a dual meaning in mind.

I intend the term *Contradict Movement* to refer to the movement of the Holy Spirit as he leads Christians to share the good news of Jesus Christ. Jesus indicates this unpredictable movement of the Holy Spirit in his often-quoted discourse to Nicodemus in John chapter 3, saying, "The wind blows wherever it pleases. You hear its sound, but you cannot tell where it comes from or where it is going. So it is with everyone born of the Spirit" (verse 8).

With this in mind, each Christian reading this book will likely be prompted to share the gospel with others in ways that I haven't yet perceived. Maybe some readers will be moved to step directly into the manner in which I have shared Contradict, using a poster at a college campus. The objective of the Contradict Movement is to counter the spirit of this age that all religions are equally valid and true, that all roads and paths lead to God.

It is more specific than this, however. A conservative Muslim could easily stand alongside a conservative Christian and boldly proclaim, "We worship a different God." Grounded in the Christian worldview, my goal is to move people not only to see that all religions can't be true, but to point them to Jesus Christ as mankind's one and only, all-sufficient Savior. Then I want to prayerfully and winsomely reason with them in the various marketplaces of life to which God has called each Christian to serve and be his witnesses.

To participate in this movement, a person is *not* required to use the Contradict logo I have made. Many people are likely participating in this movement already without having seen Contradict; in fact I think this movement goes all the way back to the beginning of humanity. God's people have always stood in opposition to the patterns of this world which lure us to exchange the truth of God for a lie, enticing us to bow down to the things of God's creation rather than worship and praise the Creator.

It is not surprising that the lies of pluralism have infiltrated the ranks of the visible church. Jesus indicated that this would happen with his parable of the wheat and the weeds (Matthew 13:24–30). Lies, the Enemy, and people who claim to be followers of Christ but are not will spring up within Christ's church (Matthew 13:36–43).

You can see Satan's sowing of lies within the church in the way that a large percentage of Christians in America have embraced certain New Age elements within their Christian beliefs and practices, as shared in chapter 1. With the lie swallowed and craved by society and even within the church, taking a stance in our pluralistic age will receive harsh criticism. This is what Jesus promised would happen. He said, "Brother will betray brother to death, and a father his child. Children will rebel against their parents and have them put to death. All men will hate you because of me, but he who stands firm to the end will be saved" (Mark 13:13).

Everyone in the church won't stand firm. Jesus promised this too. He said that when persecution comes, "many will turn away from the faith and will betray many people" (Matthew 24:10). This is why those of us who are standing upon Christ, pointing to Jesus as the only way to salvation, must band together, meet with one another, and encourage each other as we see the signs of the day of the Lord approaching (Hebrews 10:25).

Tapping into Spirit-Filled Movement

Jesus didn't leave us empty handed in this battle. He didn't ascend to his Father saying, "You can do it! Go get 'em, boys! I'll see you on the other side—I hope." What Jesus said was, "All authority in heaven and on earth has been given to me. Therefore go and make disciples of all nations … And surely I am with you always, to the very end of the age" (Matthew 28:18–20). That's Matthew's retelling of that command.

Luke also shares Jesus' departing Great Commission, as Matthew's verses are usually entitled, but he has a different focus. Luke records Jesus telling the disciples not to leave Jerusalem until the gift his Father promised was given to them (Acts 1:4). That was Jesus' last command before his ascension, as recorded by Luke in the first chapter of Acts. It's quite different from "go and make all disciples of all nations," isn't it? Luke still contains that aspect of Matthew's record, but Luke pens it as a *promise* and not a *command*. Luke has Jesus' last words come in the form of a guarantee with a specific outcome: "You will receive power when the Holy Spirit comes on you; and you will be my witnesses in Jerusalem, and in all Judea and Samaria, and to the ends of the earth" (Acts 1:8).

What I think is often missing from homilies that I have heard about Christ's command for us to make disciples of all nations are the gospel promises from both Matthew's and Luke's accounts. In Matthew, Jesus tells us that *all* authority, *everywhere*, is *his*, and he is with us *always*. Luke tells us that Jesus promised that the Holy Spirit would empower us to be *his* witnesses.

If these two promises are cut off from the command to proclaim God's Word to those who do not know Christ, we are left with our ingenuity, skills, and guts to get us by. We are left to pick and choose where we think

God wants us to go and speak. We are left to plan and scheme methods of attraction and deliverance on our own. It can become like the process of marketing, advertising, and growing a business, because after all those are things that we as people can relate to and understand in this physical world apart from God.

When the promises are attached to the command to preach the gospel and make disciples, we see that the outcome of our mission is certain. The gospel will be proclaimed to all nations, and the driving force behind this accomplishment will be the work of the Lord in his people (Matthew 24:14).

If you are sitting on the fence, wanting to share the gospel but too afraid, or too worried about what to say or how to answer people's questions, you are likely leaning on your own abilities and not trusting in God's provision. Acts 1:8 says that the Holy Spirit will empower us to be Christ's witnesses. John chapters 14 and 16 speak in detail about the work of the Holy Spirit in our lives. Jesus calls him the Counselor or the Helper who will teach us all things, remind us of God's Word, speak to us, reside within us, lead us into all truth, comfort us, and bring glory to Jesus. In Acts we see that when the disciples were filled with the Holy Spirit, they were enabled to witness, that they did so boldly, and that people were astonished.

This filling by the Holy Spirit is not a onetime event in the life of a believer either. We see mention that Peter is filled with the Holy Spirit on three different occasions in the short span of two chapters of Acts (Acts 2:4; 4:8; 4:31). Every time Peter is filled, it is for the proclamation of the gospel. On the first occasion that Peter and the other disciples with him were filled with the Spirit, they were in prayer, likely praying for the Holy Spirit that had been promised to them.

The second time Peter was filled with the Holy Spirit, he was before the Sanhedrin, on trial with John for healing and preaching in Jesus' name. My guess is that he was praying in that situation; I know I would be. Once they astonished the Sanhedrin and were released, they returned to the other disciples. All prayed for God's strengthening to enable them to proclaim the gospel in the face of their enemies' persecution.

At this point, Peter was filled with the Holy Spirit again, as were the others, and they spoke God's word boldly. Through the rest of Acts, when someone is filled with the Spirit, it is usually connected to prayer and proclamation.

The disciples' example in Acts is necessary for us to follow as we share the gospel, in light of the persecution we'll face for proclaiming that Jesus Christ is the only way to salvation in today's pluralistic age (which really is no different from the pluralism of the Roman Empire that the first disciples opposed). As we set out to share God's Word, and during our conversations with nonbelievers, we need to be in prayer and connected to Christ. We need to draw on his authority and power through prayer and reliance upon the Holy Spirit in us. To bear witnessing fruit, our role is to remain in Christ, to suck deep from the nutrients of good soil and water and sun—that is, to soak in God's Word—to live in prayer, to fellowship with one another, to walk in our baptism, and to eat and drink of Christ's body and blood.

These are the means through which the Holy Spirit works to strengthen our faith and lead, guide, and empower us to be Christ's witnesses. If we are cut off from these resources, or trust in our own abilities to share how all religions contradict each other and can't be true, we will be scared. We won't know what to say, and we won't bear good fruit in our efforts (which would be tough for us to tell, since God is the one true Judge in such matters, so we might think we're bearing good fruit when in fact we're not).

Many Christian denominations regularly pray the Lord's Prayer in church services, and if a denomination doesn't do this, its members still usually know it. It's found in Luke 11:2–4 and Matthew 6:9–13. After teaching the prayer in Luke's gospel, Jesus told a story about a man who goes to his friend's house at midnight and bangs on his door, demanding that his friend open up and give him bread. The friend doesn't give it to him because he is his friend, but because of the man's boldness. Jesus was encouraging his disciples to pray in boldness or perseverance until the answer was given, because the way Jesus told the story, it appears as if the friend didn't instantly give the man bread. Jesus then shared that if earthly fathers give good gifts to their children when their kids ask, "how much more will your Father in heaven give the Holy Spirit to those who ask Him!" (Luke 11:13). The indwelling of the Holy Spirit is the greatest gift the Father can give to us, and this passage clearly says that we can boldly ask God for more of the Spirit in our lives.

This shouldn't be taken to mean that Christians only have a part of the Spirit. This is not the case; the Spirit can't be divided. A person can't have 60 percent of the Holy Spirit and then be filled to have 100 percent.

The best way to understand the filling by the Spirit is the antithetical analogy that Paul uses in Ephesians 5:18 where he exhorts the Ephesians to "not get drunk on wine, which leads to debauchery. Instead, be filled with the Spirit." When a person is drunk, he is not in complete control of his body, thoughts, words, and actions. He might want to share a thought but not say it correctly. He might want to walk down the middle of the hallway but instead keep stumbling into the walls. He's under the influence of the alcohol in his body, and it leads him to sin.

The comparison to being filled with the Spirit indicates that when we are filled with the Spirit, we aren't in control either; we're still mentally present, thinking and acting, but we're under the influence of the Holy Spirit. When this happens, we are led into righteousness. When under the influence of alcohol, we do things that we ordinarily *wouldn't* do; when under the influence of the Spirit, we do things that we ordinarily *couldn't* do!

In my church life, I have heard very sparse teaching on how to be filled with the Holy Spirit as Paul exhorts the Ephesians. The answer to a degree has already been shared: pray for this filling of the Spirit and go to the resources of God's Word, fellowship with believers, and the gifts of baptism and communion, means by which God has promised to work in our lives.

To tap into the Holy Spirit's power, there is a key action that is required. It's so simple, yet at the same time it is a great struggle. Considering how God works, this paradox shouldn't come as a surprise. The key to being filled and led by the Spirit is revealed in the verb parsing of Paul's exhortation. "Be filled" is a passive voice. This is something that we simply receive, that we allow to happen to us. The key is surrendering our wills to the will of the Holy Spirit, allowing him to work in us, not resisting his movements.

The seventeenth-century Lutheran theologian Philipp Jakob Spener called this passive state of reception "resignation." Spener gives six chief points regarding the virtue of resignation:

1. Complete denial of everything a person can have in this world.
2. Denial of one's own will, crucifying the flesh, denying our own desires, enjoyment, and self-worth.
3. Desire nothing but what God desires for us.

4. Give no place to Satan in our lives, that we do nothing for ourselves, but only desire that the Lord do with us as he wishes.

5. Patience as we wait upon the Lord to bring about his will in us.

6. Follow God obediently where we feel his movement, yet also resign our will, understanding, and actions for him to use them as he desires.[1]

Resigning Contradict to the Will of God

Influenced by the verses I have just shared and Spener's instruction on resignation, I am praying and doing my best to resign this book, the Contradict logo, and their message into the hands of the Lord to use as he pleases. I have my dream and my vision of what I hope will happen with this book, but is it God's plan? Will the Spirit use it to stir others to set up evangelism tables on college campuses or in other public spaces? Will the Spirit use it as a teaching tool to educate Christians about the world's religions and how they are contradictory to the truth of Scripture? Will the Spirit prompt Christians to slap Contradict stickers on their cars and laptops so that they outnumber the coexist and tolerance stickers? Will the Spirit use Contradict as a tilling tool, a way to break up the soil that is not ready to receive the gospel? Will the Spirit use it to lead someone to faith in Christ? How long or short will this movement be, where will it go, where will it end, and what will be my involvement in the future?

If this book is only read by a handful of people and no one comes to saving faith through reading it, I won't lie: I'll be disappointed and likely upset. Resignation to God is difficult. But that won't mean that it's a failure on my part or that I wasted all of my time putting this manuscript together and creating a Web site for it. It just means that the Spirit had other plans.

For instance, in Jesus' hometown he wasn't able to do many miracles. The people who knew him intimately rejected his message (Matthew 13:53–58). This certainly doesn't mean that Jesus was doing something wrong, or that he wasn't supposed to go to his hometown to minister. We often judge a ministry's significance based on instant returns and quantitative measures that we can observe. But seeds bear fruit in seasons (Isaiah 55:10–11). God judges the heart and doesn't care about size (1

Samuel 16:7). He treasures the small things and goes out of the way, risking everything, even for one lost lamb (Luke 15:4).

One time "the Spirit sent him [Jesus] out into the desert, and he was in the desert for forty days, being tempted by Satan" (Mark 1:12-13). The Spirit doesn't always lead us into prosperity and comfort.

Another time, the apostle Paul and his companions were "kept by the Holy Spirit from preaching the word in the province of Asia" (Acts 16:6). Then the Spirit would not allow them to enter Bithynia. Then they went to Traos, and during the night Paul received a vision of a Macedonian begging him to come help them in Macedonia. They concluded that God had called them to Macedonia, a place they'd have to get to by sailing.

These restrictions by the Spirit must not have been easy or pleasant, because we're talking about traveling several hundred miles. This wasn't just a walk in the park each time they were kept by the Spirit to preach. We don't know the details of how they were kept from preaching, but we see that they set out several times to minister to people in the name of Christ and came into some sort of conflict. Even in Macedonia, the first town they came to was Philippi. They were able to convert a woman and her family to Christ, but then they ended up in prison for casting a demon out of slave girl who made her owners money by fortune-telling under her demonic influence!

Following Christ as the Holy Spirit leads may not always be easy. We may not always understand what he is calling us to, and for many of us, our calling may seem pretty dull compared to those of globe-trotting missionaries. But regardless, everyone who is a member of the body of Christ has a spiritual gift useful and necessary for the health of the church. With these gifts and our various vocations, we're called to serve and be witnesses of Christ for the purpose of disciple making. We will hit snags and we will face failures along the way, but we must trust that the Lord is moving us and will use all of the trying times in our lives for good (Romans 8:28).

I share all of this because, as a movement, Contradict might face persecution. We may not see any fruit. But we know that God is moving us one step closer to him through each hurdle, failure, and success. I don't want people to lose heart if they choke sharing the gospel, or don't receive the support or response they expect from their efforts and endeavors.

Therefore, since we have been justified through faith, we have peace with God through our Lord Jesus Christ, through whom we have gained access by faith into this grace in which we now stand. And we rejoice in the hope of the glory of God. Not only so, but we also rejoice in our sufferings, because we know that suffering produces perseverance; perseverance, character; and character, hope. And hope does not disappoint us, because God has poured out his love into our hearts by the Holy Spirit, whom he has given us. (Romans 5:1–5)

I would like to thank the following individuals for bringing me through life:

Jessica Wrasman, always my better half as we journey through this life together; Charles Miller (PawPaw), the greatest example of a Christ-like servant I know; Virginia Miller (Grandma), the most faithful servant who has been tested in fire again and again, but always remains in Christ and full of joy and love to share; Becky Wrasman, the lady God used to bring me both physical life and spiritual life and who has set the best example I have seen firsthand of daily devotion in God's Word and commitment to prayer; Bernard Wrasman, the man who taught me right from wrong and most importantly demonstrated how to stand and fight on the side that's right and true and to stick up for the weak no matter the cost, and to Jenny Donovan; I am so very proud of you and I am glad that you are now married to Lonnie. Jenny, I am relieved and encouraged to know how close and supportive you are to the kin and it makes it a little easier on me being so far from Rocky Top. Jeff and Donna Horn, thank you for being my second set of parents.

Special thanks are due to the following individuals whose financial support, encouragement, and prayers helped bring this book to publication:

Brett and LaVelle Johnston, Charles and Virginia Miller, Bernard and Becky Wrasman, Adam Stetson, George Allen III, Steve Busch, Jeff and Donna Horn, Connie Rios, Brian and Jenny Harrison, Bob and Claudia Tremonte, Danny Martinez, Gino and Ally Landry, Anthony Landry, Joshua and Janelle, Alan and Wendy Gonzalez, Tim and Sally Brink, the Schalm family, Lawrence and Brandy Wilson, Josh Suh, Einer Rivera, Laurie Post, Geri Robinson, Jeffrey Schneider, Carolyn Lewis, Marty and Conni Schramm, Jenn Heisey, Kevin and Christie McClain, Mark Christenson the Great, Doug and Jenny Cooper, Jack and Jennifer Brouwer, David Magruder, Daniel Harders, Ramona Brown, Marcy Crabtree, Aaron and Stephanie Wrasman, Paul Jackson, Aileen Fitzpatrick, Kathy Kendall, Sara M., Kyle Beshears, Josh Moore, and Jake Wells.

Endnotes

1: The State of Tolerance

1. Barack Hussein Obama, "President Barack Obama's Inaugural Address," *The White House Blog*. Posted January 21, 2009. *The White House:* www.whitehouse.gov/blog/inaugural-address (July 9, 2012).
2. Robert E. Van Voorst, ed. *Anthology of World Scriptures*, 4th ed. (Belmont, Calif.: Wadsworth/Thomson Learning, 2003), 35.
3. Robert E. Van Voorst, ed. *Anthology of World Scriptures*, 39-40.
4. Henry David Thoreau, *Walden* (New York: Alfred A. Knopf, 1991), 264.
5. Ralph Waldo Emerson, *Ralph Waldo Emerson: Selected Essays, Lectures, and Poems*, ed. Robert D. Richardson Jr. (New York: Bantam Books, 1990), 173.
6. Emerson, *Ralph Waldo Emerson*, 178.
7. Emerson, *Ralph Waldo Emerson*, 187.
8. Nina Baym, ed., *The Norton Anthology of American Literature Vol. C* (New York: Norton and Company, 2003), 37.
9. Baym, *The Norton Anthology*, 77.
10. Terry Gifford, ed. *John Muir: His Life and Letters and Other Writings* (Seattle: The Mountaineers, 1996), 167.
11. Swami Vivekananda, "Response to Welcome," *Addresses at the Parliament of Religions. Vivekananda: www.vivekananda.org/readings.asp* (July 8, 2012).
12. Sri Swami Satchidananda, "Woodstock". *Sri Swami Satchidananda: www.swamisatchidananda.org/docs2/woodstock.htm* (July 12, 2012).
13. Sri Swami Satchidananda, "Woodstock".

14. Sri Swami Satchidananda, "Woodstock".

15. Joel Makower, *Woodstock: The Oral History* (New York: Doubleday, 1989), 193.

16. Makower, *Woodstock*, 245.

17. Pew Research, "Many Americans Mix Multiple Faiths". Posted on Dec. 9, 2009. *Pew Research Center: www.pewforum.org/2009/12/09/many-americans-mix-multiple-faiths* (February 10, 2013).

18. "Bush: All Religions Pray to 'Same God'". Published on Oct. 7, 2007. *WND: www.wnd.com/2007/10/43906* (February 10, 2013).

2: The Multiple Religious Paths

1. Elizabeth Gilbert, *Eat, Pray, Love* (New York: Penguin Books, 2006), 13.

2. Pew Research, "U.S. Religious Knowledge Survey: Executive Summary". Posted on Sept. 28, 2010. *Pew Research Center: www.pewforum.org/U-S-Religious-Knowledge-Survey.aspx*, (February 10, 2013).

3. Steven P. Mueller, ed. Called to Believe: *A Brief Introduction to Christian Doctrine* (Eugene, Oregon: Wipf & Stock, 2006), 41-42.

4. Fouad Masri, *Bridges: Christians Connecting with Muslims* (Indianapolis: Crescent Project, 2008), 21-22.

3: Enacting the Law of Noncontradiction

1. *The Upanishads,* trans. Juan Mascaro (London: Penguin Books, 1965), 110, 118.

2. *Dhammapada*, trans. Juan Mascaro (London: Penguin Books, 1973), 63.

3. Carl Sagan, *Cosmos* (New York: Wings Books, 1995), 245.

4. *Gura Granth Sahib*, 1399. *Sri Gura Granth Sahib Ji: www.granthsahib.com* (Aug. 27, 2012).

5. Tracey R. Rich, "Human Nature". *Judaism 101: www.jewfaq.org/human.htm* (Sept. 15, 2012).

6. *The Upanishads*, 95.

7. Robert E. Van Voorst, ed. *Anthology of World Scriptures*, 4th ed. (Belmont, Calif.: Wadsworth/Thomson Learning, 2003), 193.

8. Anton Szander LaVey, "The Nine Satanic Statements," *The Satanic Bible. The Satanic Bible Free Ebook Download: www.thesatanicbiblefree.com* (Sept. 9, 2012).

9. Church of Scientology International, "What are Some of the Core Tenants of Scientology?" *Scientology: www.scientology.org/faq/background-and-basic-principles/what-are-some-of-the-core-tenets-of-scientology.html* (Sept. 15, 2012).

10. *The Koran*, trans. N. J. Dawood (London: Penguin Books, 1999), 22.

11. *The Upanishads*, 63.

12. *Dhammapada*, 40.

13. Mary Baker Eddy, "Chapter 14: Recapitulation," *Science and Health with Key to the Scriptures. Christian Science: http://christianscience.com/read-online/science-and-health/%28chapter%29/chapter-xiv-recapitulation#anchor.1.14* (Nov. 2, 2013).

14. Henry Rollins, *Talking from the Box/Henry Rollins Goes to London* DVD (IMAGO, 2001).

15. Mordechai Housman, "How Does a Jew Attain Salvation". *Being Jewish: www.beingjewish.com/toshuv/salvation.html* (Sept. 24, 2012).

16. Tracey R. Rich, "Jewish Attitudes Toward Non-Jews". *Judaism 101: www.jewfaq.org/gentiles.htm* (Sept. 24, 2012).

17. *The Book of Mormon: Another Testament of Jesus Christ* (Salt Lake City, Utah: The Church of Jesus Christ of Latter-day Saints, 1981), 99-100.

18. *The Koran,* 429.

19. *The Koran,* 225.

20. *The Upanishads*, 103.

21. *The Bhagavad-Gita: Krishna's Counsel in Time of War*, trans. Barbara Stoler Miller (New York: Bantam Books, 1986), 143.

22. *The Sermon at Benares. Internet Sacred Text Archive: www.sacred-texts.com/bud/btg/btg17.htm* (Sept. 24, 2012).

23. Church of Scientology International, "What is Auditing?" *Scientology: www.scientology.org/faq/scientology-and-dianetics-auditing/what-is-auditing.html* (Sept. 24, 2012).

24. Laurence B. Brown, *The Justice of Judgment*. Last modified on Feb. 22, 2009. *The Religion of Islam: www.islamreligion.com/articles/569* (Nov. 5, 2013).
25. *The Bhagavad-Gita: Krishna's Counsel in Time of War*, 33.
26. *Dhammapada*, 56-57.
27. *Christianity, Cults and Religions* (Torrance, Calif.: Rose Publishing, 2008), 7-23, 31, 44, 46, 50-52.
28. Huston Smith, *The World's Religions* (San Francisco: HarperSanFrancisco, 1991), 71.

4: Finding a Religious Litmus Test

1. Karl R. Popper, "Science as Falsification". *Critical Thought and Religious Liberty: www.stephenjaygould.org/ctrl/popper_falsification.html#see* (May 11, 2013).
2. John Warwick Montgomery, ed. *Evidence for Faith: Deciding the God Question* (Dallas: Probe Books, 1991), 44.
3. Jeffrey Burton Russell, *Exposing Myths About Christianity: A Guide to Answering 145 Viral Lies and Legends* (Downer's Grove, Ill.: IVP Press, 2012), 147.
4. Chauncey Sanders, *An Introduction to Research in English Literary History* (New York: The Macmillan Company, 1952), 143.
5. Sanders, *An Introduction*, 144.
6. Sanders, *An Introduction*, 146–155.
7. Sanders, *An Introduction*, 155.
8. A. J. M. Wedderburn, *Beyond Resurrection* (Peabody, Mass.: Hendrickson Publishers, 1999), 4.

5: Testing the Testable

1. A. T. Robertson, *Introduction to the Textual Criticism of the New Testament* (Nashville: Broadman Press, 1925), 70.
2. Norman Geisler and Peter Bocchino, *Unshakeable Foundations* (Minneapolis, Minn.: Bethany House Publishers, 2001), 256.
3. Lee Strobel, *The Case for Christ* (Grand Rapids, Mich.: Zondervan, 1998), 81.

4. Kenneth Samples, *Without a Doubt* (Grand Rapids, Mich.: Baker Books, 2004), 92.

5. Strobel, *The Case for Christ*, 77.

6. Paul E. Little, *Know Why You Believe* (Downer's Grove, Ill.: Inter Varsity Press, 2008), 100.

7. Strobel, *The Case for Christ*, 78.

8. Don Stewart, *What Everyone Needs to Know About ... The Bible* (Orange, Calif.: Dart Press, 1993), 79.

9. Frederic G. Kenyon, *Handbook to the Textual Criticism of the New Testament*, 2d ed. (London: The Macmillan Company, 1912), 5.

10. "Chapter 18, verses 31-33," *Fragment of Saint John's Gospel: recto". The University of Manchester Library: www.library.manchester. ac.uk/searchresources/guidetospecialcollections/stjohnfragment/rect* (Feb. 18, 2013).

11. Fondation Martin Bodmer, "The Gospel According to Saint John". *Fondation Martin Bodmer: http://fondationbodmer.ch/en/ bibliotheque/les-fleurons/le-millenaire-chretien/evangile/* (Feb. 18, 2013).

12. John Warwick Montgomery, *History, Law, and Christianity* (Calgary, AB: Canadian Institute for Law, Theology, and Public Policy, 2002), 27–28.

13. Eusebius Pamphilus, *Church History Book III, Chapter 29:14-15. New Advent: www.newadvent.org/fathers/250103.htm* (Nov. 4, 2014).

14. St. Irenaeus, *Against Heresies Book III, Chapter 1:1. New Advent: www.newadvent.org/fathers/0103301.htm* (March 1, 2013).

15. St. Irenaeus, *Against Heresies Book III, Chapter 11:8. New Advent: www.newadvent.org/fathers/0103311.htm* (Nov. 4, 2014).

16. Kenneth Richard Samples, *Without a Doubt: Answering the 20 Toughest Faith Questions* (Grand Rapids, Mich.: Baker Books, 2004), 107.

17. Samples, *Without a Doubt*, 105–108, 125–126.

18. *Letters of Pliny the Younger and Emperor Trajan*, trans. William Whiston. Published in April 1998. *Frontline: www.pbs.org/wgbh/ pages/frontline/shows/religion/maps/primary/pliny.html* (March 6, 2013).

---

19. Ulrich W. Mauser, *Christ in the Wilderness* (Naperville, Ill.: Alec R. Allenson, 1963), 56–57.

20. James T. Fisher and Lowell Hawley, *A Few Buttons Missing* (Philadelphia: Lippincott, 1951), 273.

21. Isidore Epstein, ed. *Babylonian Talmud, Sanhedrin 43a. Come and Hear: www.come-and-hear.com/sanhedrin/sanhedrin_43.html* (March 10, 2013).

22. *Historical Evidence for Crucifixion Darkness. Bible History: www. biblehistory.net/newsletter/crucifixion_darkness.htm* (March 21, 2013).

23. *Historical Evidence for Crucifixion Darkness.*

24. Kei Thong Chan, *Faith of Our Fathers: God in Ancient China* (Shanghai: 345 Xianxialu, 2006), 318.

25. Chan, *Faith of Our Fathers*, 318.

26. Tacitus, *Annals, Book 15:44. Internet Sacred Text Archive: www. sacred-texts.com/cla/tac/a15040.htm* (May 5, 2013).

27. Montgomery, *History, Law, and* Christianity, 16.

Chapter 6: The Ring of Truth

1. Henrietta Mears, *What the Bible is all About, Visual ed.* (Ventura, Calif.: Regal Books, 1999), 13.

2. Isaiah 52:13-53:12

3. Robert Kolb and Timothy J. Wengret, eds. *The Book of Concord: The Confessions of the Evangelical Lutheran Church* (Minneapolis, Mich.: Fortress Press, 2000), 45.

4. Kolb and Wengret, *The Book of Concord*, 193.

Chapter 7: Using Contradict to Share the Gospel

1. Bill Bright, *Have you Heard of the Four Spiritual Laws? Campus Crusade: www.campuscrusade.com/fourlawseng.htm* (Nov. 4, 2013).

2. *Way of the Master: www.wayofthemaster.com.*

3. Fouad Masri, *Bridges: Christians Connecting with Muslims* (Indianapolis: Crescent Project, 2008), 13.

4. C. S. Lewis, *The Problem of Pain* (San Francisco: HarperSanFrancisco, 2001), 91.

Chapter 8: Joining the Contradict Movement

1. Peter C. Erb, *Pietists: Selected Writings* (New York: Paulist Press, 1983), 84-85.

THEY CAN'T ALL BE TRUE—JOHN 14:6
WWW.CONTRADICTMOVEMENT.ORG

Visit www.contradictmovement.org for:
Videos
Small Group Discussion Guides
Facebook Community Page
Andy Wrasman's Blog
Contact Information
Contradict Stickers and Gospel Tracts
Contradict Shirts, Mugs, Cell Phone Covers,
and more…